MW00962550

Suite 300 - 990 Fort St
Victoria, BC, Canada, V8V 3K2
www.friesenpress.com

First Edition - 2016

Cover design concept by Eleanor Deckert and Krista Thomas
Author's web page: DADEM Studios
www.dademstudios.com

Graphics: chapter breaks: Eleanor Deckert
Front cover photo: Krista Thomas
Young Eleanor photo: Daddy
Author Portrait: Kevin Deckert
To protect privacy, names of people and places in this memoir have been changed.

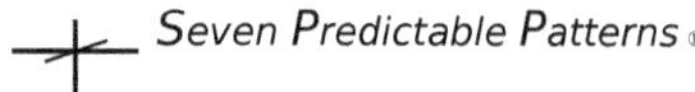

Photos illustrating each chapter can be found on the author's web page:
www.eleanordeckert.com

ISBN
978-1-4602-9710-0 (Hardcover)
978-1-4602-9711-7 (Paperback)
978-1-4602-9712-4 (eBook)

1. *Biography & Autobiography, Personal Memoirs*
2. *Family & Relationships, Ethics & Morals*
3. *Self-Help, Green Lifestyle*

Distributed to the trade by The Ingram Book Company

Dedication

Somehow the Lord can bring people into your life just when you need them. Father Emil Sasges has been such a person for me. As a newlywed twenty-year-old bride, I came to the wilderness of Canada to live thousands of miles away from my home, church, friends and family. Father's pastoral visits, caring wisdom, warm humour, meaningful songs and ever-ready smiles have nourished me over the years. He has heard my whole story. He was witnessed major turning points. Friend, Guide, Mentor, Priest, I could not begin to write any of my memoir until I had the experience of wholeness brought about after many hours of his skillful listening.

Father Emil Sasges
February 6, 1931 – August 5, 2014
57 years a priest

Acknowledgments

Where to begin?

Every person who crosses my path adds to my story, is my teacher, shares their point of view, impacts my life in some way.

This is not an historical journal or photographically accurate biography. It is a memoir, a sketch, a collection, an impression.

Seven people are in my family of origin.

I asked my parents about their dreams, and how they did or did not become reality. I wanted to trace what happened when disappointments and conflicts complicate the Path. I wanted to understand the influences and interactions that shaped my world view, my view of myself, my spiritual Journey and my Quest to find healthy relationships with my Father, Brothers, Sons and most significantly, my Husband.

I tried to be mindful about how I shaped my own children.

And, maybe, I would come to a clearer view of my Self.

Along the way I have had skillful Counsellors: Dean Nicholson, Kathy Green, Phil Janicki, and I am giving Lorina Traub lots of practice as she works towards her counselling certification. Father Sasges gave me more time than all the rest put together!

Thank you to everyone in the 'Helping Professions.' You are willing to go to the places where your clients experience pain and bring them hope, resources and patience while the miracle of transformation unfolds and their inner balance is restored.

This is 'Book 2' and now I know why authors thank their spouse in the acknowledgments. Mountains of patience! Heaps of encouragement! Stacks of dishes! Careful listening! Thank-you, Kevin!

Foreword

While writing this memoir, I puzzle over these interconnected reoccurring questions: Is it possible to know your own Mother, Father, Brothers, Sisters as real people? Or are we stuck in roles and patterns, some assigned to us even before we were born, some gender specific, some set in place by 'birth-order,' some cultural, some echo across generations, some determined by the decade we were born in? And from there another question silently waits to be asked: Can you ever really know your Self?

I have tried to pay attention to my own inner dialogue, turning points, listened to what is influencing me, tried to remember the thought process that went into my decisions, kept my eyes and ears open to observe the people around me, made an attempt to notice the point of view each person has.

Woven throughout my life is a keen interest in very young children. Heavy messages about 'who I am' came to me at a very young age. I did not get a clear understanding of my very early fragmented memories until I was 52 years old.

What happens to the memories of a young child? Can they impact the person's life decades later? Do the family dynamics surrounding a very small child really matter? Is it helpful to try to piece the fragments together to gain a clearer picture?

It's hard work. It takes time. But it strips away the isolation. 'It only happened to me' is simply not true. Others have moved from darkness to light.

Daddy did.
Mother did.
I can, too.
You can, too.

Table of Contents

Photographs to illustrate each chapter can be found on the author's web page www.eleanordeckert.com

Chapter 1
Tuesday, January 25, 1966
Daddy's Birthday

Think of everyone as a child
in need of friendship and love.
—*John Bradshaw*

* ** *** ****

Friday, January 21

"Mommy, may I have some coloured paper? And blank white paper, too? I'd like to make a birthday card for Daddy. Like a book. With pages." There is not much time between arriving home from school and suppertime. There is not much time between suppertime and bedtime. But, if I start a few days early, I think I can make my plan work out.

"Certainly, Dear. Look in the bottom drawer under the telephone." Mommy was busy in the kitchen making supper. The thick beef and barley stew smelled good. The bread would be out of the oven soon. "Could you go look at the Job Chart and see who's turn it is to come and set the table? Then call them."

Mommy was very organized. She had to be.

* ** *** ****

We live eight miles from the nearest store and twenty miles from Colorado College where Daddy works. At first he took the blue Ford station wagon to work. That was our 'covered wagon' when we drove in all the way out west from Pennsylvania three years ago. But now we have an icy-blue-green Dodge van. Daddy goes to work. Mommy stays home. Our brand new house was built just for us on the property Daddy bought from his Uncle Allan. Two-story high beams shaped the walls and roof into a flattened 'A'. The floor plan was a giant 'T.' Great glass walls and sliding glass doors at the end of each branch of the 'T' allowed the spectacular surroundings to be seen: mighty Pikes Peak behind the green mountain ridge, closer hills changing with the seasons display, wispy spring grasses, summertime fragile flowers and brightly painted autumn shrubs as well as prickly pear cactus, spear-like yucca, and of course, winter's blanket of deep, silent, untouched snow.

The centre branch of the 'T' was a large, open living room downstairs and a big playroom upstairs with a balcony railing overlooking the living room. The branch towards the entryway from the driveway was the main entrance with the kitchen downstairs and my brother's bedroom upstairs. The branch towards the hillside was nestled into the slope allowing the sliding glass doors of my parent's bedroom downstairs to open out onto a cozy alcove rock garden. Through the upstairs bedroom windows my sister and I enjoyed watching the scampering chipmunks.

Such a unique design had caught the eye of a photographer who came to prepare a feature in the 'American Home' magazine.

With three children in school and a preschooler and new baby at home, Mommy had to have a schedule to get through the day. She got up early to get the coffee perking and make a nice breakfast and pack lunches for Daddy and the three of us going to school. Meanwhile, Baby Carol needs to be changed and her bottle ready. Julie needs help getting dressed, brushing her hair and tying her shoes. James and Andrew and I have to catch the bus at 8:00 at the end our driveway.

Mommy always makes a hearty breakfast. Sometimes she makes sourdough pancakes. Sometimes, French toast. Soft boiled eggs, scrambled eggs or sunny-side-up and of course breakfast includes stacks of toast. Oatmeal, corn meal or cream of wheat are wintertime possibilities. Mommy used to walk us down the driveway, but this winter, with the new Baby, now we get a ride with Daddy who waits with us beside the highway until we have safely boarded the big yellow school bus.

Mommy organizes more than her time. With Daddy's payday once a month, she has to carefully budget the money Daddy gives her, plan ahead for special days and make a really careful grocery list.

With a not too generous well, she has to ration water, too, take all the laundry to town on Saturdays and make sure we take turns flushing the toilet and share the shallow bath water.

Managing the household is another area where she keeps organized. A 'Job Chart' is on the refrigerator to keep track of who has which job each week. There's also a 'Mark Chart' taped inside the kitchen cupboard door where we each keep a tally of the jobs we do: 2¢ each. We get paid once-a-month, just like Daddy. When it's shopping day Mommy piles the grocery cart high as we help push it down the aisles. It takes two carts to bring home enough food for seven people for a whole month. We have a big pantry and a double fridge-freezer as well as drawers for flour, sugar, potatoes and onions.

* ** *** ****

"Andrew! Come and set the table! Mommy said!" I call up the stairs.

Art supplies are not abundant. It is a big responsibility to plan the project and be trusted not to waste paper, glue, or crayons. I gather supplies to make my plan. "Mommy, is there Scotch tape? May I use the stapler?" I can make one page before supper. I go up to my room. Daddy's birthday is on Tuesday. I'll have time to work on my project over the weekend.

Julie and I share a room. It is upstairs right above Mommy and Daddy's room. We each have a built-in bed up against the wall on opposite sides of the room. We each have a closet by the head of each bed and a window at the foot of each bed. Through the window we can see the hillside, pine trees, yucca, tall grasses. Sometimes we see deer and often little chipmunks. Under each bed is an air vent. It is to let the warm air come up from downstairs. Julie's bed is over Daddy's study, which is where the Baby's crib is set up. We can hear the Baby cry and Mommy's soothing voice as she takes care of her in the night. My bed is right above my parent's bed. I can hear them, too. The alarm clock, the water running, the toilet flushing, the closet door opening, the tone of voices as decisions are made in the early morning. Mommy goes to the kitchen to start the coffee pot. Daddy sings while he shaves.

But, for this birthday project, I need some privacy. I don't want anyone to copy me. My closet is pretty big and there's a string I can pull to turn on the light. So I set my supplies on the floor and pull the door shut. First: I decide to make the booklet. With two blank white pages folded in half I'll have enough pages. A blue piece of construction paper will be the cover. I'll staple it together when all the pages are decorated.

The first thing I want to make is the last page. That's what I need the tape for. Daddy is turning 36. So I want to tape on 36 pennies.

I have saved quite a few. The 'Mark Chart' for the end of December had more than the usual tally. I usually have two chores a day, but since it was recently Christmas time, I helped in the kitchen even more. Baking, washing, helping with the Baby added up to 80 times 2¢. Plus, Daddy has been paying me 'a-penny-a-minute.' He's writing a book and I can help him proofread. I'm in Grade 3 and an excellent reader.

'New par, cap, quote, end quote, decimal, comma, semi-colon, period' I learned to read the punctuation aloud as I stumbled over words like 'Gross National Product' and names of foreign countries and 'interest rates' and 'wage and price control' and 'inflation.' Daddy is a Professor of Economics. When I try to understand, all I can think of is the $1 bill Oma gives me every birthday, the slow earnings I collect, the cost of treats I am allowed to buy and my pledge to put some of my own coins in the collection plate at church. 'Economics' seems to be about money and I guess it means 'how much does each person or country have.' So, I think Daddy will like it that I am giving him some.

I have just enough time to count out 36 pennies and tape them down in a nice big oval on the page. Now I hear the dog bark. Daddy's van comes up the steep driveway, the door slams and his feet stomp snow off his boots. Rex, our black lab, can come inside now. He wags, sniffs and settles on his mat. Mommy clangs the bell to tell us to come for supper.

Holding hands around the table we smile and look at each other while the traditional song-blessing fills the room.

need and know they are guided and protected. That's what Fathers do.

Now we each sit comfortably, but pay attention as Daddy reads aloud. He already taught us that the Bible is a collection of books written at different times by different people and collected together from long, long ago. He also told us that the Word has an inner meaning which was revealed to a man in Sweden about 200 years ago. The writer is called a 'The Seer' because he could see the Spiritual World. The books The Seer wrote are also holy. Not very many people know about these books, so it is very special that we belong to this Seer-Book Church. Daddy is named after the first ordained minister in America to read, believe and teach from these Seer-Books.

Today Daddy is reading about Samson.[2] God made him especially strong as long as his hair was not cut. A woman tricked him into telling her the secret so she could tell Samson's enemies how to make him weak. They cut off his hair, jabbed out his eyes and tied him up in prison where they made him do the work of a donkey grinding at the mill.

But his hair grew back.

One day there was a great feast for a large gathering of the enemies. They decided that for entertainment they wanted to make fun of Samson, now blind, weak and no longer a threat. Samson was brought into the great hall. The crowd laughed and called out rude jokes. He was tied between the two pillars that held up the building. He called out to God for help him and pulled the pillars down. All the people in the building and on the roof watching and also Samson were crushed.

It feels scary to imagine this scene: an evil woman, a captive hero, a jeering crowd, the stone work crumbling, the screams and then: silence. Why is this gruesome story part of this Holy Book?

"May the Lord add His blessing to the reading of His Word."

Now Mommy goes to the piano. I picked a song we all know by heart. Daddy likes to march us along and sing it while he puts us to bed. But Mommy thinks it's too rambunctious for bedtime.

March on, march on to victory
with the light of the Lord before us,
from His throne above He looks down in His love and
His holy arm is o're us. And His holy arm is o're us! [3]

It's hard, even for me, to not march and stomp but rather maintain a steady, respectful posture. The boys are grinning and tapping their feet. Julie can't stop herself from moving in a lively march to the compelling beat. Next time I'll choose a more reverent song, maybe *The Church in the Wildwood.*

Now we stand up, bow our heads and Daddy says, "May the Lord bless us and keep us, Amen."

We stay standing and silent while he closes the Word and Julie snuffs the candles.

Now we get to colour a picture. Mommy has the pages and crayons ready on the dining table. We get lessons in the mail from the Seer-Church school in Bonnie Hills, Pennsylvania. Each lesson is three pages: the Bible verses with a short explanation, a page of questions to be sure we listened to the lesson and understand the main ideas, and a picture to colour. This one shows Samson with long hair and big muscles and the chains and the pillars. Daddy decides to join us. He starts to sketch the scene with a pencil. James and Andrew leave their project to watch the scene unfold. We didn't know that Daddy was so good at drawing! It's exciting! People screaming, the balcony falling down, the dinner guests with their platters of food and wine glasses spilling. The royal canopy and fancy gowns make it seem pretty while the fine people are sneering and laughing with ugly faces. But suddenly, they are conquered by the dirty, ragged prisoner they thought was incapable of action.

Mommy notices the time, has to calm us down and sends us upstairs to get ready for bed.

Daddy is reading to us from Mark Twain. Sometimes he starts to cry when he reads sad parts, like when Jim realized that his little girl was deaf. He sits with the overhead light on in the playroom at the top of the stairs that separates the boys' bedroom from the girls'. I fall asleep pretty fast so I don't get how the whole story goes. Something about Tom Sawyer painting a fence and getting the other boys to help. While I snuggle in, I get a new idea for Daddy's birthday card. I think I can draw 36 books!

Daddy loves books! He is writing one! Grammie wrote one! Grampa translated one! Yes, 36 books will be fun to draw. Text books, library books, dictionary, encyclopedia, travel books, animal books, fairy-tales, real and pretend, and of course, the Word.

'The Princess and Curdie' and 'The Wind in the Willows' and 'Just so Stories' and 'Mary Poppins' and 'Peter Pan' and 'Black Beauty' and recently 'Huckleberry Finn' and 'Tom Sawyer.' So many pages! So many characters! So many books! Great-grandmother read aloud to Grammie and she read aloud to Daddy and he reads aloud to us and someday I will read aloud to my children. There is a long line of book readers stretching backward and forward in time. I feel safe and wealthy and connected.

Daddy likes to make up stories, too. The best one ever was for the boys' birthday two weeks ago. He put all the characters and plots together into one long tale called 'Little-Snow-Cinder-Hood and the Seven-Eleven-Dwarfs.' I hope he writes it down and makes a book for us!

Sometime in the night, with my heart pounding, "Mommy, I had a bad dream!" I stand beside her side of the bed. "The Samson story was too scary!" The deadly scene all came back in vivid detail: enemies gouging out his bloody eyes, the screaming people falling from the roof as the thunderous stones collapsed. Mommy lifts the covers and lets me crawl in for a snuggle. But, just then, she also needs to get up give a bottle to the Baby. So I ended up in-between Mommy and Daddy. Safe. Snug. Warm. Sleeping.

Saturday, January 22

Saturday is Room Cleaning Day. We strip our sheets and bring them to the laundry pile downstairs. It only takes me a few minutes to tidy up the rest of my side of the room. After breakfast on Saturdays, Mommy usually goes to the laundry mat. Since Baby Carol was born, she often invites me to come along to help. I am eight and a quarter years old. I can rock her and make her laugh and sing songs she likes and hold the bottle. I can fold the towels and match the socks. I can carry loads in and out and bring Mommy things from the diaper bag. While Mommy works, I can keep myself out of mischief. Today I bring the crayons and paper and keep working on Daddy's birthday card. I don't mind showing Mommy what I'm making. She likes to draw and make presents, too. And she has good ideas.

"Mommy, remember when you used to let me iron Daddy's handkerchiefs? I watched Captain Kangaroo on our big black and white TV. How old was I then?" I felt so grown-up to be allowed to sprinkle the wrinkly cloth, slide the hot iron, fold exactly in half, iron again, fold again and make a stack of clean, white handkerchiefs for my Daddy. He always looked so handsome as he left for work: black suit, white shirt, striped tie, shiny shoes... and he was just as tidy when he came home from teaching at the college. Imagine how smart my Daddy is. He is teaching grown-ups!

"You were about four years old when you started. That was before the two cousins came to stay with us." Her hands are moving rapidly to fill the washing machines and measure the soap powder. I get to lay the quarters in their slots and push the slider in to start the machine.

Mommy's mother and father ran a laundry business in their basement. Opa drove a big, black car with his name painted on the side. He had customers for each day of the week. He came on time to pick up piles of dirty laundry in wood-slat laundry baskets and deliver the clean laundry on time, neatly ironed and folded and wrapped in brown paper bundles. Oma and a helper ran the ringer washing machines. The hot steam of the mangle filled the house with a soapy smell. As they reached high school age, all of their eight children learned to hang, press and fold the sheets and other linens. Mommy had learned to be very precise about how to do things properly.

"Why did the cousins come for such a long time?"

"Your Daddy's sister, Aunt Madeline, was in the hospital. The older two cousins went to live with their grandmother. The younger two came to our house."

"Why was she in the hospital? Was she sick? Was she going to die? Did she have an operation? Was she in an accident? Did she have a baby?" I couldn't think of any more ways a person might need help. But every answer was, "No."

"She just needed to rest," was the unsatisfactory answer. "Let's get you set up with your art project," she smiled and settled in with the Baby on her lap, holding the warm bottle.

"After the pennies and the books, I've decided to draw 36 candles. One for each year since Daddy was born," I announce to Mommy's approving smile. Chuckling and patting the Baby's head I wonder, "It's hard to imagine big, tall Daddy as a little baby! Will you tell me stories of his life?"

As the first load swishes and the machines spin and my crayons fill the page with a line of candles, I hear some things I already know, and hear some things that are new to me.

"Well, you already know who is in Daddy's family. First Little Eleanor[4], who died when she was four years old, then Grace, then Daddy, then Madeline and later Ronald. His mother and father moved a lot. Daddy lived here on our property when he was a little boy and again later as a college student. Besides Colorado, they lived in Minnesota, Texas, Massachusetts, Vermont, Illinois, New York, Michigan, Maine, and Pennsylvania.[5] Grammie believed every child should have violin and piano lessons and they listened to classical music on the radio. Wherever they lived, Grampa was always in the church choir. The family loved to sing together: patriotic songs and hymns, the popular radio songs and songs they heard on records. Sometimes your Grampa was a teacher. Sometimes he was a translator or proofreader. Grammie was a kindergarten teacher until she had children. Then she taught Sunday School and directed Bible Pageants at the Seer-Church summer camp in Maine. She started a community library and wrote lots of letters. So Daddy always had reading, writing, music and going to one of the Seer-Church groups all his life, no matter where they moved."

"No wonder Daddy likes books! Grammie sends me a new book every birthday and Christmas. And she is a good storyteller, too," I add. I remember the stacks of papers in Grammie and Grampa's house. Unfinished projects, unwatered plants, untended cats, unmade beds, unwashed dishes. Reading was a job. Housework was an interruption.

I've finished the first row of ten candles. Now Mommy tells me about Daddy's teenage years.

"Your Daddy was very smart in school. He and Madeline both skipped two grades. That meant they were younger than the other students in high school, but they could do the same school work. He went to the Seer-Church high school and college. It was war-time. Daddy's classmates went off to fight in the war, but Daddy was too young. There were lots of girls but not enough boys to take them on dates, so Daddy had fun at dances and school outings with so many girls around. He also got to star in the musical plays. Daddy could sing an entire musical operetta by himself! They used to call him, 'The Professor of Trivia' because he knew so many things. The special books written by The Seer were very important to him. He also did odd jobs like any teenager: babysitting, cutting the lawn, painting houses and jobs to help out old people. Later he went back to Colorado College because the Seer-Church College didn't have the courses he needed to become a professor."

"Look, Mommy, I am drawing at the same speed you are talking! I'm done 20 candles just in time for you to tell me about when you and Daddy first met!"

"Daddy's best friend married my older sister. She asked me to be her Maid of Honour and Daddy was the groom's Best Man. The wedding preparations, rehearsal, ceremony and party afterward all brought us together. We got to know each other, date and have a very nice time together. In a few months he asked me to marry him and I said 'Yes.' My older sisters were all getting married and it was just the next thing to do. I was still nineteen years old, but that was quite an ordinary time to get married in the 1950s. Daddy was twenty-four. For our honeymoon we drove out from Pennsylvania to Colorado so I could see the property he loved so much and learn about where Daddy wanted to live. Both of us very much wanted to have a lot of children. So, here we are!"

"But, you like living here, too, don't you, Mommy?" I wonder what it was like for her to leave behind all of her family, familiar places and friends. I wonder if I will like it when I get married: to walk away from everything familiar so that my husband can live his dream. Maybe I will find a husband with a dream that matches my dream?

"Oh, yes, Dear, and I especially like to be a Mother no matter where I live," she interrupts the biography to make progress on the work of the day, moving the wet laundry from several machines to the dryers. She keeps out Daddy's shirts, my school dresses and the boys school shirts to iron. I continue colouring. She continues with the story. "First we travelled for three years. Daddy was a Bank Examiner. He went from one city to another and he entered the vaults to count all the money to make sure the records matched the actual count. It was great fun to travel. We drove from the east coast all the way to California and all kinds of places in-between. Then we settled down to have a family and lived in two places in Pennsylvania while Daddy finished some courses and started teaching college."

Now the Baby needs her. I have coloured 30 candles now. I can finish the last 6 candles with my own thoughts. I know how the rest of the story goes anyway. Because I am the oldest, I can remember the most.

* ** *** ****

"I am the First-Born Son of the First-Born Son of the First-Born Son! Can you say that seven times?"

Daddy was shaving. His striped pajamas, black wavy hair, thick eyeglasses, big nose and posture of confidence looked back at him from the small mirror above the bathroom sink. I was sitting on the toilet tank where he lifted me each morning, watching the predictable sequence: whip up the soapy lather in the china cup with the bristly brush, dab and smooth the white froth all over his stubbly chin, grimace this way and that to keep his cheeks, neck and upper lip as flat as possible while the scrape of the razor shaved off last night's growth.

"If the Church was a Monarchy, I'd be King!" His bold, grandiose exaggeration loudly proclaimed for all the world that he had a special position, ancestry, esteem, a place in the grand scheme of things, a sense of entitlement.

But wait. I've seen the family portrait. Daddy is the third child, born after two sisters. How can the third-born be the first-born? I am the first-born child in our family, but, the seven minutes between the first-born twin boy and the second is repeatedly reinforced. If our family was a Monarchy, I would be third in line... unless the next baby is a boy. That would have bumped me even lower on the scale.

It's only a comment, never intended to do harm, but it is a signal of an underlying hierarchy, a competition that I can never win, a struggle for attention and approval and significance that will constantly plague me.

"What is that red place on your neck, Daddy?" my observant eyes could see a large ouchy looking place just at the hair-line where Daddy's collar and tie would cover it when he was dressed.

"You gave that to me," he gave me a frowning sideways glance over his white foamy chin. Puzzled and alarmed I gasped. I would never try to hurt my Daddy. "You brought this infection home from the hospital when you were newborn. Your boil got better. I can't seem to get rid of mine."

And so, I was handed my script. Before I could tie my own shoes or button my own coat, I had been assigned a role. I was a girl: like my Mother, I would do domestic tasks. I was a descendant of clergy, professors and academics: I would be expected to achieve. I was an inconvenience: having brought Daddy this annoying skin condition he was having trouble eradicating. Although first-born, I was female and automatically, no matter what my in-born talents or future achievements: I was less important than the boys.

Before they could roll over or sit up, I was already jealous of my brothers, both of them, but especially the oldest. Oldest by seven minutes.

Other than that, life was perfect.

Daddy had finished his Masters Degree and was working on his PhD while I was a tot. The sound of the typewriter keys peck-peck-pecking was a sound of security and stability as I fell asleep in my crib. Now he was stepping forward in his career. And along came twin boys! What could be better than that?

Mother was a capable housewife with everything neat and tidy, nourishing meals, safe places to play, educational activities and outings, and of course, her piano playing. Although I was only fifteen months old when the twins arrived, I helped her by fetching the cloth diapers from the changing table upstairs to bring them to her in the living room. "Hold your hand on his tummy," she would say to me, passing on motherly skills, "so he won't roll off the couch." So I did.

We made a silly game when the boys were old enough to stand up and form their first words. With Mother's strong support, up on the dresser, first one, then the other looking at himself in the mirror, "Who's is that, James?" we would ask again and again. "Andrew!" he would answer. Then the other identical twin was hoisted up to see in the mirror. "Who is that, Andrew? Who do you see?" I held my breath, waiting. "James!" was the answer which kept Mommy and I laughing no matter how often we repeated the prank.

Employed as an assistant professor, Daddy moved us from an apartment in the hill country of Pennsylvania, into a house near the Bonnie Hills Church Community just outside of Philadelphia[6]. Sometimes we took the train into the city to see where he was teaching. Baby Julie arrived when I was just past three years old. At that time, Daddy's sleep was disturbed by dreams of endless doors opening to hallways branching off into alcoves with more doors. In his dreams he was continually finding more babies who needed clean diapers, a bottle, comfort, a song, or rocking, or another blanket. And no wonder. While his sister was hospitalized for six months, the two youngest cousins came to stay. Six children under five years old was a challenge every day and all night. Mommy relied on me to help fetch, deliver messages, tell her what happened when one of the little ones was crying, keep watch (more than play) in the backyard, stand on guard to keep the other five children safe. "Set a good example." "You're the oldest." "What happened?" Another role was assigned me: Reporter.

When I turned five, at last, Daddy's lifelong dream came true. All of the pieces were fitting together. Daddy was accepted for a position as Assistant Professor at Colorado College, his Alma Mater. He already owned 52 acres of land near his childhood home that he bought from his Uncle Allan for $300. When we first arrived, Uncle Allan's old three-room cabin was sufficient. Five people shared one bedroom with Mommy and Daddy's big bed, bunk beds and a cot. One of the twins slept on another cot in the living room. The wood stove in the living room kept us warm, although there was only crumpled-up newspaper in the walls for insulation. The kitchen had a wood cook stove, a pantry and a big, white enamel sink. Mommy gave us baths in the sink when Daddy brought 5-gallon metal jerry-cans full of water from a spring. Each room had a window and a string to pull to turn on the light bulb. Mommy could sweep right out the door and off the front porch. We had a rain barrel, an out house and a wood shed.

Two years later, Daddy engaged an architect to design a house for us. That's when my youngest sister, Carol, was born. It was like Daddy was on the top of a mountain. His achievements and goals were fulfilled: smiling wife, lovely home, well-behaved children, and a view of Pikes Peak. Camera at the ready, Daddy frequently took pictures of our family. Life was 'Picture Perfect'! It was a lot to accomplish in just less than ten years of marriage. I felt a deep sense of family loyalty and security.

* ** *** ****

One-by-one the dryers stop and warm laundry, neatly folded and stacked into the baskets is loaded into the back of the van. Carol lays in a little nest on the floor. We're hungry for lunch. We have to hurry home. I must leave again this afternoon for my ballet lesson at the college.

But our arrival home did not go smoothly.

When we pull up the steep driveway, Rex announces our arrival. We can see the boys and Julie playing in the snow. For a minute I wish I had stayed home. The fort is so much fun to play in. Daddy helped us make it with the branches from the Christmas tree. When we searched all over our property for the perfect tree to fit right up to the second story balcony, it was so exciting to drag it home, shove it through the open glass sliding doors and decorate it. When it was time to take it down, the needles were dry and falling off so easily. So, Daddy brought a saw inside and sawed off the branches one-by-one. The fort we made is up against the dirt bank that was dug out for the driveway approaching the new house. It is so much fun to pretend to be pirates, or pioneers, or robbers, or orphans.

But, I see the look on Mommy's face. Somebody is in trouble.

"Are you finished cleaning your room?" Mommy asks.

"Daddy said we could go outside," comes the reply.

Keeping an eye on their play through the sliding glass doorway, Daddy has the table covered with students' papers he is grading. As I pass the kitchen door, I can see open bread bags, lids off the peanut butter and jam jars, coffee mugs and milk glasses here and there. The kitchen counters look like a whole troop of monkeys had recently had a field day.

The jolly fun the younger ones had while we were gone was immediately chilled by Mommy's icy glare.

"And the ham! I was saving that for your birthday dinner!" she tried to control her voice so the Baby would not be startled awake.

"I only made one sandwich," Daddy frowned.

Taking control of the situation, Mommy calls the trio inside to hang up their wet snow pants and march upstairs to get those rooms clean. Saturday was always Room Cleaning Day. Daddy unloads the laundry while Mommy finds enough counter space to make a sandwich and apple for me to eat while Daddy drives the van down the two-lane road through narrow Ute Pass. Daddy can do more work in his office at the college during the time I am on the same campus at my ballet lesson. As we leave, Mommy is rolling up her sleeves to get the kitchen put back together. I grab the bag with my leotards and ballet slippers and we are off.

* ** *** ****

The noisy changing room filled with chattering girls is a contrast to the quiet of the orderly studio. The long room has a wooden floor, a wall of windows, two walls with ballet exercise barres and one wall of mirrors. The piano and resin box are in the corner. Black leotards, pink tights, black slippers unify the girls.

Mrs. Gray is teaching us the beginning exercises for ballet: stretches, barre work, positions, porte de bras, and how to turn, leap and curtsy. Part of each class is an introduction to folk dances and there is always time for creative movement. Our class is making a story about 'Frost Fairies.' We dip our paint brushes into our paint pots and then reach and twist, turn and leap, bend and twirl to pretend to paint the frosty patterns on leaves and windows. Soon we will perform on stage. For my eighth birthday, Daddy took me to see 'Kismet' on this same stage. Someday I hope to dance a part in the annual Christmas production of the 'Nutcracker.'

It is almost dark by the time we get home. The family is quiet, orderly, not wanting to repeat the strain of the first reunion this morning. Mommy slices bread and grills open-face cheese sandwiches under the broiler. Tomato soup and tall glasses of milk complete the supper.

It's bath night. Mommy scrubs and shampoos Julie and I, wraps us in towels and calls the boys to come and wash in the same shallow water. Nobody wants the well to go dry, so this is the way we do it. Sometimes Daddy gives us baths. Mommy scrubs hard like Oma. Daddy kind of splashes and dabs, like Grammie.

While I put on my brand-clean PJs, and watch after Baby Carol, I remember the time before the baby was born when Mommy let me stay up later than the others. She wanted to tell me something special.

* ** *** ****

Mommy was pregnant with 'Baby Dear' and before she told the younger ones, she had a very gentle conversation with me in the kitchen at the telephone desk.

"When a husband loves his wife very much the Lord makes it possible for them to help Him make a new baby!" She told me. "Once each month, the wife's womb prepares a soft nest inside in hopes of a new baby, but if one does not begin to grow, then the womb washes and empties to be ready to begin again."

She told me that the "husband loves his wife so much that he wants to give her the best gift of all, his seeds, to make the baby grow." She drew very accurate pictures of both male and female parts with the correct words as she was explaining. "When it is time, the seeds leave the husband and travel up the wife's birth canal so the baby can grow safe and warm in the mother's womb. Everything has to be just right so the Lord can make the new baby grow. That's why every person is new and different and precious and carefully made."

She showed me the newly published 'Time Life' photos of the embryo and foetus[7].

Deep inside my heart I knew that is a was kind, good, sweet and honorable thing for a husband to give to his wife in this way. I remember being full of gladness and wonder that this potential was within me. I felt pleased that someday I, too, would marry, participate in this miracle and conceive, grow and give birth to a child.

* ** *** ****

On Saturday after supper, Daddy lays out newspaper and gets the shoe polish box out. We all bring him our school shoes and church shoes and he rubs the black or brown paste over any scuffs and then buffs them with a soft rag.

Everyone picks out their church clothes. Mommy already put clean sheets on every bed. The whole world seems clean after our baths, fresh sheets, tidy bedrooms. All is in order. It is

Saturday night. The only way to gain a day of rest for Sunday, is to finish all of the work on Saturday.

Daddy's voice reading tonight is a monotonous drone and I soon fall asleep after this busy day.

Sometime during the night I hear crying and blink my eyes from the bright lights. Julie has sore legs again. Daddy has the ointment that makes muscles warm. She cries and he comforts her. She cries and he soothes her. From across the room I feel sorry for myself, to be awakened by this ruckus. I feel my heart squeeze tight. I'm thinking she's just doing it for attention like all the other special attention she gets. 'I have a sore throat'... so she gets cherry lozenges. 'I feel car sick'... so she gets the seat by the window. 'Wait for me'... so she gets carried. I turn away and shut my mouth and my eyes. But I still smell it. The ointment must be working, or the massage Daddy has been rubbing and rubbing on her legs is helping. She is quiet, hugs Daddy and he shuts off the light.

Sunday, January 23

Sunday morning is all about getting ready to go to church. Mommy has ironed our clothes. Daddy has polished our shoes. The breakfast is ready. The house is tidy. Mommy had curlers in her hair last night. I entertain Baby Carol on Mommy and Daddy's big bed while Mommy brushes her hair-do, pulls on her girdle, fastens the garters to her stockings, and zips up her Sunday dress. Her Sunday coat has a real fur collar.

The boys have to be inspected: shirts tucked in, no missing belt-loops, cowboy-style bolo necktie, hair slicked down. Daddy looks trim, the same as every day, with his suit and tie. Julie and I stand still while Mommy brushes and braids our hair. Julie's curls are all in a tangle from squirming last night while her legs hurt. Mommy forgot to use the creme rinse so now there is a fuss and coaxing, whining and pleading to get the job done. Julie is wearing my old blue Sunday dress and I have a green one from my older cousin.

At last we are away. The highway down Ute Pass weaves and winds beside Fountain Creek. The winter roads and sky are clear. When we arrive at the church, Mommy settles Baby Carol in the nursery. She and Daddy are in the choir today. I lead my brothers and sister to the front row. Mommy told me to sit there so she can keep an eye on us. But she can't see that James and Andrew are playing tic-tac-toe on their bulletins! I nudge and frown. But they keep it up. Next time I should sit between them. Julie needs to go to the bathroom. I blush as I lead her down the aisle and return. I can read the words of the songs in heavy red the hymn book, but not the others.

It's hard to pay attention to the minister and look after everything else. But the little old ladies come up and make a fuss over us after the service. "The children are so well behaved," they say. Cookies and friends and the grown-ups talking are next. Then we drive all the way back home.

In the summertime we often change into play clothes before we leave the church. Mommy packs a picnic and Daddy takes us to the Garden of the Gods. Climbing the rocks, hearing about his college days, exploring the pathways, finding deer tracks, wondering what it was like for the Indians to live here, and helping Mommy with the picnic are all part of a summertime Colorado Sunday.

But, in the wintertime we just drive through the park, slowly, the familiar formations have features usually unseen which are now outlined with snow.

* ** *** ****

Family outings! That gives me another idea for the birthday card. I can draw 36 balloons and think of the many places Daddy has taken us: swimming and sledding, skating and hiking, under the highway through the culvert to explore the rest of our property, wade in the creek, to the top of Bald Faced Mountain, to the zoo, parades, fair grounds and movies, to the top of Pikes Peak and the Empire State Building. He came to school to hear me recite a long poem and also heard the boys give their Science Fair presentations. He takes us to the bus stop and always brings a camera along to capture our childhood adventures, golden moments, preserving memories.

* ** *** ****

Mommy left the timer on to heat the oven and the roast beef is ready when we arrive home. The brown, onion-rich smell fills the house. Quickly she turns on the burners to bring the potatoes to a boil. Frozen mixed vegetables fill another pot. The peas, carrots, green beans, corn and lima beans make a colourful combination. Everyone changes out of their Sunday clothes and comes to the table.

Sunday dinner. Then a long afternoon of free time. Sometimes Daddy teaches us how to play 'Careers.' He has to read all the cards for the little ones. Sometimes he teaches us how to play Chess. He has to coach us and show us how to plan good moves. Sometimes Mommy gets out a puzzle. But today, I'm eager to finish the birthday card project. So, I head back up to my closet art studio.

I plan to use all eight colours to draw the balloons. Well, maybe not the brown and black. Who ever heard of a black or brown balloon?

Red makes me think of Valentines and Christmas poinsettias and visiting Santa when Daddy took us to the park called 'The

North Pole, Colorado,' to see the reindeer, feed the goats, ride on the Ferris Wheel and watch the magic show. White reminds me of the icy North Pole in the middle of the park where the elves and storybook characters lined up so Daddy could take our picture. Yellow is the colour of my Flower Fairy ballet dress that Mommy made last year with her sewing machine. Daddy took my picture. Orange, of course, is the colour of Jack-o-Lanterns. Daddy drives us through the streets of the nearby town with our costumes on so we can shout 'Trick-or-Treat.' Mommy stays home to pass out goodies.

The green balloons represent the forest all around us. Daddy takes the family for hikes among the evergreen cloaked mountains. We've seen crags and cascades, steep trails and grasslands, dry gullies and soggy lowlands. Mommy hasn't been coming on the hikes since she had the Baby.

* ** *** ****

Suddenly I have a tight feeling in my tummy. The last hike we went on was not so fun. Mommy stayed home to rest with the new Baby. It was in the fall before the snow. Daddy took us four kids on a rock climbing hike. Mommy has a rule: "If you can't get up by yourself, then you can't get down by yourself. So I am not going to lift you." But Daddy started to lift up little Julie, then each of the twins. But I stepped back. "No, Daddy. Mommy has a rule. I don't want you to lift me up." It's very important to me that I obey my Mother, especially when she cannot see me. He tried to convince me that it was alright, but I refused.

He got kind of mad at me when I kept saying, "Mommy said, 'No'!" For a moment it seemed like he didn't see me, but in his frustration, he saw his wife saying 'No' to him.

I'm just a kid! I don't know what to do! It's too scary!

Finally, he got fed up. "What is *wrong* with you?" He climbed up himself and frowned down at me. "Well then, you can wait here or go back to the van!" And they were out of sight.

At first I felt kind of lonely and sorry for myself. It was an impossible problem to solve. If I can't do the thing I have to do, what shall I do? Can I figure this out some other way? I tried to find another way that I could climb up by myself. I noticed a shelf-like place. I thought I might be able to go across and then up, instead of the steep way that Daddy had taken with my brothers and sister. With my back against the rock wall, moving cautiously to the right, I started to take side-steps out along the shelf. But the ledge began to get narrow. And the rock was not solid. It crumbled. My footing was getting worse, but I thought I was almost across. If I could just slide a few more steps the ledge would open up again. And then I stopped.

The gravel was like marbles under my feet. The ledge was no longer wide enough for my feet. My hands were pressed against the rock behind me. The way back looked very far. The distance to the grassy pathway below me was very dangerous.

I don't know how long I stayed there. I was really scared that I would slip and fall. I wondered if I would die. Or be so badly broken. Or maybe the others would never find me. Somehow I had the idea that I could ask God for help, or at least look over my life and ask forgiveness in case I died, or say to God, 'If You let me live...'

I said the Lord's Prayer. I tried to remember each of the Ten Commandments. Had I lied? Had I stolen? Had I broken the Sabbath Day? Or taken the Lord's name in vain? "Dear Lord, I do not want to disobey You. If I ever have, I am sorry. Please forgive me so I can go to Heaven." I didn't know anybody in Heaven. My Aunt Eleanor died when she was only four years old! Opa died when I was a baby! I believed that little children went to Heaven, but I was pretty big. Old enough to 'know better.' So I might not be good enough! What if I went to Hell because I did not obey my Daddy? But if I did let him lift me, then I would not be obedient to my Mommy! Have I honoured my father and my mother? Quite clearly: no. I had to pick one or the other.

I was terribly stuck.

Then a man came. He was below me. He saw me. He looked up for a long time. I was quiet. He didn't speak. From where he was it looked like I was OK, that the shelf was a good place to be. I was so scared that I might fall. Scared to go back. Impossible to go forward. But now, even more scared of this stranger. I waited. He left.

Finally I decided: I have asked God to take care of me, so what ever happens, He is the One who is making it turn out how ever it turns out.

Slowly, one little shift at a time. I eased my way to the left, back the way I came. It felt like it took hours. But I made it back to a pathway. I climbed back down and got into the van. I locked the door. My heart was pounding. I was scared and mad and thankful and lonely and embarrassed all at the same time. I had never been alone like this and so confused. So abandoned.

It wasn't long before I could hear and then see the rest of the family. Happy voices. Fun time. As my siblings clamoured into the van, Daddy looked at me with this strange expression on his face, but I didn't look up. "I hope you're satisfied." He said. And we went home.

I wanted to run into his arms. I wanted him to know how scared I was, how dangerous it was, how alone I was. I wanted to be protected and valued and respected for being obedient to Mommy. But, my mouth stayed closed. My eyes down.

Usually after an outing I tell Mommy all about it. She missed the fun! If I describe everything then she would still be included. But this time, I said nothing. I never told anyone about that day.

* ** *** ****

Maybe I should draw a black balloon? But then, if I do, someone might ask me why...and then I would have to remember and tell about that frightening day. I think I would rather stuff the memory back down inside and never talk about it. It might seem small. They might laugh at me. I might have to stay home next time. I might get Daddy into trouble with Mommy. The others might say it never happened that way. No, I can't do it. 'The Day on the Cliff' is my own, personal story. It doesn't fit with the rest of my life. It is all too mixed up inside me. Scrambled, mismatched pieces that just won't fit.

I'm only eight years old! I can't figure this out.

* ** *** ****

Looking back, fifty years later, now that I have been pregnant, taken kids on hikes, made rules, felt tensions between myself and my husband as we say 'yes' and 'no' to our children, I realize a few things that I had no way of knowing as a child. First of all: a pregnant or newly postpartum woman should not be lifting the four older children. Secondly: it is appropriate for Mothers to say, “Be careful!” and Dads to say, “Let's do it!” That is part of the blessing of having both parents. There is a 'sweet spot' of taking risks... safely. Thirdly: I can see how Daddy was stuck that day, the same way I was. Three children are up ahead. One child is now behind. What to do? He had to solve a problem, too.

We all get stuck. We all have 'I can't - I have to' problems to solve. No one knows the future. So, we take a step. Nobody had dark motives. Each person did what they did. Gladly, everyone got home.

* ** *** ****

I think I need to take a break from drawing for awhile. I count. There are 28 balloons so far. I'm almost done. I go out of my creative, cozy privacy to see what is happening with the rest of the family.

The boys have their door shut. Daddy has those college papers on the table again. Carol is sleeping in her crib. In Mommy and Daddy's room I hear quiet voices and I knock on the door. "Don't come in!" Julie's voice sounds alarmed. "I'm making Daddy's birthday present!" Mommy is helping her.

So, I go back upstairs to finish drawing. But it doesn't feel as much fun anymore.

Blue. The Colorado sky is blue. The wild columbine are blue.
Brown is OK after all. It is the colour of my Brownie uniform.
Purple! I start to hum.

O beautiful for spacious skies, for amber waves of grain,
for purple mountain majesty, above the fruited plain! [8]

Daddy told me that the lady who wrote this national anthem was inspired when she stood at the top of Pikes Peak and looked down over the scene. I've been there. I saw the sign with the words on it. We sing this song often at school after we say the Pledge of Allegiance every morning. I love being on the top of Pikes Peak. I can see my school, the highway, our house. And, when I am on the school bus, or going to church, I can see Pikes Peak. It's kind of like God. He can see you where ever you go. You can know He is nearby where ever you go. It feels safe.

Mommy's voice calls upstairs to everyone. "It's almost 5:30. Time for 'Lassie'! Put your PJs on!"

Everyone scrambles cheerfully and arrives in the playroom for this once-a-week TV program. Lassie, the beautiful, fluffy collie, will certainly find the lost child, or pull the heavy branches off the little lamb, or lead the pony home, or find her way through the storm, or bark a signal to bring help to the old man up on the hill. At the end, when the music plays and all is well, Lassie sits and raises a paw. "Come on, Julie!" I help her reach up. Julie loves to pet and stroke the picture of Lassie and say, "Good girl, Lassie! Shake a paw!" It is pretend, but I like to do it, too.

Next comes 'Walt Disney.' Tinker Bell signals the start of the show with her fancy flight and magic wand sprinkling pixie dust. Sometimes Mr. Disney introduces the program. Sometimes we see amazing views of Nature, wild animals or birds or funny little baby animals. Sometimes it is cartoons of Mickey Mouse and Donald Duck or a two-part movie like 'Lady and the Tramp.' Sometimes we get to see how Mr. Disney and his workers make the drawings, rehearse the songs, or use the cameras.

Mommy seems to have left the room. Then I hear her footsteps on the stairs. Look! She has a tray with bowls, spoons, Cheerios and a jug of milk. We get to eat supper in front of the TV! "Thank-you, Mommy!" we all chime together. After cereal comes popcorn! "Thank-you, Mommy!"

Mommy has taken the Baby downstairs. I can hear her washing up in the kitchen.

It's bedtime. And we've had enough stories from the TV. So, instead of reading, Daddy is going to sing. That gives me another idea. It would be easy to draw 36 music notes for his birthday card. Then there will be something on each page and I'll be done.

Daddy lies down on each bed with the person who requests the next song.

James asks for a silly campfire song and Daddy belts it out. It's not exactly a soothing bedtime composition.

Oh, Johnny Rebeck, how could you be so mean.
I told you you'd be sorry for inventing that machine.
Now all the neighbours cats and dogs
will never more be seen.
They've all been ground to sausages in
Johnny Rebeck's machine.[9]

Andrew asks for the song in the operetta that Daddy performed on stage when he was in college. It's a great long tongue twister. There's a solo and then the chorus repeats the same line. Daddy makes a funny high falsetto voice when there are ladies singing.

I polished up the handle so perfectly
that now I am the ruler of the Queen's Navy.[10]

Julie's turn to make a request. "Daddy, sing the one about the river."

"You mean, *Old Man River* or *Deep River* or *Michael Row the Boat Ashore* or *Swanee River* or *Down by the Riverside* which one? There are a lot of songs about rivers, Honey."

"The sad one, Daddy," Julie tries to explain. "The lonely one."

"Can you sing part of it, Honey, or remember a few more words?" Daddy is puzzled. He knows so many songs.

"It has a daughter... and a long time... and they go across the wide muzoorie," she fumbles to recall.

"She means 'Shenandoah,' Daddy. But it always makes her cry," I offer.

Daddy's voice fills the house and we are transported to long ago and far away, scenes of river rafts, pioneers, and parting from loved ones. Always, always, the river flows on. Leaving home. Seeking new lands. This is how America came to be. We are a part of this story.

Oh, Shenandoah, I long to see you,
Away you rolling river,
Oh Shenandoah, I long to see you.
Away, we're bound away, 'cross the wide Missouri.[11]

"Why do you want this one, Honey, if it makes you cry?" Daddy is holding her and rocking her gently.

"I don't know," she sniffles, "I just do."

"It's my turn, Daddy, but you can stay with her," I don't want to miss my opportunity. And so the final song for the night begins.

There were ninety and nine that were safely laid
In the shelter of the fold;
But one was lost on the hills away,
Far far from the gates of gold.
Away on the mountains wild and bare;
Away from the tender Shepherd's care.

"Lord, Thou hast here Thy ninety and nine;
Are they not enough for Thee?"
But the Shepherd made answer:
"One of Mine has wandered away from Me."
Far out in the desert He heard its cry;
Fainting and helpless and ready to die.

Then all through the mountains, thunder-riv'n,
And up from the rocky steep,
There arose a glad cry to the gate of heav'n,
"Rejoice! I have found My sheep!"
And the angels echoed around the throne,
"Rejoice, for the Lord brings back His own!"[12]

Now it's my turn to wipe away a few tears.

* ** *** ****

Lights. Voices. Someone is crying. Someone is helping.

I rub my eyes to shelter them from the bright light. "Mommy, what's wrong?"

"Go back to bed, Dear. I just have to change the sheets and give your brother some dry pajamas. Everything is OK."

Monday, January 24

Monday. Button up my dress. Breakfast. School bus.

Attendance. Pledge of Allegiance. Sing together.

My country 'tis of thee, sweet land of liberty of thee I sing.[13]

In the morning we have regular classes: reading, writing, spelling, math.

This week I am the Monitor. I wear an orange sash and belt. I stand beside the door to ring the brass bell for recess and lunch.

In the afternoon we might have science or social studies or art.

Today, Mrs. Thompson is reading aloud to the whole class from 'Little House in the Big Woods,' by Laura Ingalls Wilder.

It's a tradition. She reads it to her Grade 3 class every year. I love to hear about the food that Pa and Ma grow, hunt, gather and preserve for the winter. I love to hear about Ma teaching Laura and Mary their school lessons. I love the Saturday night baths and quiet Sunday of rest that Ma insists on, even though they live far from a town or church. I love the way Ma and Pa respect each other, do their work, relax in the evening, share child rearing.

I wonder if I could do those things someday? I love the mountains, but, I'll need to marry a man who knows about tools. Daddy rented a chain saw to cut our firewood and returned it to the store when the teeth got dull. My husband will have to know how to fix things.

I also love hearing Mrs. Thompson read about Annie Sullivan and Helen Keller. I wonder if I will be able to help children learn someday?

I know eight years old is pretty young, but there are so many times I feel like I know 'what I want to be when I grow up' so I think I should pay attention, listen, learn, collect, remember.

The school day is over. Time to bundle up for the trip home. I hope no one will notice. Wearing my school shoes, I have to slide my foot into a plastic bread bag, then into my leaky boot. Line up for the bus. Walk with my brothers up the long driveway. Winter is almost over. I'm glad. The back of my legs have a sore, red, chapped line where the rubber boots rub against my bare skin when my socks slide down inside my boots when I walk.

Home.

I hurry to finish. Tomorrow is Daddy's birthday! Drawing the music notes goes fast. Just a round dot and a stick pointing up. All black. Nothing much. But still, important. Daddy has so many records he likes to play on the stereo: Mozart and Beethoven, musical plays and patriotic songs, funny and sacred, Christmas for church and Christmas for fun. He sings in the shower. He sings while he's shaving. He sings in the car. He sings while we hike. He sings in church. He sings at bedtime. Yes, this is the last page of the birthday book. I hope it will make him smile.

It's time for supper, but, Daddy's not home yet. We have supper without him. Sometimes he's late. Is he still working? Did he have a meeting? Or appointment? If he knew he'd be late while he was still in his office, then he would use the black dial telephone on his desk to let Mommy know. But maybe there is a problem on the way home? Of course he can't contact us if he's in the car. Is there a delay on the highway? Was there heavy snowfall? Or a truck blocking the lane? Or, worst of all: could it be that Daddy is hurt? Mommy seems anxious. My brothers and sister try to stay quiet.

Chores. Homework. No family worship. Daddy's not here to be the leader. Mommy coaches us as we learn a new memory verse. "Thy Word is a lamp unto my feet and a light unto my path." Psalm 119:105. It means that when you are making a decision and you aren't sure what to do, you can remember something you learned from the Word and then you'll know what is right and wrong. The Lord will help you as you go along in your life if you listen for His guidance. Mommy says that the whole reason she wants us to learn how to read is so that we can read the Word for ourselves to be strong in what we believe.

It's bedtime. Daddy is still not here to read or sing to us. Mommy isn't familiar with Mark Twain, can't do the voices, hasn't been following the story line. We look at her expectantly.

"Will you read us a story?" Julie asks.

She sorts through the stack of library books and picks one. She knows everyone will enjoy the marvelous stories and illustrations by Bill Peet. Which one did she bring home for us this time? We've already read 'Huge Harold' the overgrown rabbit who helps the neighbours. 'Hubert's Hair Raising Adventure' was about the poor lion who had his mane scorched off and he wanted to grow a new, full mane. Then there was the circus performance of 'Chester the Worldly Pig.' And who could forget the Griffin that hatched out of 'The Pinkish-Purplish-Bluish Egg'! Tonight is the newly published 'Farewell to Shady Glade'[14] featuring a posse of little forest folk who realize that the nearby sound of engines comes from giant machinery which will soon crush their home! Stow-aways on the train, they pass through cities, farms, prairies and mountains and finally see the perfect place to hop off and call home. Ecological awareness is a new topic. The 1960s is a time of ever-expanding urban sprawl. I want to be one of the people who takes care of the Earth.

Squeezed tightly on the sofa so we can all see the pictures, we enjoy Mommy's voice, the clever illustrations, the teamwork of the squirrels, rabbits, frogs, the leadership of the raccoon. Story time is soon over.

"Mommy, I don't think I can go to sleep without music," I quietly ask.

"I can't sing all of those songs your Daddy knows," she answers.

"Could you play the piano?" I suggest.

"How about this," she is inspired. Since everything is different tonight, it might as well be fun! "If you each take turns looking after Baby Carol, I will play the piano while you take turns getting your PJ's on, brush your teeth and get ready for bed. How's that?"

"Yay!" Four faces grin. Four voices shout in unison.

"You two girls stay and help first. Julie, you get to pick the first song!"

Mommy has a book of children's songs from her sister, Anna. They are not the usual British Nursery Rhymes. They're from Holland. "I like *Ponto* best!" Julie announces. *Ponto* is a poor old doggy. His tail gets stuck to the ice, but a clever boy comes to the rescue.

My turn. "That was so short! Please, my choice is for you to play the other ones in that book, too." So Mommy adds the other favourites, *Tiny man what are you doing at my door?* and also *The stork has brought a little brother into our house today.* Julie claps her hands and dances to entertain Baby Carol. I am allowed to hold her, so I pick up the Baby and rock her gently on my lap while Mommy plays, *All the ducks are swimming in the water fol-de-rol-de-rol-do.*[15]

Now the boys come tromping down the stairs, washed and dressed for bed. Julie and I head up, wanting to hurry and return.

"We'd like *Golliwog's Cake Walk*!"[16] they boldly proclaim.

The boys perform: prancing, marching, spinning, exaggerating the long-legged tugging and pulling while walking on top of a sticky cake. They play peek-a-boo with Baby Carol during the quiet parts. Their jumping stunts are still happening by the time I return to the living room.

Now Mommy props the baby so she won't roll of the sofa while she comes upstairs to tuck us in. "Oldest to youngest!" I make the first bid.

"Put your hands up!" she commands while I lie on my back. She pulls the sheets and blankets up over my face. "Now: suddenly, put your hands down," and the covers fold neatly across my chest. "Now I'm going to tuck you in as snug as a bug in a rug!" and she tightly tucks in the blankets on both sides of my bed so I can hardly even move! It is her special way. It feels good to be wrapped up tightly. I hear the others chuckle and squeal as she gives the same commands, then blows kisses once more before her soft footsteps return down the wooden stairs.

The Baby must have dozed off.

Beautiful, familiar, soothing music drifts into our ears and hearts and off we go to dreamland. I try to stay awake and savour every note.[17] But, eyelids close and ears can no longer concentrate, although the music resonates for many more minutes.

* ** *** ****

Headlights approach up the driveway. The dog barks. Daddy's home. Far away, I hear and turn in my sleep, glad he's home safe. Sleep returns.

* ** *** ****

Again, crying in the night. It's not the Baby calling to be changed and fed. It's not my sister, sleeping so still across the room. It's not upstairs at all. It's coming from the vent under my bed.

Is it Mommy's voice? I wonder if I should go downstairs? But then I remember that Daddy is home. I wonder. Did Daddy come home late with bad news? Is there a problem with money? Or Daddy's job? Is Mommy unhappy to live here? Are we going to move again? Is the Baby sick? Or someone else? Is there bad news from a relative?

But Daddy's voice does not sound calm, comforting, or reassuring like he was when Julie was crying. His voice sounds angry, like that day on the hike when I said, 'No' to him. Mommy's voice does not sound like sad crying. Her voice sounds like how I felt when he left me alone that day. I wonder if he told her what I did? I wonder if this is all my fault?

My two little sisters are soundly sleeping. My brothers' bedroom is way over on the other side of the house. None of them can hear this sound. I feel very alone. What is happening? There is no way for me to know.

Alone. I curl up tight and bring the blankets up over my head. I scratch the pillow near my ear so I can hear the scratching sound more loudly than the voices. I don't know what the trouble is. I don't know what to do. Grown-ups know what to do.

Sleep returns.

Tuesday, January 25

"Happy Birthday, Daddy!" one by one each morning voice conveys the greeting.

Mommy always makes pancakes for Birthday Breakfast. She makes them in the shape of the Birthday Boy or Girl's initial. Backwards! So when she flips them, they are the right way 'round. But this morning the routines and voices and coffee and pancakes and lunch boxes and boots all jumble together.

Daddy goes to start the van, but I notice that Mommy did not look at him and he did not give her a good-bye kiss. Since no one else heard what I heard, no one else can see what I see. My eyes and ears feel very large. My mouth is tightly shut. I wait, but neither of them speak to me. I guess I'm not the one in trouble.

The boys can't figure out which boot belongs to which boy, or on which foot. Julie wants another pancake. The Baby is whimpering about something. My coat sleeve is turned inside out.

But, somehow we all get to where we're going.

* ** *** ****

When we get home after school, the smell of the baked ham and sweet potatoes welcomes us. Mommy put a special cloth on the table and I see the traditional glass plate with the birthday cake on the counter. Julie has an apron tied on. She's standing on a chair putting little pinches of coloured sprinkles on the cake.

I hurry upstairs to my art studio. I just have to write 'Happy Birthday' on the cover, staple the pages together and then sign my name at the back of the birthday book.

"I love you, Daddy. From Eleanor" is what I had planned to write. But I hesitate. There are other feelings now, too. I don't know what to call them. His frowns, me feeling alone, his shouting and me feeling unimportant. The unhappy voices in the night. It seems impossible not to say, "I love you" but if I do, it also feels kind of fake. Right now, my heart feels like a closed gate.

"To: Daddy

From: Eleanor"

That will do.

"Supper's ready!"

It is a delicious feast. There are second helpings. Daddy slices more meat. Mommy smiles when we say, "Please" and "Thank-you."

In the kitchen, I hear her strike the match and James turns off the lights. Wow! 36 candles is a lot of candles! Julie has a big smile and rosy cheeks as we all sing "Happy Birthday." She made Daddy a card with colourful x's and o's. James and Andrew cut a slit in the side of a round oatmeal box and covered it with pink paper and drew a face to make a piggy bank. I made the birthday booklet. And Mommy made the feast and cake.

"Another trip around the sun!" Daddy announces. "Now I'm more than half way to 70!"

Yipes! I look around the table at Baby Carol, active Julie, clever James and Andrew, talented Mommy, academic Daddy, even me...Where will we all be when another 10-20-30-36 years go by?

REFLECTIONS

Necessary conditions for a healthy relationship:

- Congruence – inner feelings match outward display; genuineness.
- Unconditional positive regard – acceptance of the other person is not contingent on performance.
- Empathetic understanding – temporarily entering into another's world without prejudice; non-judgmental listening.

—*Carl Rogers*

Chapter 2
Monday, January 5, 1981
Twin Brothers: Competition

> One can choose to go back towards safety
> or forward towards growth.
> Growth must be chosen again and again;
> fear must be overcome again and again.
> —*Maslow*

* ** *** ****

3:00am

I am in limbo: neither 'here' nor 'there.'

It is neither morning, nor night. I am neither a self-sufficient adult, nor a dependent child. I celebrate having everything I ever hoped for and at the same time I strain while enduring tremendous loss. I have returned to my childhood home, but soon my family will scatter. Since 1978, I have my own precious husband, but right now there are 3000 miles between us. A new generation has begun with our new baby daughter, just as my parents' marriage crumbles apart. I am safe and secure, warm and well provided for here in Ontario, while my own tiny log cabin in the woods in British Columbia is too isolated and cold for me to stay with the baby. I am surrounded by urban sprawl and the hurried pace of the city, while my husband is alone in the silent mountain wilderness.

Christmas? New Years? Celebrations? It feels more like heavy, dark, dreary sadness.

I'm awake in the wee hours of the morning to take care of my baby, Elise. Today she is exactly six months old. Today we have been here in Ontario for exactly one month. Today my sisters and brothers will start back to school. Today my twin brothers will turn 22 years old. Today, as she always does on this date, my Mother will take down the Christmas tree. Today my Dad, who has been living alone, will be invited to come for birthday cake.

That is a lot to think about all at once!

It is 3:00 in the morning here, midnight where my husband, Kevin, is in British Columbia. Right now he is outside at work on the railroad as Night Patrolman. No matter how low the temperature or how high the snow, from 11:00pm until 7:00am he pedals a 3-wheel rail bike, cycling along the tracks, through the wintery darkness, past hazardous rock cuts, beside the rushing river, through a narrow gorge, protecting two scheduled passenger trains. With a kerosene lamp swinging from the handlebars, his lunch and 2-way radio in the basket, his layers of clothing, face mask and parka giving some semblance of shelter, he makes his way first north in front of the east-bound passenger train, waits an hour or two in the warm-up shack, glad of the propane furnace, then plunges back into the frigid dark to pedal south to protect the west-bound passenger train.

Drenching rain, swirling mosquitoes, bitter cold do not keep him away from his duty to go in front of the oncoming train looking for avalanche, rock or mud slides, fallen trees, any defect in the rail, high water or a wash out. Moose, bear, coyote as well as smaller forest folk have crossed his path.

I can hardly allow myself to think of it! The steady income that this job provides, his sense of satisfaction to work alone, the adventure of it all, these are the things he likes about the position. Shooting stars, Aurora Borealis, ducklings following their mother, salamanders, bear cubs, waterfalls, the changing seasons, soaring eagles, these are the perks of the job. Every bite of food I eat, every drop of gas for the truck, every piece of clothing I wear are paid for by my husband's efforts. Having a steady income is a huge step forward after that first year as newlyweds, when we built our cabin only to have winter plunge us into bitter cold, which seized up the engine of our VW van resulting in unemployment, hunger and isolation.

* ** *** ****

Kevin and I were married in June, 1978, in southern Ontario, where I was raised in the Arbor Vale Church Community. About 40 families built homes near the Seer-Church and School. By limiting contact with other religions, educating the young, emphasizing expected behaviour, and encouraging young adults to marry within the Community, it was hoped that the next generation would accept the Teachings and The Church would grow and flourish. When curious neighbours asked, “What are your plans?” I gave them all the same answer, “I want to get married, go out west, build a log cabin, raise a family, teach our children about the Lord, volunteer in my community and then write a book about it!” And so we did! The outdoor daisy filled wedding, the VW van set up for camping, the trek across the vast Canadian landscape, the search for land, the welcome and help from new neighbours, the income from my waitressing job, the challenges of building a dwelling place with limited time and money, the effort of one man to work alone, all of these things are part of our story.[18]

That first bitterly cold winter in our tiny uninsulated cabin, heated only with a kitchen wood cook stove was such a dreadful experience. We had to set the alarm clock for every one-and-a-half hours to get up and feed the fire. We had to melt snow for water. We had to cut firewood daily because every day of the autumn months were spent building the cabin with no time to gather wood for the winter. My waitressing job paid $2.57 per hour, so there were no savings. The temperature dropped to -40°C and lasted for three weeks. The van would not start, so I lost my job. With only that last pay cheque to spend, our food supplies ran so low that we had only two small meals a day for most of February and March.

Things improved in the springtime when Kevin found work on the railroad. My parents and sister, Carol, came for a month in the summer of 1979 to see what the 'Back-to-Nature' lifestyle was all about. I hired on with a 'pine cone picking' crew in September and earned enough money to buy a pickup truck. Now that we had a larger wood stove, a chain saw and firewood stacked, a truck, an income and Kevin brought water jugs every day in the truck, we thought it was a good time to start our family.

The second winter in the cabin we were so much better prepared. I was pregnant. Kevin went to work. I napped and dreamed of my new baby. Elise was born at the hospital 45 miles away in the summer of 1980. We spent that summer building a warmer dwelling. Kevin's brother, sister-in-law and their little daughter came to see our progress. But, the summer months brought so much rain that we did not have time to complete our larger, warmer house. A baby needs to be washed and dressed so often every day. The temperature in the cabin would be below freezing during a cold snap, so, I realized that it was not sensible to stay in the cabin for the winter. That is why I decided to return to Ontario again, but only for the cold months. I eagerly look forward to springtime when I can return to my log cabin in the mountain forest.

On the first day of December, Kevin flagged the train to stop. I felt my heart rip when I stepped up onto the train, carrying Baby Elise, and turned to wave to my husband. 'Good-bye' is not my favourite word!

I booked two seats in 'Coach' so she could lie down and sleep while I could recline beside her on my seat. I brought food for myself, was nursing her and had everything in my luggage for the four day trip. First, through the narrow river valley to Jasper, gradually exchanging mountains for foothills, then, the wide open prairie.

In Canada, there are two rail routes from west to east. The northern route was the one I was on: from the Pacific coast of Vancouver, British Columbia, north between mountain peaks, to the hub city of Kamloops, still north winding along the North Thompson, Albreda and Fraser River valleys, turning east towards Jasper and Edmonton, Alberta, then on across the prairies, through Saskatchewan, to Winnipeg, Manitoba. The southern route branches off to the east at Kamloops, steeply climbing over Roger's Pass, through tunnels to Calgary, across the prairie to meet up with the northern train in Winnipeg. After the cars from both trains are united into one, the train passes along the northern rim of the Great Lakes to turn south, entering increasingly dense population, and arrives at Toronto, Ontario.

Unless there is a disruption.

As it happened, the day I was travelling, the southern passenger train was delayed. All of the passengers on the northern train were told to wait in the Winnipeg train station. It was late at night. The train we were to board would not arrive for eight to ten more hours. Because I was travelling with an infant, I was given a berth! I was so snug behind my thick blue curtain. It was so comfortable to lie down and have the rocking sensation when the train began to move clickety-clack over the joints in the rails. After a restful night, I returned to my coach seats. But, I learned that the price of two seats was almost the same as the price of the berth! So, I plan to return to the west in the springtime in this luxurious accommodation!

I befriended some children! Two brothers were travelling with their parents and grandmother. I tried to guess their nationality by listening to their language: not Spanish, French, German or Dutch. They seemed to be Polish, Czech, or Russian? I could not speak with them, but they enjoyed playing with my baby. Nursery rhymes sound much the same in any language! I set up little puzzles for the boys to solve. I gave them math problems. I played hide-and-seek with grapes under paper cups. We shared food. The mother and grandmother looked after Elise so I could stand up and walk around.

It took four days and nights for the train to travel from the mountains of British Columbia to the CN Tower in Toronto. As I travelled the miles across the land, I also travelled in time. As I relaxed and enjoyed scenes through the window, I could also recall scenes of childhood memories. But those were scenes from the past. A lot has happened since I left home two-and-a-half years ago. I need to try to envision scenes of the present! Family? I wondered how my siblings had changed since I left after my wedding. Parents? I tried to comprehend the raw fact that my parents were no longer living together. Christmas? So sweet as a child, tension between parents now. Siblings? I have unresolved conflict with my sister, Julie. I have treated my sister, Carol, like a cute little pet. The twins and I have mostly experienced competition. Community? It will be amazing to see how the children I used to babysit have grown and also greet my childhood friends again. Church? There is a tug-of-war within me about The Seer-Church. 'I can't – I have to' keeps struggling within me.

I wavered between idealized pictures of family bliss and anxiety about re-entry.

The miles and the hours passed by. Prairie became dense forest. Forest merged into farm fields. Fields became overgrown with towns. Towns knit together into unbroken urban sprawl. I could see the city looming larger. CN Tower was an unmistakable landmark.

I got ready and stepped off the train. I found my way through corridors to the high vaulted ceiling, stained glass windows, swirling crowds and confusing echo of the Toronto Station waiting room. I held my baby in a blue carrier up against my chest. A heavy brown backpack was full of my clothing and necessities. In my left hand was a bulging tan duffel bag full of baby clothes and in my right hand I gripped a red diaper bag. My tickets, ID and cash were zipped in a flat pouch inside my clothing. Feeling out of place with my mountain parka and manly felt-pack boots, looking like a koala with my baby strapped to my front and a turtle carrying my home on my back, I found a place to rest on a long wooden bench. The baby asleep, my feet throbbing from carrying the heavy load, I leaned back, closed my eyes and silently braced myself for what would be next.

A month ago, when I spoke with my Mother on the telephone, my voice eager and bright, I asked, "I'd like to come home for Christmas. Wouldn't you like to see your first grandchild?" She told me, in a voice like heavy, black ice, "You're Dad won't be living here by the time you arrive." My glad heart and my sad heart kept dipping and soaring like a roller coaster ride all day and all night as we crossed the continent. The anticipation over, I kept reminding myself, "Now it is time to enter this drama."

I felt someone touch my head. Startled, I sat up straight and turned. It was my Dad wearing a long, tan trench coat, looking very glad to see me and eager to help carry my baggage. It was a little awkward. Me, with a baby and overflowing with questions. He, with the multi-lane traffic and overflowing with questions. It was an hour long drive to the Arbor Vale Church Community near Kitchener.

The community was built on rolling farmland, donated by a deceased Church member. In the 1960s, full of hope and pledged to renewal, a school and church building were built overlooking a forest of beech and maple, and crops of corn and oats. One-by-one families built individual homes on half-acre lots. Walking to church, the elderly greeted the families with young children. It was a time of prosperity and dedication, traditions and a bright future. The visions of pleasant community life which The Seer had observed while visiting Heaven could be lived out on Earth! It was worth striving for. Our family had participated in every way. It felt good to return and drive the quiet streets and see familiar places. Up ahead, near the top of the hill, I could see 'Home.'

Like a visitor, Daddy walked me to the door and brought my luggage. Saying good-bye to him and entering the home he no longer lived in was like a warped dream. I don't know how much or how often I will see him. I don't know how much he will want to tell me, or how much I will want to know about the break-up.

There are so many people who will want to see me while I'm here: Mother, four siblings, Kevin's Mom and brother and sister-in-law and daughter. I have childhood friends and classmates, the Arbor Vale Church congregation, people I used to work for and people who helped with our wedding. They all want me to come for a visit. And of course, the needs of my baby come first.

* ** *** ****

This morning I can look back and realize that I arrived one month ago. It has been the strangest Christmas I have ever heard of. My Mother changed the locks. My Dad doesn't live with the rest of the family. Mother is selling the house.

These facts change everything... for the whole family... not only in the present and for the future... we may also have to re-write the past?

My brothers have been attending University where our Dad is a professor and Chairman of the Department. Instead of driving in together, now they have to buy their own car to get back and forth each day. Their architecture program offers a co-op term. They are moving to Toronto to work for a semester. But, instead of taking along a few necessities, now they have to strip the house of their possessions, figure out how to transport or store their things and vacate the premises. Both have a future unknown. Both are puzzling about what to keep? Suddenly, childhood interests, hobbies, books, treasures are all clutter. The floor to ceiling wall of shelves holding teddy bears, rocks, trophies, model airplanes and hot rods with elaborate decals, school art projects and popsicle stick Cub Scout inventions are all at once 'keep or trash' decisions. Treasured artifacts? Useless junk?

Disassembling the layout for the HO model railroad was already done. They had taken the model buildings off of the 4x8 sheets of plywood and displayed them on shelves. The train cars were in boxes, the room they had been using was bare and hollow sounding.

Julie will soon be 20. She graduated from the Bonnie Hills Church high school and now goes to the Seer-Church college. She came home for two weeks over the holidays. She just announced her engagement. Her dreams are buoyant and bright, just as Mother's have come crashing down.

Carol is only 15 years old. Where will she live while she finishes high school? With Mother in some unknown far-away place? With Dad in some unknown local place?

No one seems to have specific plans. Every family member will be moving out. Each will have to sort every single piece of clothing, childhood keepsake, books, sports, school and hobby items.

I find private moments to ask my siblings, 'What happened?' But, like sailors on a sinking ship it's 'every man for himself.'

If it wasn't confusing enough at home, I also had invitations to come and spend time during the holidays with Kevin's relatives. And there were a lot of them! Kevin's Mom, Adele, has eight brothers and sisters, an older son with a wife and daughter and an unknown tally of cousins. I know them a little because I knew Kevin for four years before we married, yet, our 'Back-to-the-Land' lifestyle is so different, it is hard for me to smoothly fit in.

6:00am

I hear Mother running water and then quietly go slipper-soft down the carpeted stairs. She likes to begin each day with Bible study in early morning solitude.

I asked Mother once, why she was so dedicated to daily Bible study as an individual. In the Seer-Church, people usually waited for group instruction from the Minister. She said, "When

I was growing up, my parents and teachers and siblings and the neighbours and the kids at school said mean things about me. I thought they were true. I thought I was unimportant. I am reading the Bible because I want to learn what God says about me. Look at Psalm 139! He made me on purpose! I am precious to God! I am not hurt by those old messages anymore. I am not who they said I am. I am who God says I am!" So, I did read Psalm 139. It gave me something valuable to believe.

Our house is big. Four bedrooms and a bathroom are upstairs. The main floor has a large living room with couches, carpet, picture window and enough room for a piano, electric organ and drum set. Across the hall, Dad's study is lined with book shelves. There's a small bathroom and laundry room. The big, open family room, kitchen and dining area are also on the ground floor. The basement is mostly unfinished, used for the freezer and canning jars, storage and play space on rainy days. The twins' bunk beds are in a paneled, shelved, good sized room in the basement. Each separate room has its own separate purpose. Each person has their own separate territory.

But, the family room is where everyone and every activity comes together. The hallway to the rest of the house, the big pantry door, one exit through the garage and another exit through sliding glass doors to the patio show that this room is a hub for all coming and going. The brown brick-like floor and daisy-pattern wall paper, the fireplace and book shelves, the record player and telephone, and of course, Mother working in the kitchen, all combine to spell 'Family.'

You can always tell who's home by what records are playing on the stereo in the family room. James and Andrew turn up 'Led Zeppelin' and 'The Guess Who.' Julie stacks up the 'Beetles' and the 'Beach Boys' and 'Herb Albert and the Tijuana Brass.' Carol has a small black and white portable TV that Kevin gave her. I don't think she listens to records much. I like

'Harry Belafonte' and 'John Denver' and the musical plays like 'Brigadoon' and 'My Fair Lady.' Mother listens to 'Carole King' and the 'Carpenters.' Daddy has a vast array of classical music as well as a recent favourite: 'Jesus Christ Super Star' which he blasts so loudly I have to go outside.

The family room brings a sense of security and stability where we can all be together. Until now. Now the echo of 'Family' feels faintly fake. The shadow of 'scattered' is beginning to take hold.

Dad has gone to live in the city. Julie left yesterday to return to the college campus. The twins will leave for Toronto in a month or so. I will be gone in three months. Mother is selling the house. That leaves Carol, with still two years until high school graduation. It's all so hard to comprehend.

7:00am

Alarm clocks are beeping.

"Happy Birthday, James! Happy Birthday, Andrew!" Mother is ready with the initial-shaped birthday pancakes. A tradition which, I realize with a jolt, is probably being repeated for the last time.

Carol is up and out to catch the school bus. She walks to the bus eating a piece of toast. An apple and sandwich are in her backpack. The twins, as a team, pack a lunch and head for their car. Mother is finished Bible study and coffee, goes to get dressed. We sit down for a more leisurely breakfast and make plans for the day together.

"What are you going to make for the boys' Birthday Dinner?" I ask, although I'm pretty sure I know the answer. The boys always ask for Mother's special baked chicken.

"Well, chicken, of course," she chuckles, "with tossed salad and pilaf, although Andrew prefers corn, so I'll make both. James asked for a Boston Cream pie and Andrew likes Chess pie."

"O, good, I'll learn how to make them," I reply. When I left home I was a vegetarian and health food nut so I didn't pay attention to meat and dessert preparations. During this pregnancy I began to crave meat and since I had no support from older, experienced vegetarian ladies, I decided it was too high a risk to continue and I began to eat some meat again. And, now that I'm a Mother, I want to learn how to make the traditional treats for celebrations.

"We'll need to pick up some groceries. The fridge is getting empty after the holiday meals and everyone home," Mother reaches for a pencil and paper from beside the telephone and begins to plan. "Maybe you'd like to visit with Kevin's Mom while I do the shopping? You can phone and ask what time of day would be best for her."

10:00am

After making arrangements, I need to put Elise down for a nap. Mother borrowed a crib for her and set it up in Dad's old study so I don't have to go upstairs.

I hear the phone ring in the kitchen. Mother's voice sounds like it's someone she knows and is glad to speak with. Suddenly I can tell by the questions she is asking: it's Kevin!

"Hello, Darling!" I am gripping the phone, pressing my ear to catch every scrap of information from his tone of voice, trying to envision him so far away. I glance at the clock and subtract three hours for the time zones. It is 10:00 here. He has just come off work at 7:00am.

"Hello, Lady Person!" He sounds tired after his night patrol, but happy to hear my voice.

"Where are you? How was your night? How cold is it? Is everything OK? Tell me everything!" I eagerly rush all at once.

"Cheryl gave Jim a ride to work and she invited me back to the farm for breakfast, so I am going to warm up a little before I head back out and get the fire started in the cabin. The temperature has been holding at about -15° Celsius, but it is expected to drop to 40° below in a few days."

"O, Darling! I am so sad that I am not there to keep the cabin warm for you to come home to! What are you eating? How do you manage? Are you warm enough without me to help keep the fire going while you sleep?"

"Don't worry. I'm eating OK. I have eggs and cheese and canned stew and plenty of food. I make spaghetti and French toast and pork chops and pork and beans. It is the same as winter camping. I bring the dog with me every night. When I get home, I get the fire going, fill it up, shut it down and go to sleep. That heater stove from Howard lasts about five hours. I crawl into my sleeping bag and put yours on top. I wear a toque and socks, of course. " He sounds so confident and brave. "I bring water every day and we have plenty of firewood, so there is nothing for you to worry about. It's OK."

I can hear Cheryl's two small children making a racket in the background and Cheryl scolding. Now I hear her one-year-old banging his spoon on the high chair tray.

"Kevin, I need to talk to you," I want him to focus, although there are distractions in Cheryl's kitchen and Mother is in this kitchen. "Can you hold on a minute while I get the phone upstairs?" Turning to Mother I ask, "Will you hang up this phone?"

Now that I have some privacy, I can share what I was thinking about this morning.

"Kevin, I am the only one here with a permanent address! I know where I live! Our fourteen by fourteen foot uninsulated cabin, with newspaper stuffed in the cracks in the floor, single pane windows salvaged from a scrap pile and roof built of only lumber and tar paper is a castle compared with the uncertainty of every person in my whole family!" I feel so upset, but I have to say it out loud. It has been all bottled up inside me.

"Kevin, my Dad lives in a one-room garret up on the attic of a 100 year old house! It's nuts! Mother is getting ready to sell the house, but she doesn't really know where she is going to go. Maybe to live near a sister in Pennsylvania. Maybe to return to Colorado where she has a best friend. Maybe back to Florida. It is hard to ask, wait, listen, suggest. It is like an ever shifting kaleidoscope. Maybe this? Maybe that?" I am dizzy with all of the possibilities.

"My brothers have school, but no real plans after that. My sisters are still in school. This is the last time any of us will come home for the holidays. How will they be able to concentrate? Where will everyone go after this?" My confusion and heart break spill out.

"How is it possible that we will never have Thanksgiving, Christmas or family gatherings with everyone present? Everything my Mother worked for is dissolving, the customs and traditions. Everything Dad hoped for is collapsing." It's hard not to cry. "Our family feels like puzzle pieces broken and scrambled and scattered!" I want to keep talking to my husband.

"You and I are the only ones who know where we live, know our permanent mailing address and have a 'tomorrow.' Darling, this is so terribly sad!" I try to control my voice and keep the tears back, but I can't stop the sobs.

Kevin has been part of our family for the four years that we knew each other before we got married. He knows each person and it hurts him to know that everything is such a tangle. I can hear him sigh deeply. He can't fix it. If it was an engine or home repair, he would know what to do. But people problems are an entirely different realm.

"You don't know how things will turn out right now. I'm sure that each person will figure it out. These things take time," he speaks reassuringly.

"Yes, I suppose so, but, Darling, it also feels so scary! How do these things come to be? What if our marriage ends? It makes me feel like everything I thought was solid is actually fragile." It's hard to find words for my tumbling feelings. Part of me wonders if the 1950's expectations of marriage my parents started out with could not withstand the 1970's 'Women's Lib' movement. Did Daddy expect Mother to be like the women on television ads: sexy, smiling, happy to be scrubbing the laundry, pots and oven? Does marriage crumble when the woman earns an income? owns a car? makes up her own mind? What happens between a husband and wife if one says 'No' to the other about decisions? or in the bedroom?

"And, if they actually get divorced, if their marriage should never have happened, then I should never have been born! I feel afraid of bursting into molecules or of being vacuumed up, or dissolved, or evaporated and cease to exist!"

"Now," Kevin's tone becomes firm and confident, "There is one thing you will never have to doubt: our marriage. I am not going anywhere. You are stuck with me. I said 'forever' and I meant it. 'Twogether' remember?" I feel myself become calm with the certainty of his pledge. "Now, tell me about Elise. Tell me about your day. Tell me about you." He is very good at taking care of me, even from so far away and infrequent phone calls.

"Well, Elise couldn't quite sit up by herself when I left, and now she is so strong. She started to eat solid food. I make soft sweet potatoes, bananas, apples, and mashed vegetables for her. She loves my Mother and she loves the bathtub but she is pretty shy about everyone else and all of the outings. We are going to your Mom's place this afternoon. It's the twins' birthday today. Daddy is coming for supper and birthday cake. The temperature here isn't so bad but the wind is awful! I put Elise in the Snuggli and wrap my parka around her but I also cover her face with a blanket so it's not so shocking when we go out for a walk." Again I hear the noises of Cheryl's farm kitchen so far away. "I'd better let you go. We're running up Cheryl's phone bill."

"Yes, OK, but I love you!" Now I really have to hold on to my emotions.

"I love you too, Darling! More and more each day! I'll give Elise a kiss from you, too! G-bye." And it's over. I have to take a few deep breaths before I can leave the room and re-enter my day.

I phone Daddy and ask him to bring his camera to take birthday pictures and some of Elise so I can have them developed and mail them to Kevin. What else can I do?

10:30am

The mail has arrived. There is something from Avola! It is a homemade card addressed to 'Miss Elise.'

I sink into the reclining chair to savour every clue of my husband's creativity and message. On the front, Kevin has drawn a cluster of six tiny flowers: two tall and four shorter ones. Each one is simply a plain pencil line for a stem and little round red flower. Inside he wrote:

> Precious...Lady:
>
> If I was a priest, I would call
> from Heaven myriad blessings
> and heavenly gifts befitting of you;

Twin Brothers: Competition

If I was a doctor, I would use
such skill to guard your health
and keep good care of you;

If I was a teacher, I would strive
to teach you all that you
longed to learn;

If I was a farmer, I would raise
fine food for you,
to nourish you;

But alas...

...I am none of these,
I am but a humble man;

But by the Grace of
the Lord I have become
your earthly father;

A father to be true must
be a priest and a doctor,
a teacher and a farmer, but mind,
I could be none of these
without your mother;

Together we pray that the Lord
will show us how to care for you
in a way befitting
His great gift of you.

We ask, Precious Lady, that we may
grow with you and become like you,
that together we may share our home
in God's Kingdom for a time
and times to come.

Much Love,
Your Father, Kevin Deckert
January 1979

Now silent tears flow. In this delicate message, I find the solid foundation I had so recently doubted.

11:00am

Elise wakes, nurses and the day begins anew, fresh and bright. I take her upstairs for her bath. In the cabin I could only wipe with a wash cloth with water from the basin. Now, with a whole tub and running water, what an amazing discovery for her to enjoy the sounds and sensation of the water trickling, to trust the buoyant feeling, to relax in the tightly wrapped towel, to anticipate the routine of getting dressed.

As we leave the bathroom, I hear strange sounds from the living room downstairs. Mother is taking down the Christmas tree as she does every year on the boys' birthday. But, what is this? I peek around the corner. She is smashing the glass ornaments!

"Mother? Are you OK?" Her back is to me and I am not sure what is happening. Was she using the time I was out of the room to express her anger, rejection, disappointment, fear of the void in the future, grief of her loss by destroying the very symbol of family togetherness?

But, no, her face is calm. "I am breaking the chipped glass balls. I am packing up each person's treasures, like I did for you when you left home. I am only keeping a very few things for myself. The other things I will put in the rummage sale." She has a logical plan.

12:00 noon

Bundled up, with questioning eyes, I buckle Elise into the car seat. Mother is taking me to Adele's place for lunch while she does errands. I never did get my driver's license and I can't really take the city bus in wintertime with all the gear I need to carry and the baby.

Adele is a restaurant cook, so I anticipate a fine meal. I see my sister-in-law's blue hatchback car in the drive way, so the two little cousins can be together, too. Peggy is one year older than Elise. I wonder if they will ever know each other with so much time and space separating them.

I come in through the back kitchen door, and pass through to the front room. The house is always kind of dark, with rooms leading into rooms with closed curtains and low ceilings. What has been furnished recently as the 'front room' used to be a store front. Little Kevin grew up in a playpen while his Mom tended to the customers and local news. Now the huge windows, right up against the sidewalk, have hanging plants and Adele's collection of glass figurines and in wintertime, fluffy white 'snow' and a Santa display. Adele cooks and serves lunch at the hotel across the street. Since her husband died ten years ago, she has had a live-in named Bill. The close quarters, loud city traffic and constant in-coming people make me realize how much Kevin wanted a different lifestyle. However, there is much to learn from the in-laws, so I settle in for an afternoon together.

Deviled eggs, my sister-in-law's specialty, green beans, mashed potatoes and a savoury meat loaf are served. Little Peggy eats bright pink 'Strawberry Shortcake' cereal pieces off her high chair tray. Elise is in the car seat reclining near the window so she can see the red and green ornaments there.

Adele hands out two gifts. She made her two granddaughters matching smocked dresses. Peggy's is a lovely shade of aqua-blue. Elise's is apple-red. It's fun get the little cousins dressed and line them up for Adele to snap photos. It's interesting how I can share some parts of my life with 'family' and other parts of my life with 'Church' people.

But, I don't have a very relaxing time today. The comings and goings seem to be overwhelming and make little Elise very upset. She didn't like the car ride. She didn't like so many new noises and voices and faces. She didn't like getting picked up and bounced by so many people. She didn't like the stuffy hot rooms, the cigarette smoke, the city smells, the noises and interrupted sleeping schedule. Since I arrived a month ago, I've learned that if I go out for one day, I have to stay home for two or three days afterward for her to settle down and relax. I knew I was suffering from 'Culture Shock' but I hadn't realized it would have such a strong impact on such a small baby. Then there are the repeated questions each time I meet another relative. "Where's Kevin?" I don't like the raised eyebrows when I explain the situation. "Kevin is working. The cabin is too cold. Our new house isn't finished. I am here for the winter months." Yes, I want to add, I am still wearing my wedding ring!

My lunch is interrupted by Elise starting to fuss. I excuse myself from the table and begin to lift her, looking for a quiet place we can go to nurse and maybe nap. But the comments begin. "Maybe she needs a bust in the mouth," which seems such an ungrandmotherly thing to say. "Maybe she's teething," followed by a dip of a finger into whiskey to rub along her gums. Then my sister-in-law, "Maybe you should just let her cry. You don't want to spoil her." I am a first-time Mom. I feel bombarded from every side. Retreating to Kevin's former bedroom I close the door and feel guilty for 'wasting time' that I had agreed to spend with the in-laws.

I hear my Mother's cheery voice, so I zip up Elise's snow suit, say, 'Thank-you' and make an exit. I feel like a failure. But I don't see how I could have done anything differently.

2:00pm

Unpack the car. Unpack the groceries. Start to cook. Mother sets Elise in the kitchen sink, propped up with soft towels. A six-month-old baby can reach, grasp and put things in her mouth. I'm fascinated to watch how confident Mother is, while I am so hesitant to try anything new.

Mother measures and stirs, seasons and slices. She keeps adding interesting things to Elise's collection. First a yellow plastic measuring cup, then samples of each vegetable she is preparing. "A baby can put her whole fist into her mouth, so as long as the objects or chunks of food are bigger than that, she will be safe. Babies are curious explorers. It's important to give her a variety of new experiences," she advises.

Mother has already told me my own birth story: how she searched for a doctor who would allow her to go through labour and delivery without any drugs. In the 1950s it was standard hospital procedure to give the woman something called 'Twilight Sleep' just as she was about to deliver her baby. She would be semiconscious, forget, or have a blurry memory of the experience. The mother would not be able to participate in the birth, so more interventions were needed. The drugs would pass through the placenta so the baby would be sleepy for hours. The mother could not see or hold her newborn while she recovered. The babies were taken to the nursery where nurses woke them every four hours for feedings. But my Mother thought differently. She wanted to learn and understand, to participate and remember, to see and touch and comfort her newborn. She wanted to breast feed and not have to wait four hours to see her baby.

"I remember when you told me about how brave you were to find a doctor who would agree to not give you drugs when I was born, but tell me about when the twins were born." I love having heart-to-heart talks with my Mother. She pays attention and has such a wholesome point of view.

"Well, let me think. I had the same doctor as when you were born, so, he agreed to let me progress through labour without drugs. The first baby was born head first and the second twin was born feet first. It was the middle of the night. Your Daddy was home looking after you. But the doctor was so kind. He went to stay with you so that Daddy could come and see his new sons. I was unsuccessful nursing you. Of course I didn't try to breast feed twins! I wrote in a log book every time I fed each one and how much formula they took from the bottle," she explained.

"I always kind of wished that I had a twin," I confided. "It is amazing to have a built-in best friend. I remember when you explained to me how one seed and one egg split and two babies are formed with identical genes! It seemed kind of creepy, though. The Seer says that the soul of the child comes from the father's seed. Does that mean that they share a soul? When a baby dies before it's born, where does the soul go? And what about all the seeds that don't ever fertilize an egg? Where do all of those souls go?"

"Now you're asking me questions that no one can answer," Mother smiled at me, knowing how I often do that.

"OK, let's talk about your other births," I change the subject back to more practical matters. "What about Julie?"

"Well, we had moved by then, so I had a different doctor, but it was the 1960s so ideas were beginning to change. It was not so unusual for me to request a non-drug birth. In fact, since natural birth was actually a more calm experience for everyone, the fathers were beginning to be allowed to attend the birth. Your Daddy came and he had a whole new appreciation for his children after that."

* ** *** ****

Maybe that's why he seems to have Julie as a favourite, I thought to myself. I was only three-and-a-half when she came home from the hospital and everyone made such a fuss! How sweet she was! How darling she was! How adorable she was! What was everyone so excited about? Mommy, Daddy, grand-parents, favorite Uncle Ronald, everyone wanted to hold the baby. No one was paying any attention to me. I felt my heart shrink up hard and shrivel with cold.

When we got older, no matter what the topic, Julie and I seemed to be on opposing sides of every argument. How could two people raised by the same parents have such opposite points of view? I was modest and wore long skirts and no make-up. She liked colour and style and miniskirts and trendy hair-dos. "Why do you do all that fake stuff?" I criticized her for wearing make-up. "If you love Nature so much, why don't you take off your glasses?" she would fire back a witty reply.

And so it went. There seemed to be no way out of the strain between us from that first day. Even just now, over the holidays when she came home from college, I couldn't find a topic that was safe to discuss. I loved the Seer-Church school environment and she felt stifled by all the rules. I was married by the time I was her age, and she has been dating one boy after another. I preferred volunteering and she picked up shifts where she used to waitress to earn money over the holidays. I liked babies and she liked business. I couldn't get done with school fast enough and she has set her sights on a degree, or two.

With our family about to split to pieces, Julie and I didn't do any better while she was here. She was only home for two weeks. She came and went with jobs and friends. I came and went with relatives and Church activities. She shut the door and used the upstairs telephone. I shut the door and took naps with my baby. Except for some evening meals, Christmas morning and family photos, we hardly saw each other. She left yesterday for the eleven hour drive back to college. I wonder when I will ever see her again?

* ** *** ****

"And, Carol?" I prompted Mother to continue. "I can remember some of this part of the story. You used to let us put our hands on your belly and feel the baby move! We called her 'Baby Dear'... of course, not knowing if it was a boy or girl. And Aunt Barbara was your nurse. That's how you got to be friends, right?"

"Oh, yes! She told me that she never attended a birthing mother who was so peaceful and calm. She had two sons of her own so she knew what giving birth was like, plus she had years of observing others give birth while she was a nurse. She admired me and I admired her. We became friends and later we were your Girl Scout leaders. Then she married my younger brother and became your aunt!"

I am so glad my Mother is willing to share her experiences with me.

* ** *** ****

Yet, I always have unanswerable questions babbling in my head.

No matter how many books about pregnancy and birth that I have read (and I read a pretty tall stack), no matter how many women I ask to share their birth experience (and I have interviewed a long list), no matter how many questions I ask the Ministers or try to research in the books that The Seer wrote, no matter how many theories and observations that psychology can compare, there are always questions that no one can answer.

When do you become 'who you are'? At conception? Sometime before birth? Or do you become 'a person' the moment you take your first breath? 'Who are you'? And how did you get to be 'you'? Is it predetermined? Or do your experiences shape you? 'Nature-Nurture' they call it: Gender, Culture, Decade, Society, Birth Order, Resources, Media, Education. Do the genes from the parents control everything through heredity? Does it matter what the parents attitudes and emotions were at the time of conception? When they realize there is a pregnancy? At the time of the birth? Does the birth experience shape the child? Where does the soul come from? At the time of the birth is the child innocent? Or contaminated by hereditary evil? Or doomed by original sin? Or returning to earth from a previous life? Am I who you say that I am? Or am I somehow separate from all of this; somehow my own imperishable Self?

3:00pm

Mother has the baking out of the oven so there will be time for the cake to cool before the custard and chocolate layers are added to make the Boston Cream Pie. I wish I could capture the fragrant smells like you can snap a photo and preserve the sights. Pie crust browning. Buttery-sugar filling simmering. Cake rising. Custard bubbling. Chocolate sauce melting.

Elise is ready for another nap. I will join her upstairs in the quiet.

* ** *** ****

There's so much to think about. Does birth order matter? I didn't need to wait for psychology class in university to tell me, 'Yes!'

So there I was, happily content, minding my own business when suddenly not one, but two small brothers arrived. I was only fifteen months old. What do I remember? Only very few glimpses. Mommy said, "Put your hand on the baby's tummy so he doesn't roll off the couch," and "Fetch another diaper."

Mother took the twins in the two-seater stroller and people passing by always made such a fuss over admiring the twins. She decided it was not good for me to be entirely ignored and took another walk with only me as often as possible.

Birth order. My Dad was always talking about it.

First thing in the morning, while Mommy looked after the twins, I would watch him while he was shaving. He would sing or tell me a story or answer my insatiable questions. "I am the First-Born Son of the First-Born Son! If our family was a monarchy I'd be the King!" and out into the work-a-day world he would go to catch the train. Then there was the Bible, always talking about the First-Born Son. Plus fairy-tales.

The oldest boy gets the biggest inheritance. Puss in Boots is one example. The oldest got the mill. The second got the donkey. The third got the cat. So, what does that make me, second? No wait, there are two sons. I'm third! Birth order: it was an ongoing message. Hard to ignore. Not possible for one so young to override the pressure with the fact that we live in a democracy and there are no special privileges legal or otherwise associated with being the First-Born Son... unless the family around you thinks there are?

And, to add insult to injury, there is no special status for the First-Born Daughter in any of the stories. It is the youngest daughter who is the fairest, most virtuous, gets the handsome prince and the wealth, status and wardrobe to go with it. The eldest daughter is the bossy self-centered one, the most vain, most self-seeking, most demanding.

Type casting. That seemed to be the way our family was. Dad goes to work. Mother stays home. Bossy Big Sister. Special identical Twin Brothers. Whiny Middle Sister. Adored Baby Sister. It seemed as though each person had been handed a script entitled: 'Expectations.' How were we each going to play out the roles? I've heard of 'sibling rivalry.' But, maybe it's not all the children's fault that it happens? Maybe the parents setup the scenario and the children have to sink or swim?

So, although they were barely seven pounds, wrapped up, sleeping, crying, wetting or slurping, and I was an active fifteen-month-old with baby-needs of my own, my brothers were immediately 'Competition.'

My Mommy had only one lap. My Daddy had only one pair of hands. The babies needed immediate care. I could wait.

And, besides competition for parental attention, I was also in competition with them. Built in playmates, they didn't need to interact with me. Mischief, twin-talk, boy interests, bath-time, all kinds of sibling togetherness was primarily 'the boys' and me as the side-kick. Ask anyone who has twins in the family. The single child feels like an outcast, a less-than. They are the novelty. I am the dull one.

Two sisters joined the family. The boys came along while I was too young to have an opinion. The youngest sister was born when I was eight years old and able to understand, help take care of her and feel proud and glad. But that 'middle child' sister arrived when I was three-and-a-half. It was probably the worst time as far as early child development goes. I could achieve great things: answer the phone, bring Daddy a cupcake at the church picnic, curtsy and say and do cute things my Aunts and Uncles found charming. I could iron Daddy's hand-kerchiefs. I could sing and dance and print my name and draw a face. When my parents brought my 'Little Sister' home from the hospital, I must have been expecting a playmate. But, what ever was this wrapped up bundle of yellow blankets with a scrunched up red face inside?

It's strange how powerful these first impressions are, how embedded they become, how much they warp future interactions. Is it possible to find a way out? Are there stepping stones from a deep, dark valley to rise up to become a bright, clear meadow? Can these puzzle pieces be rearranged to form a more cohesive family portrait? Are we locked in? Or can we change? Will silence or talking bring about more healthy relationships? Who would dare to disturb what is already in place?

Then, as we grew, talents became apparent. Because I was older, if one of my younger brothers shone with a specific skill at a young age, I couldn't go back and prove myself equally proficient. So, I tried to excel at everything... just in case they got good at it later. Math, reading, sports, public speaking, music, art, the list of possible things to be good at is very long. It was a lot of pressure, especially with two worthy opponents. And they were clearly in competition with each other, too. Penmanship, reading, spelling tests, these were ways that measurements were written down. Comparisons could be made. Tally sheets and report cards are permanent records of achievements. The boys compete week by week. I am up ahead by two grades. I am always the ice breaker ship, going ahead into unknown territory. They always have each other. New school? No problem. They already have a friend. Boarding school? No problem, they already have a room mate. Dating? Who cares? Lots of girls are flocking around two handsome, talented, funny guys. Team sports? They both get picked early on. Individual sports? They are their own competition. Who cares about the other challengers?

So? What can I be good at that they can't compete with? This nagging question is underneath much of my effort.

4:00pm

I hear Carol come home from the school bus. She is playing the piano when I carry Elise downstairs. Mother to calls me from the kitchen. "I forgot to pick up ice cream! Come with me. There's a new grocery store not far away."

I start to gather the baby's winter wraps. "No, no. Carol can look after her. We'll only be gone for fifteen minutes!"

"I'd love to," Carol offers, coming into the family room.

But I have never left my Baby! It feels very scary. 'What if...' floods my mind. I have to keep pushing back frightening scenes: fire, burglars, deadly fumes, kidnappers, choking, falling, spiders! Being a Mother is a lot of stress! I didn't know I would be so nervous.

I watch the houses go by, the snowy road bright in the headlights. What if we are in an accident? Or something blocks our route? Or the engine suddenly won't run? Or Mother suddenly can't drive? Or there's a train blocking the crossing?

It only took fifteen minutes on the clock, but I rushed back inside as though we had been separated for ages, scooped up my baby and held her close as if she had been rescued from certain doom, searched her face for any signs of trauma, and then, realizing I had greatly exaggerated the situation, thanked my sister for watching her.

5:00pm

Another car pulls into the driveway. The Birthday Boys have returned!

"Sure smells good, Mom!" they greet us and come stomping into the house.

"It will be ready in an hour. Your Dad will be here at 6:00," Mother always has everything organized. The Boston Cream Pie (which is really a cake) has been layered and iced. The Chess pie is ready. Golden. Mother slides the tray of chicken pieces into the oven: sage, thyme, garlic, celery salt and parsley have been generously sprinkled. The pilaf has been toasted and is now simmering slowly on the stove top.

I make the salad. Mother whips the dressing. Carol sets the table. The boys report on their day. Uncles play with their niece. The 'family room' is full of family. The comfort of everyone safe at home is filling my heart at this moment.

Will I be the Mother someday with adult children gathered around? Grandchildren?

6:00pm

The front doorbell rings. "Must be Dad," James steps away to open the door. "I can help you with these boxes," he offers. Mother has emptied the shelves of books from Dad's old study. Every time he comes to visit there is another pile at the door for him to take. Every time he comes to visit he brings more empty boxes. He also has to pack up and move out.

I can feel Mother change. Kind of stiff. Kind of turned away. Kind of busy.

"Well, well, well, three holes in the ground," Dad greets the group. Still dressed for his role as professor, but not bringing in his brief case, not really at ease to sit in his recliner or choose a record to put on the stereo, he does not deliver the usual hug to Mother, but crosses the room to pick up the baby. "And what have you been up to today, Little One?" he camouflages the awkwardness with Mother by taking the 'Grampa' role.

Now he can sit. Now he can interact. Now he can ask and answer questions.

Dinner is ready. Delicious and generous. Dessert is served.

Julie phones to say, "Happy Birthday." Mother heads upstairs with the baby. Carol has homework. I start the dishes. Dad and the boys enter conversation.

I can never follow the conversations between the Dad and the boys very well. For them, politics, history, economics and current events somehow all fit together. For me, it all doesn't make any sense. Dad loves theories. He reads a lot. He often takes a differing point of view. He compares and contrasts various positions and adds in a previously unmentioned alternative. I can never find a solid starting point he is defending or a specific end point he is driving towards. The whole world seems to be built on 'Maybe.' Pros and Cons line up and remain unresolved. Translations are questioned. Sources doubted. Unrelated fragments seem to fit together. Established norms are taken apart. He finds it intriguing. I find it distressing.

The three sit at the table. My back is turned while I am at the sink. Once again I try to follow along, but end up lost in the fog. Oh, well. They are happy to be together.

Look at the time! Dad heads out.

8:00pm

It's a birthday tradition for Dad to prepare a slide show for the evening entertainment. But not tonight. Tiny baby boys, cute twin mischief, Easter eggs, 4th of July parade, Halloween costumes, Christmas trees, toddlers with birthday party hats, first day on the school bus, big boy denim jackets and manly 'coon skin caps, Cub Scout uniforms, family gatherings, sports events, graduations...all of these pictures are so familiar. Storytelling, 'remember when' and 'I never knew that' are all part of our family birthday tradition. But Dad's case of photos is not here, nor his projector equipment, nor the invitation to stay longer.

* ** *** ****

One series of pictures I will be glad not to see: Christmas morning, 1958,[19] was eleven days before the twins were born. I was a toddler, only fifteen months old. My parents so young and happy and full of hope gave me twin dolls in an attempt to prepare me for the new arrivals. Although I see in the photographs, colourful snap-together beads, a miniature red piano, a stuffed blue doggie and other small items all unwrapped near the tinsel draped Christmas tree, the dolls were clearly my favourite thing.

"What will you name your dolly?" Daddy asked.

"Zheezuz," I answered, knowing the name of the Baby in the manger.

Chuckling, snapping my portrait with his camera, he picked up the second doll and asked again, "And what will you name this baby?"

"Zheezuz," came the confident answer.

"No, Honey, you can't name two babies with the same name!" Daddy retells the story every year, making use of his acting skills.

And then I squirm in my chair when he gets to the part I don't like to hear about every year on my birthday.

"You put your doll in the oven! It melted! Why did you do that?" Every time we get to this part of the slide show Daddy stops and turns to me looking directly into my eyes, quizzically, with a mixture of scolding, bewilderment, and dread. Was she actually trying to destroy her siblings? Before they were even born? Is it possible that an act of violence could come from one so young and tender? Is this the first signal that his daughter is headed for insanity? A criminal?

Of course I cannot answer. How can I remember why I did it? No one can remember being fifteen months old! Nor what they did on a specific day! Nor the motivation for one specific action! Why does Daddy bring it up again and again? It seems like I can hear the echo of his voice, "What is *wrong* with you?"

For a moment it seems like he doesn't see me, but in his frustration, he sees his sister long ago and the nightmare of her unpredictable behaviour as her mental health problems became undeniable. His unspoken question hovering over me: Is insanity linked to heredity?

So, I'm just as glad to skip the slide show part of the birthday celebration.

* ** *** ****

Still, reminiscing is meaningful. So, with my brothers, I start to stimulate a trip down Memory Lane.

James has finished putting the left over food away. Andrew is drying and putting away the dishes. Neither has class tomorrow, so I'm not keeping them from their studies.

With all the confusion and disruption and unknowing, we siblings try to bond by retelling our own stories. Knowing we would be going our separate ways soon, we revisit the past and laugh about childhood antics. Even the sibling rivalry feels more like a bond. We are woven into each other's life stories.

Like a litany or recitation, one after another the stories came tumbling out.

"What is the earliest moment you can remember from your childhood?" I prompt.

"Well, it's always a little hard to tell. Dad's pictures and retelling stories are decoys for my own memory. What do

I remember because he told me and what is actually my own memory?" James ponders.

"Except rolling your doll's head down the stairs!" Andrew chimes in with a huge grin. "That I remember!"

"Oh! You guys! How could you laugh about such a gruesome thing and keep doing it while I'm screaming, 'No! Stop! Don't!' I guess I was about four years old," I quickly do the math, "so you were two and a half or so." My domestic sense of matronly responsibility was very different from their mischievous sense of glee as they repeated the incongruous scene of the smiling, hair flopping head bouncing down the stairs. Boys (teaming up to repeat the stunt with endless bouncing variations) stimulated by my helplessness. Me (holding a headless, life-sized doll dressed in a girly, pink, ruffly dress) in agony over the butchery.

"Moving on!" I attempt to change the subject.

"I remember lots of stuff after we moved to Colorado: walking to the school bus and how we would chase the girls after Brownies," James recalls.

"And I was so offended when you passed me in piano playing skills. Mother was a good teacher, but I was always distracted and didn't practice. You stayed focused. I just wanted to magically be able to play beautifully, not have to stumble along on those early exercises," I shake my head, wishing I had behaved differently.

Rapidly we continue to more memories. Naughty pranks, daring 'Mountain Man' activities, climbing Bald Mountain, swimming farther and deeper, daring bicycle stunts. Boys' play is overflowing with a sense of adventure. These things I had no intention of keeping up with, yet I felt the tug of competition. They were not scared on hikes, near the edge, or other rugged, new activities. I wanted to stay safe, obey Mother, be cautious about how far to go and when to come home.

It felt like there was favoritism. Dad explained and coached more when they were learning. "Remember when we visited Uncle Allan out on the hot, dry, sagebrush prairie? Dad taught you how to shoot the .22. When I asked for a turn, he barely showed me what to do. I got to shoot one time! You guys had the whole afternoon!" What a wide gap between boy and girl activities.

"That's pretty good... for a girl," James looks at me with that familiar grin.

"Yup, you two said that every time I tried something new: golf, badminton, hockey, baseball, Frisbee... It sure took the fun out of it for me!" I pout.

During the year that we lived in Florida we went swimming nearly every day. There were trips to the ocean and searching for sea shells and feeding the seagulls. At the nearby lake there was a high platform to jump off. At the university where Dad was teaching there was a big chlorinated pool with diving boards. Flips and high dives, tricky twists and hand-stands, diving for pennies and learning to do a jack knife or swan dive or cartwheel off the diving board were all part of that year.

When we moved to Canada, the Arbor Vale Church School was so small that I was in the same classroom with four grades. My brothers were with me all day long. Now academic accomplishments entered the competition. The two boys vied for the highest score on spelling and math tests, and track and field events. I saw their scores. I wanted to do as well or better. I wanted to be first and best and win. There were ten boys and five girls in our classroom. The girls were all so ladylike and reserved. I wanted to achieve.

Twins just automatically drew attention. A well behaved girl did not stand out. The boys were popular. I got picked on. The boys were handsome. I was plain. The boys excelled. I did well.

"I'll tell you another thing that drove me crazy," I eagerly launch into a new story. "Remember when Mother took us to Colorado that summer? I think it was 1970. Dad was on some other trip and Mother packed us up with a tent and sleeping bags and cooler and we drove for four days, camping all the way. She gave us each an allowance: 10¢ a day. That was enough for one purchase: a comic book, ice cream, or a chocolate bar, candy, chips or pop. It was clever. She could give out money once every morning and we could choose how and where to spend it when she stopped at a gas station. With five children in the van, she would not have anyone whining, 'Mommy, can I buy this?' all day. It was a great system, but you two figured out how to double your treasure. You pooled your resources, or traded half of your goodies with each other. Sometimes you had both chips and pop. Or shared an ice cream and a comic! I couldn't get Julie or Carol to agree to such a deal. I felt jealous every day!"

"But the feuds were fun!" Andrew points out. "After we watched the Disney movie, 'Parent Trap,' we got the idea from the tricks those twin girls played on each other at camp: the web of string in the cabin, the toilet paper all over, the water bucket over the door."

"Yes, having a feud over Spring Break became a custom for quite a few years," I chuckled. "Boys Against Girls!"

The rules we agreed on included: no wasting food (like putting dry cereal or crackers in the bed sheets), no ruining anything (like cutting clothing or throwing books), no harm to a person (like anything heavy or hot or dangerous). You had to be clever. You had to set booby traps. You had to show your opponent, 'I was here' and you had to get away without being seen.

James can hardly talk he's laughing so hard. "One time Julie snuck downstairs at night. She had perfume or lipstick to put on us while we slept. But we were ready. I had tied a string to the vacuum cleaner so if the door was opened, it would turn it on as an alarm system. But, she felt the resistance and tiptoed back up the stairs to get scissors and she snipped the cord. So slowly, so quietly, she came towards me thinking I was asleep on the bunk bed. But, just as she reached towards me in the dark, I clicked on the flashlight! 'Hello?' I said. She was so shocked and ran away, tripping and frustrated and already planning another sneak attack."

"You tied all my clothing in knots," I shake my head and grin.

"You put an open puzzle box above my door which spilled 1000 pieces when I came home," Andrew scolds with a twinkle in his eye.

"Carol's favorite trick was putting a large book into pillows. That was a pretty good one," I remember.

* ** *** ****

Later, when we were teens, the gap between the boys and the girls became wider. I had all babysitting jobs while my brothers got hired to work on a farm. I depended on my employers for rides to and from their homes. The boys both got driver's licenses. One learned to monkey wrench to set up the travelling carnival rides. The other worked at an all-night gas station.

Then I started dating. My brothers and their friends found ways to embarrass me, tease and pester.

I knew that the boys would end up stronger and faster and better than me at physical work. I thought I would be about even at the academic part. But, with art, I thought girls would always be better than boys. When it became clear that both brothers excelled at the arts, I felt the worst.

Both brothers' designs and drawings became exquisite. Nature and fantasy, portraits and historic buildings all filled pages in their sketch books. And music. I was in the high school band with my clarinet, but James mastered the piano, even composing. Andrew bought a drum set. The boys had their friends over with electric guitars and bass and practiced with their band in the living room.

Mother and Dad gave James a beautiful new classical guitar. The golden wood, smooth body, sturdy case and sweetly tuned strings resounded with warm chords and clever arpeggios. When did he learn to play? Why did no one acknowledge my guitar playing? I bought my own instrument. I was never given lessons. *Where have all the flowers gone?* and *Blowin' in the Wind*, were the first of my ever expanding folk song repertoire.

Jealousy also flared up within me when the twins were popular on the Bonnie Hills Church high school campus. Not me. I decided long ago neither to follow the other girls with the primping and preening to make myself look attractive, nor to participate in wide-eyed flirting. But, the twins' handsome looks, trendy hair cuts, shy, yet clever, mannerisms, and the endless question: 'Which one is which?' was irresistible to all the girls. Popularity had been a pattern for them where ever we lived, but is seemed especially powerful now that teenagers were actually pairing off. Marriage was just a few years away for many.

I guess that looking back at this one aspect of life, I can see part of my motivation to walk away, leave the education and choices leading towards a profession. Fed up with the competition, knowing I'd never be able to be first or best or win, I took a 180° turn and headed for the rustic log cabin life: 'Back-to-Nature' and 'Self-Sufficiency' and 'Do-it-yourself.' No one else was going that way, so, I could be best at something, even if it was digging potatoes.

When I first came home a month ago, I kind of over did it, though. I was bursting to 'prove' my success. Eager to joke with my brothers like 'the good old days' and simultaneously overwhelmed by the break-up of the family, I did not know that they were coming home from pulling an all-nighter to finish a project at the architecture studio before the Christmas break. Unfamiliar with the pressures of university deadlines, I burst forth with a speech that I had been composing while travelling on the train.

And so, rather boldly, on my first day at home, the first time I had seen them since my wedding day two-and-a-half years ago, the instant they walked through the door of the family room, before they had taken their boots or coats off, I demanded, standing with my baby on my hip and my 'Big Sister' scolding frown, "What have you been doing since I left? My husband built me a house! He built it with his bare hands! He chopped down trees, sawed them up, stacked the logs, hammered down the roof. I haul water and chop firewood and build fires and cook dinners and have babies. What have *you* been doing? Huh?"

I wanted to play my trump card, sink the basket, score the goal, reach for the trophy, hear the applause!

But I misfired. Sleep deprived, dumbfounded, both brothers gave me a withering look, obviously insulted. Apples and oranges. There was no real comparison. I had a mean little sense of 'got-ya' but revenge was not as sweet as I had anticipated. It was a sour way to start a reunion.

* ** *** ****

Tonight, we banter and tease, recount and compare. Yes, we have hurt each other's feelings. Yet, the bond is strong. The years have passed. Competition is not helpful towards building family ties. And family ties is what we will need if there is any future ahead, while time and miles will try to keep us apart.

"Another piece of cake? pie?" and we sit together. Actually together. I think we can sense the 'yesterday' and the 'today' and the 'tomorrow.'

I have no words, but I can borrow from others who have been in similar circumstances.

> When one door of happiness closes, another opens,
> but often we look so long at the closed door
> that we do not see the one that has been opened for us.
> —*Helen Keller*

There are still a few weeks before my brothers go to Toronto, before I get back on the train and before Mother sells the house. I can feel the security in the past, the turning points we each are living through now and the completely unknown, uncharted territory ahead. In a field of newly fallen snow, we each get to make our own mark. There is no prescribed path to follow. No guide. No longer a home-base. So, the time together is bitter-sweet. I can feel how much I want to hold on. But the pages turn. The story continues.

10:00pm

The kitchen is clean. Lock up. Lights out. Good-night.

REFLECTIONS

Prayer of Thomas Merton

God, I have no idea where I am going.
I do not see the road ahead of me. I cannot know for certain where it will end. Nor do I really know my self, and the fact that I think I am following Your will does not mean that I am actually doing so. But I believe that the desire to please You does in fact please You. And I hope I have that desire in all that I am doing. I hope that I will never do anything apart from that desire. And I know that if I do this You will lead me by the right road, though I may know nothing about it. Therefore, I will trust You always though I may seem to be lost and in the shadow of death. I will not fear, for You are ever with me, and You will never leave me to face my perils alone.

Chapter 3
Wednesday, January 24, 1996
Papa-Joe

Maybe you can afford to wait. Maybe for you there's a tomorrow.
Maybe for you there are one thousand tomorrows,
or three thousand, or ten,
so much time you can bathe in it, roll around it, let it slide
like coins through your fingers. So much time you can waste it.
But for some of us there's only today.
And the truth is, you never really know.
—*Lauren Oliver*

* ** *** ****

Wednesday, January 24

The man standing beside my mother must be her husband.

Besides a quick hug for her and a 'Nice to meet you' to him, there is no time before the memorial service begins. I cannot juggle the conflicting thoughts and feelings that clamor for my attention as I see my 'step-father' for the first time face-to-face. But I block them all. I have to go into the chapel now.

The funeral is for my Father.

* ** *** ****

Four days ago his heart was still beating. Newly repaired, the surgeon did an excellent job. A quintuple bi-pass is not a small achievement. In a major Canadian hospital, Daddy was in good hands.

Six days ago each of his five children were waiting beside the telephone, expecting to hear the post-surgery message from his wife, Shirley, sharing the 'all is well' message.

Thursday, January 18

The telephone rang, later than expected. My blood ran cold. It was not the voice of Dad's wife, Shirley. My sister, Julie, conveyed the information. "The surgery went fine, but Dad is not waking up. They think it's a stroke. His left side is unresponsive."

My children were in bed. My husband waited silently, knowing I was not getting good news. I phoned a friend in Vancouver. "Can you pick me up and take me to the airport? Can you book my ticket?"

I brought my husband up-to-date as my brain rapidly put the pieces together. "If I get on the 9:00am Greyhound tomorrow morning, let's see, that's Friday, I will be in Vancouver in twelve hours, catch the over night flight, and be in Toronto at 7:00am on Saturday. That's my plan. Uncle Ronald is already travelling to be there. He and my brother, Andrew, and his wife, Lisa, and my sister, Carol, and her two children are driving together all night from New York City and Philadelphia. Julie and her husband and children are driving from New York City tomorrow. James is coming all the way from England. Kevin! I just have to go!"

We are his five children, each with a husband or wife. We three sisters each have children. My body turns to ice when I recall that Daddy's motivation to agree to this surgery was this: his first-born son's wife was expecting their first child. Daddy wanted to be present for the infant baptism of his first grandchild who would bear the family name. And, yes, the ultra sound revealed: a son! The First-Born Son of the First-Born Son of the First-Born Son! The family name will carry on!

Friday, Saturday, January 19, 20

The preparations, the bus ride, the airport, the flight, were all a blur of childhood memories, anxiety for the future, bracing myself to re-enter the city pace, cope with the hospital atmosphere, face difficult facts and the emotional strain of 'Hello' coupled and contrasted with the possibly of 'Good-bye.'

Zipping through traffic from the airport to the hospital, I was aware that 'the end' could be for any one, at any time, in any place. The forces of Providence are always at work. My mind was whirling, 'Is my father on his deathbed? Or will there be a miraculous recovery?' Words? Silence? Prayer? Science? Information? Decisions? Action? Waiting? The Greek goddesses are always at work: One spinning, one measuring, one will make the final cut. The three 'Fates' can not be persuaded to change their course.

Time felt so heavy... and rushed so fast. The gladness of seeing my family and the seriousness of why we have come together clash painfully.

By Saturday afternoon, the tests were in, the doctors met with us to explain the situation. Daddy's brain had not received adequate blood supply the entire time of the surgery. An error was made before the surgery even began. The shunt which circulates blood through a pump while the heart is stopped had not been inserted into the vein carrying blood leaving the brain (as is the normal procedure), but into the artery bringing oxygen to the brain. Such a tiny error. Such drastic consequences. The heart repair was excellent. However, the brain had been starved for nearly four hours.

It was highly unlikely that we would be caring for a disabled, aging, Dad, unable to communicate, move or function. There was only one way for this to end.

We re-entered the hospital room, knowing now that we had each been prompted to travel in order to say 'Good-bye.'

"Oh, Sweetheart! Please don't go!" Shirley sobbed, tightly squeezing his unresponsive hand. "Being married to you has been the happiest ten years of my whole life!"

Deathbed. It is not a place I had ever expected to be. All night Saturday we stayed in Daddy's room: my two brothers and two sisters and I, Shirley and her brother and sister and Uncle Ronald. The Minister came as much as he could. I met my two sister-in-laws for the first time, two brothers-in-law and little nieces and nephews I barely knew.

Slowly, slowly, life was leaving organs, systems, the body was shutting down.

"Is it OK with you if we sing?" I suggested in a whisper. "Daddy sang to us at bedtime so we could go to sleep. It seems a gift we can give him now while he goes to sleep."

Hymns and patriotic songs, musicals and operettas, one after another, our voices continued for over five hours. Uncle Ronald knew all the verses. We all joined in the choruses. Then there were the Old-Time Spirituals and folk songs. So basic. So simple. So true.

Deep river, my home is over Jordan,
I want to cross over into camp ground.

Swing low sweet chariot
comin' for to carry me home!

Michael, row the boat ashore
Halleluia![20]

Sunday, January 21

At last, Sunday at noon, the stillness came. Not even the machinery could detect rhythms of heart or lungs. Four days before his 66th birthday, my Daddy's life on Earth was over.

Monday, Tuesday, January 22, 23

Monday and Tuesday were a blur of sleeplessness, tears, floods of memories, savouring faces and soaking in voices, listening to decisions being made, and certainly not being able to eat. I had kept my Mother up-to-date using the hospital pay-phone. Although they had been separated, divorced and both remarried, it still seemed necessary to include her. After all, they had been married for nearly 30 very significant years.

I was depending on others for transportation, meals and lodging.

Wednesday, January 24

All day today, the clock tells me where to go and what to do. Dress, ride, stand, see the casket. See the familiar face, so still, so cold. Shudder at the thud and finality of the closed lid. Hear the Minister read age-old Scriptures. Watch the impossible scene: the casket carried into the crematorium. Evening comes. Dress, ride, remain tightly in control of posture, face, voice, breath. Do what is expected. Just let it all go by.

Now I enter the church. My eyes are down. I don't really want to greet anyone. My Mother! Reaching for a hug, I realize that the man standing beside her is her husband. How can I possibly add to all of this once-in-a-lifetime heavy emotion? Do I call him, 'Dad' or 'step-Dad' or by his name? Too much. Block it out. Just go into the church and sit with my siblings. Each of them has a spouse or children here. I have no one. My family is 3000 miles away. My Mother sits way in the back. She has no role here.

And now. It's time. Flowers, candles, silence, hymns, prayers, Scripture, readings, biography, ritual.

* ** *** ****

James carefully prepared thoughts to read aloud as part of the eulogy.

> How are we to reconcile ourselves to such a tragedy? This death so unexpected, so accidental, so unnecessary? How can we accept the monstrous disproportion between the minuteness of the causes and the enormity of their consequences?
>
> Tragedy enlarges the soul. The terrible pain of tragedy is the torment of a soul being racked and stretched to a more capacious size, until it is deeper, broader, larger, capable of embracing more emotion, more compassion, more wisdom, more love.
>
> Perhaps my father's final hours were his greatest masterpiece. How could something he never intended, something he desperately didn't want, be regarded as his masterpiece? And yet, he

> had been composing, quite unconsciously, throughout his entire life. The cast -- his family gathered around him during his final hours. The score -- the last songs he ever heard -- were the songs he taught us. The script -- the stories, the poems, the passages of Scripture which we recited at his bedside -- were the words he taught us when we were children.
>
> Tragedy enlarges the soul. Perhaps this helps to explain why an all-merciful, all-loving, all-wise, all-powerful Creator could have chosen to create a world which includes sin, suffering and death. Perhaps it even sheds some light on one of the most inscrutable mysteries of the Christian religion itself: that the infinite, incapable of enlargement, became finite, that God himself became man in order to suffer and to die. And if tragedy expands our experience, if the richest life is that which embraces the fullest breadth of emotion, then perhaps... those of us who witnessed the tragedy of my father's death most intimately and suffered from it most painfully will emerge, in time, most profoundly transformed by it in their assessments of the meaning of his life and perhaps of life itself.

* ** *** ****

I wipe my eyes. I control my face. I tightly clench my hands.

The reception downstairs offers a chance for others to speak. It is strange to hear people tell things I did not know about my Father. It is strange to hear his older sister tell about Little Daddy. It is strange to learn of the impact that Daddy's work has had in important places with important organizations and important people. It is strange to have his wife receive all the condolences and my Mother leave because she has no place. It is strange to eat a familiar cookie with familiar people all around me in such a familiar place with such turmoil within me.

Thursday, January 25

We went to his apartment. Shirley let us look and choose things we had given him to take home as mementos. As if my heart did not hurt enough already, not enough tears had been shed, not enough conflicts and contrasts and confusion, there was one more detail. January 25, the day after his funeral was Daddy's birthday. We had cake. We sat for a family photo. We said, 'His Earthly birthday,' We said, 'His Heavenly birthday.'

People, started to leave. Hugs. Last looks. Pledges to keep in touch. Driving. Flying.

While we were together for this 'Good-bye' I had wanted to collect the sweetness of every moment with my siblings. Yet, I am a stranger to them. I have been gone for seventeen-and-a-half years. They interact with each other frequently. Their children don't know me.

I stayed to help Shirley sort Dad's belongings... to sort my own memories and feelings. I stayed to walk again in familiar places: the Arbor Vale Church Community I loved and left, our old house, the places I used to play, swim, skate, go to school, where I met and married my own husband, beginning our own branch of the family tree.

Thursday, February 1

Today I travel back to the airport. Back across the continent. Back on the Greyhound. Twelve hours of looking out of the window. Back to my little town, my little home, my little family. Back to my husband. Back to my own life story.

During the long hours of travel, I allow my thoughts to wander back through time, collecting pieces, trying to fit things together.

What about my Mother? What about her husband? How will I ever have an idea of him when they live in Florida and I live in British Columbia, Canada?

I didn't go to my Mother's wedding. It was in December, 1994. How could I make travel plans when unknown weather could close in, dumping snow on the mountain highways I would need to travel to get to the airport? Why would I leave our children: Elise (now fourteen), Michael (twelve), Nicholas (seven) and Toby (six) just before Christmas? Why would I spend hundreds of dollars for a one hour ceremony? And, if I did go all that way, how could I pretend to be happy when the groom is a complete stranger to me?

Instead of attending the wedding, I decided to make a counselling appointment close to the day and time of the ceremony.

Friday, December 2, 1994

"Instead of going to the wedding, you would rather be here to talk about your feelings?" my counsellor prompted me when I explained my decision.

"Yes," I brought every part of my thought process to that hour. "I need to allow every emotion and unanswered question to flow out, unobstructed, in this safe environment. I need to untangle many confusing memories. I need to make a way in my mind for this to be possible, for me to accept someone who is not my Father to kiss and hold my Mother!" I was already speaking fast, as if I it would hurt less if I could get it over with quickly. "Are you willing to help me do that? It feels so scary!"

It kind of felt the same way as going to the doctor or dentist. I don't know why it hurts. I need to ask for help. I might experience something worse. But, in the end, I will feel better.

"You're feeling overwhelmed and need someone to stay with you while you sort out your feelings?" He is very good at understanding what I mean. It is such a relief to be heard.

I had been keeping my observations under lock and key for thirty years, never telling anyone what I had experienced. Now I felt like I had to make my parents' divorce a permanent reality, instead of avoiding the fact. Since I moved so far away, I didn't watch it unfold. I only talk on the phone. It just didn't seem real to me.

I had been seeing my counsellor for three months. He listened. I talked about anxiety, fear, self-doubt, depression. My patterns of self-talk were so negative, so out of proportion to the situation. It had been a very worthwhile experience to read, journal and talk about my inner thought process, feelings and memories of my life.

"You're feeling anxious to say things that you have kept bottled up since you were a small child," he was welcoming me gently to begin. "Where in your body do you feel the tension?" He had often asked me to stop and notice my physical signals of stress.

"My heart is pounding. My jaw and shoulders and fists are tight. My breath is tight, too." But I wanted relief. I wanted there to be a safe person to tell. I wanted to not be alone with this painful confusion. For me it was the most terrible thing. For someone who has training and focus and skill, it would be all right to say nasty things, to lance the wound and allow the ugly to drain, to hope for a soothing balm, to be relieved of the dread.

"Let's pause a moment to see if you can deliberately relax the muscles and draw in a few deep breaths. This is a safe place.

I will stay with you. Together we can explore your memories and questions and see where they lead."

"I feel that if I can lay out all of the pieces and fragments, instead of keeping them locked up, then I might be able to see the whole picture and better understand things that I could not comprehend at the time that they happened when I was a small child. The fear seems to be keeping everything tangled up. When I talk to you, everything seems to get smooth."

"Yes. You might see meaning instead of confusion. Are you ready to begin?" His manner communicated both gentleness and strength.

And so I began the history as I understood it.

"When I was about eight years old I overheard my parents' loud voices in the night. I felt the tension. I wondered about what happened between them that children cannot understand. I heard my Mother crying in the night. Was she sad? Hearing of unfortunate family news? Was anyone ill? Or dying? I heard my Father's voice, not comforting, but demanding. Each voice seemed to disagree about something and refuse to back down.

"My bedroom was directly above their bed with air vents under my bed allowing sounds to pass unobstructed.

"I was confused. Sleep is more powerful when a child is small, so it is a foggy, blurred memory. I scratched the sheets near my ear. The sound of the nearby scratching was louder than the further away voices. I didn't understand how there could be any problems. Dad had brought us to Colorado. His dream had come true. Dad had the job he had always wanted. We had just moved into the new house uniquely designed by an architect. Then there was the new baby, darling, healthy, growing. Even the book Dad wrote would have been something good. What could possibly be so bad that my Mother's tears would wake me up in the middle of the night? Why wasn't Dad helping to make the crying stop?" I remembered the tumbling confusion. It just didn't match. Happy times and sad voices.

"So, you made a noise to block out the sound." He was paying attention. I felt like a life raft was nearby to rescue me.

"Yes, but that didn't make the problem go away. None of the others heard it. I felt so alone." My counsellor's face is calm and relaxed, yet, focused on my story. I took another deep deliberate breath and continued.

"When I was about nine, I heard them quarreling in the living room. Both seated across the room from each other, lights on, the sound filling the house. I stomped down the stairs, crossed my arms over my chest, frowned and fiercely shouted, 'Why don't you just get divorced!?' With a disgusted face, I turned on my heel and marched loudly back up the stairs. Things were quiet after that. Then we moved to Florida.

"The year in Florida I did not hear voices at night. My bedroom was down the hall. Besides, grown-ups don't get stuck, I thought. Whatever the problem was it must have been resolved."

"Do your muscles feel more relaxed now?" he asked, "When you remember more peaceful times?"

I quickly scan my own sensations. "No, actually. I just noticed something. The tension feels just the same as 'The Day on the Cliff' when I felt 'I can't – I have to.' Even when the situation is over, the sensations of resistance are still there. When someone is making you do something you don't want to do, your body stays 'on guard.' Like it could happen again. Unexpectedly. And here's another thing. The tension I feel matches the tone in my Mother's voice."

"So resistance is a pretty strong feeling. It doesn't just go away." Seeing me tense up again he suggested, "How about another deep breath? Are you ready to go on?" I am grateful for his guidance.

"When I was twelve, we moved to the Arbor Vale Church Community in Ontario. Our first house was unusual. The ground floor was a car port, entrance, laundry room, family room, bedroom, and stairway. The upstairs had the kitchen, dining and living room and two more bedrooms. My parents took the downstairs family room as their bedroom since it was the largest room. My little sister, Carol, and I shared the other bedroom right beside theirs.

"One night, after my Dad came home from a men's meeting at the church, the dreaded sounds began again. I decided that I was old enough to understand. What do they disagree about that is so dramatic that it becomes this loud unhappy scene? Is someone in trouble? Is it my fault? Or can I help? Why can't they agree to disagree? Why can't they get help if it is a money problem? A health issue? A family matter? What is needed that is not available? What cannot be changed so must be accepted?" I gestured and shook my head, my eyes darting about.

"I was up on the top bunk bed, right beside their bedroom, with my door open. I decided not to scratch the sheets to cover up the sounds. I decided to listen. After all, we had moved twice. I knew that Ontario was a step up for Dad's career. I could not imagine that we had money problems, or Mother had done anything to upset Dad with her management of the home, children, or activities within the Church Community. There couldn't be illness or problems in the extended family which would still cause tears after so much time had gone by."

Confidentiality is a necessary part of the counsellor-client relationship. I said out loud to my counsellor the words I had heard. The tone. The emphasis. The high voice. The low voice. Tangled up. Overlapping. Resistance. Pressure.

"And then I heard him say what he sometimes said to me, 'What is *wrong* with you?' Suddenly the door burst open, my

Dad strode past my room, pushed open the outside door, slammed it and spun gravel out of the driveway. 'Never mind!' he shouted."

Recalling the scene brings back the sensations: ears stunned, wide-eyed, my jaw clenched, my fists tight. What could I do? Go? Stay? Speak? Silence? Let her know that I heard? Let him know that I heard?

"How did you feel then? How do you feel now?" My counsellor had walked with me, steady through the storm.

"I felt trapped. Stuck. I knew couldn't speak about this. I forced myself to keep it bottled up. But, now?" He waited for me to find words to describe what I was experiencing inside. "I feel relief from the release of the turmoil. When it's bottled up it stays and festers. Now it has been spoken and seems less intense. At the time I thought adults knew what to do about every problem. But, I am the age now that they were then. I don't know everything. People didn't know very much about healthy communication back then."

Aware of the time, I moved quickly over some more family history and influences which formed my views of marriage.

"My Mother told me, when I was older, that my parents had gone to the Minister for counselling, but my Mother put a stop to it when Daddy pressured her to take 'Prozac' or 'Valium.' It seemed to him that she was to blame for the unhappiness. If she would simply cheer up, everything would run smoothly for him."

* ** *** ****

There is also so much cultural influence woven into the backstory of every marriage.

Movies show that falling in love is sweet and good, gentle and kind. Both the man and the women are smiling. My Mother had told me that sex was a valued gift God gave to people.

In the 1950's, when my Mother and Daddy got married, the expectation for marriage was pretty simple. The man earns the money and the woman stays home to cook and clean and take care of the children. The man will provide for her and stay within his marriage bonds as long as the women stays within hers: by being available to him.

In the 1960's, when my siblings and I were growing up, television and movies brought both extremes into view: wholesome marriages, cheerful families and 'white picket fence' homes. In contrast, there was also unlimited visual stimulation for the roving eye.

In the 1970's, my siblings and I began to date and make decisions about our own adult lives. Women voiced their 'equal rights.' Contraception and sterilization had made an entirely different ratio in the bedroom. And now legalized abortion shifted what happened between men and women even more.

In the 70's, when I was a teenager, I gradually learned more about problems people might have in their lives. While reading the Ann Landers column I learned what 'rape' meant. It was a topic in the news at the time. Women were enrolled in university and entering career paths. Women went walking across the campus, or to their cars after work, in the dark. Women were wearing miniskirts. Women seemed to be 'asking for it.' The courts were harsh. The laws were not helpful. A man forcing a woman to have sex? What does force have to do with giving and receiving love? How frightening!

Each of these decades and social trends impacted my parents as they moved through time.

* ** *** ****

I continued my monologue. "Although there was tension, I never heard my Mother cry again. First me, then my brothers went away to the Seer-Church boarding school and college in Pennsylvania. It came as a rather shocking surprise when our Minister came to tell my brothers and I, 'Your parents may not be together by Christmas.' I decided to drop out of college to come home. But, somehow they stayed together." I sat back, relaxed.

"A year later, when I was engaged, my Mother let me know, 'We might not be together by the time your wedding date arrives.' Yet, they were all smiles for our wedding day. The next year it was my parent's 25th wedding anniversary. They came out west to stay in the cabin with my husband and I. It seemed that our wedding had a positive effect on my parents' relationship. They smiled and laughed and held hands. But, a year later, after I had a baby, I phoned Mother, asking to come home for the winter months. 'Won't it be nice to have Christmas with your first little grand-daughter?' But my Mother replied with a voice as heavy as lead. 'It won't be what you imagine. Your Father and I will not be living together by the time you arrive.' And this time, it was for real."

"How did you feel to be going home under those circumstances?" My counsellor seemed to be able to empathize with the shifting emotions as I related the sequence of events.

"Hope and dread. Not a comfortable mix! I quietly asked each of my siblings, 'Why are Mother and Dad breaking up?' They told me that Mother moved out of the master bedroom and now slept in my old bedroom, that she pushed him away.

"I asked Mother, too, when the time was right. 'Why did you and Daddy break up after so many years?'

She was blunt. 'When trust is gone, there is nothing left,' was her compact reply.

"Then I asked my Dad. 'Why did you and Mother break up after so many years?' He had invited me to see where he lived. It was a room on the top floor of an old Tudor-style mansion near a park.

I could still imagine the scene. A statue of Queen Victoria dominated the view. 'The Victorian Era' with its straight-laced views of modesty and proper behavior seemed a discordant setting for the renovated mansion where co-ed university students were living common-law. Dad had a bedroom like Cinderella up in the eves. He had to wash his dishes down the hall in the stainless steel kitchen sink installed in the bathroom that was shared with the other renters on the top floor. He had a two-burner hot-plate to heat up food, a chair and table and a bed. What kind of situation is this?

"I suppose it was difficult for you to go there. And even more difficult to ask him directly." Like firm footing while crossing a turbulent creek, I felt my counsellor's sturdy presence.

"When I look back," I mused, "I can feel opposite forces within me. Courage and determination to uncover the truth, and swirling uncertainty and risk of the unknown. 'Do you really want to hear this?' Daddy asked me. He sat on the only chair. I sat on the bed with my sleeping baby beside me. He looked up at me with this strange expression on his face. It looked to me like a combination of sadness (from the loss of the marriage, family, home), guilt (from the facts he knew and I was yet to learn) and eagerness (to confess and face the truth). His expression was twisted by conflicting emotions.

"I said, 'You know what you are about to tell me and I don't. If you want me to know, I am listening. I'd like to understand, because I know you two have had problems over the years. Are you separated or getting divorced? Why now?' I couldn't keep eye contact. I kept rearranging my baby's blanket while she slept. It was very confusing. I was thinking 'now or never' and knowing that what ever he said would change my view of everything in our family. Yet, deep down inside, I might already know.

"He took a deep breath, looked down at his hands and simply stated the facts. 'I was on a trip making speaking engagements. I stopped to visit an old flame... one thing led to another.'

"I still didn't understand. 'But that was a long time ago, Dad. Why did you split up now?' I questioned.

"Now his head came up and he looked off in the distance. 'Well,' he paused. He cleared his thoughts and took another breath. 'It wasn't the only time.' I had to make it stop. 'OK, I don't want to know any more.' And the conversation was over." I couldn't speak. My face down. My face frozen. My voice very quiet.

"And that was thirteen years ago," my counsellor brought me back to the present time. "But the feelings are still very strong," he indicated that I could continue, or pause, or stop.

I was shaking. But I wasn't finished. New realizations were popping in my head. "Before I asked, I wondered. On the way up those stairs, I carried the burden of not knowing. I saw things. I heard things. Tiny scraps. Little pieces. I didn't known how they fit together. Or maybe they were unrelated fragments. I was a child! Then he told me. Then I knew. On the way down those stairs, I carried the burden of knowing. It is a heavy burden. Now I know something my siblings do not know."

"What else?" my counsellor's perception told him that perhaps now the pieces would start to fit together.

"Two huge shifts happened within me. Buoyant, I felt new confidence that my intuition had been accurate. Anxious, I felt hyper-vigilant about every boy-girl interaction around me which might impact my own marriage." Since I had never told my story, I had never become fully aware of these inner workings of my heart and mind. And, I realized these memories still had an effect on me and my own marriage.

"But, now I was also stuck again. I couldn't expose the facts, but I had to acknowledge the impact. I couldn't tell my siblings, but they needed to know how much our parents have tried to shield us from their troubles. I can't hate my parents, but I have to try to understand, perhaps hope, somehow forgive. I can't allow fears to grip my heart, and I have to continue to trust my own husband. No wonder I struggle so often with self-doubt!"

"Each person in the family has to sort through and make their pieces fit, each in their own way," he gave me a kind of map.

* ** *** ****

In previous sessions we had already worked through how I felt on the day of my parents' divorce.

Five years after they started to live apart, after all hope of reconciliation was dried up, on the day of their divorce, I stood still, expecting that at the moment the judge hammered his gavel on the bench and declared the official dissolution of their marriage, I would cease to exist. If the marriage was a 'mistake' then I was also a 'mistake.' I waited. I thought that the chromosomes I had from each parent would separate, that the DNA that came to be me 27 years ago would shatter, that I would never have been born, erased, withdrawn, unraveled, sucked back up into the vast unknown void of nonexistence.

But, I lived.

And, since that day, way deep down inside, I have felt like I had to do good deeds to 'pay the rent' since my existence was probably a 'Cosmic Mistake.'

In 1985, Daddy remarried. The day that he phoned to tell me the news, I was putting icing on my daughter's 5th birthday cake. Elise had grown into a darling, clever, intelligent person. Her birthday was always a very special day for me. Happiness I could hardly contain was funneled into special details of her celebration. Her existence was my joy. The phone was tucked up under my chin, held by my left shoulder while my hands continued to dip and spread the icing.

"I'm getting married," my Father's voice began.

Instantly an avalanche of feelings spilled from my imagination: I hope she is disgusting. I hope she is obviously a horrible mismatch. I hope everyone laughs and is embarrassed by this.

Then frightening images of destruction flared up inside me. I wanted to scratch and yell and smash and ruin everything. Feelings bubbling up. Feelings pressed down. Feelings on a rampage. Feelings squelched.

I just could not accept this thing. Marriage? Holy? But it has all been so polluted.

Then Dad told me the name of the person he would wed. It was Shirley, a woman I knew. She had been a kindergarten teacher at the Arbor Vale Church School. She was nice. She was modest, pretty, ladylike, well known, charming, nothing to be embarrassed about, 'a catch.' Actually she was someone to look up to! When I was a teenager, she had allowed me to volunteer in her classroom. She taught me how to design wholesome educational projects for the very young. I couldn't hate her. She was too nice. But it was still very confusing to accept.

My siblings attended their wedding. I still couldn't fathom such a thing and stayed away.

Meanwhile, my Mother had spent the years in Florida working in an all-night kitchen, trained as a holistic health provider, and then worked as a Nanny. Recently, in the spring of this year, 1994, my Mother told me of her friendship, courtship and engagement to Joseph. She was so happy. It was an entirely different relationship than she had with my Dad. She told me that Joseph had made a list of 26 topics for them to discuss including: background information, family history (parents, siblings, children), religious beliefs (they had both recently became Born Again Christians), health (problems, insurance, habits), preferences (hobbies, interests, entertainment), and plans for the future (travel, wish-list, retirement plans) and then the two big ones: where to live and finances.

Mother told me that in her first marriage she had never had these discussions so openly and comfortably before. She and Joseph listened to each other. They learned from each other. They laughed. They confided in each other. I was so happy for her, because I felt that I already had such a good marriage partner myself, and I was glad that she would have a satisfying companionship experience.

And yet, her wedding is still too much for me to comprehend. While all of my siblings, their spouses and children planned to attend, I just could not force myself to go.

* ** *** ****

Returning from my thoughts, I continue with my counselling appointment. "But, here it is. Tomorrow is their wedding day. My Mother sounds happy, confident, well prepared and content. They each have had lives with painful marriages. Now they approach marriage with the help of a Pastor, a model to strive for, a guideline about the role of the Christian husband and the wife."

"And the tension in your muscles? You seem quieter now," my counsellor observed.

"I can't say if it is good or bad. It is not my life. It is not my Path. All I know is that my Mother won't be alone, trying to earn a living and pay the rent. She will have a friend and support system. He is retired military so they will have a steady income, medical insurance and other benefits for life." Yes, I notice that I do feel physically more relaxed, and mentally more accepting of my own emotions, my own family history and the present reality of the lives of my family members.

Sitting up straight, leaning forward, I speak in a brighter tone. "So, here is what I think right now: If (as the Seer-Church teaches) *only* the marriage of one man and one woman is holy, pure and clean and lasts to eternity... then my parents are an utter failure. But, *if* the entire thing we are each trying to do while we live on Planet Earth is to 'grow' and 'mature' and become 'the best version of yourself' then, each of the things my parents did is part of an over-arching lifelong story. Instead of seeing one single event or one specific action as 'right' or 'wrong,' maybe it is the lifelong development that matters. Each person is on their own Life Path. Each person's heart can change, turn away from darkness and dare to reach towards brightness. It's like a plant sprouting up through a crack in the pavement. It wants to live!" I hurry on, words tumbling out rapidly.

"When I look at the whole story, like a big panorama or map, I see that it was brave and worthwhile for my Dad to propose to my Mother, and brave and worthwhile for her to accept. They married. They deliberately conceived and brought each of my brothers and sisters and I into the world. They provided necessities, education, myriad outings and opportunities and experiences for us. They continued through the decades and made decisions, moved, adjusted to the Church Community, took part in local traditions and enjoyed the middle-income lifestyle.

"Then, when the strains and difficulties within their marriage became unendurable: they separated, then divorced. This also takes courage. If it is dead and you try to keep it alive, there is a stench of decay. If you admit, 'this is dead' then you can bury it. You can grieve and move on. Realizing 'it's over' is actually a brave thing to do, too.

"So they did.

"Whatever they each suffered, whatever they each continued with or left behind, changed or remained, they each had the courage to remarry. That is amazing, to commit again when the first marriage was so painful.

"Now, I have to say, that the comfort my Dad has with his second wife, the relaxed and enjoyable outings and shared interests, this is a very good thing to see. I do not sense the tension there. He's happy! It makes me wonder: is it possible that my Dad learned how to care for another person in a cooperative relationship that they can both enjoy? That would be a good thing! Worth the struggle! Worth the effort!

"When my Mother tells me about the man she will marry today, she says they talk about things she never talked about with my Dad. She feels comfortable making decisions together with her new husband. It makes me wonder: is it possible for my Mother's life to make a change for the better and for her to have years of participation in a healthy relationship? That would be a good thing! Worth the struggle! Worth the effort!

"If it is possible for the second marriage to be fulfilling, comfortable and sweet, then I have to step away from my hope that my parents will ever get together again, forget about 'one man and one woman to eternity' and make there be room in my own personal belief system that the second marriage could be the nourishing one." I sit back, spent, but feeling like a whirling wind has calmed down.

"You laid out all of your puzzle pieces," my counsellor summarized. "When you started, they seemed all in a jumble. Now they seem to be making a more complete picture?"

"Oh, dear," another disturbing thought begins to spin. "What about me? If my parents are no longer married to each other, am I now an illegitimate child? If God arranges every pregnancy, did He make a mistake? Should my husband have married someone else? Should my children even exist?"

Oh, I feel all dizzy again! I just don't know what to do with all of these questions!

"Time for another breath. Notice the muscles in your hands. Notice the muscles in your face. Feel the security of this place." His soothing voice brings me back to the present.

When my mind slows down, I can speak again. "I have to believe: It all happened as part of the 'Big Picture.' We all exist. We all learn. We all choose. We all have a part of the story to live out in the 'Grand Scheme of Things.' There is uncertainty because we are always 'in the middle somewhere.' But, there is clarity sometimes, too."

I remind myself that Daddy made it through the rough parts. He is so cheerful and eager and comfortable with his new wife. He and Shirley travel and go to concerts and attend lectures and Seer-Church gatherings. They went to Europe!

And Mother came through those unhappy chapters, too. Her voice sounds mellow when she talks about her new husband. They have friends to play Bridge with, go to baseball games and fishing in the ocean. They have activities at church and Mother sounds so content. They listen to each other and help each other make plans and reach goals.

Then I say, more to myself than to the counsellor, "In a way this second marriage situation seems 'easy.' Neither of them have a first job, a first boss, a first car, a first house, a first debt! They have routines and systems that suit them and no leaky roof or naughty pets or babies waking them up at night. It seems pretty easy compared to getting married at age 20!

"It also makes me think about my own life: the struggles and tiredness and minor complaints and 'if only' and 'maybe someday' feelings that I have sometimes in my marriage."

A brand-new thought is forming in my mind. "Now, I have hope. The thing I have learned and intend to focus on is this: 'What if I could have the second relationship with the same man?' What if I could get through these years of drab, on-going sameness: paydays and bills, meals and laundry, summer and winter, firewood and school bus, repetition and only the empty nest coming up ahead? What if I could stay with Kevin long enough to have the comfortable, calm, companionship with my same first husband, the person I have known since we were sixteen?"

"So, all of this time when you have been anxious about your parents' marriage breaking up, it gives you feelings of fear that your own marriage could come apart?" Now my counsellor has uncovered something deeper that I have never even realized myself.

"Wow! I guess that's true! But now, instead of asking myself: Shall I stay? Are we OK? Will my marriage last? Is it crumbling? Now I can look towards tomorrow this way: What would I need to do to make it possible to stay long enough to have this second, comfortable relationship with the same husband?"

I feel tall and strong and confident now! I feel like there is a tropical island up ahead and the bright abundance is beckoning me to come and enjoy an adventure!

My appointment ends on this positive, hopeful awareness. I sense a new dedication to my husband and home. I want to reach, and learn, and focus, and appreciate, and continue, and stretch, and strive, and 'keep on keeping on.'

Thursday, February 1, 1996

Returning to the present, still on my way home, I feel so glad that the counselling session, just over a year ago, has had such a lasting positive effect. I was able to see my parents as people, each doing the best they could with the resources they had. I could communicate with my Father. It gave me the courage to meet the man my Mother married face-to-face. Just as my own Father leaves this Earth, I have another person in the role of 'Dad.'

Maybe, if I get to go visit from time to time, I'll get know him. Maybe I will hear his stories and look at pictures. Maybe I will participate in outings and events. Maybe I will play games or watch movies or help with the dishes. I may even have a few good conversations with him. Maybe I'll call him 'Papa-Joe.'

But, I'll never be a child. Papa-Joe will never push me on the swings. I'll never invite him to my dance recital. He'll never carry me in from the car when I fall asleep. I'll never get out my crayons and make him a birthday card. He'll never take me to go see Santa.

My Daddy did those things with me. Now he's gone. My future will not have him in it. He'll never see his grandchildren graduate, marry, succeed. He'll never read the newspaper articles and books I write. He'll never appreciate the ways that the decision Kevin and I made to 'get married, go out west, build a log cabin' and all the rest of our goals and ideals have actually been fruitful.

But, maybe Papa-Joe will do these things?

I can know Joseph, little-by-little as I observe and listen. I see that Mother is happy, content, relaxed. She has a companion, security and trust. She feels at home. So, who ever he is, this new 'stepfather' must be OK.

And what ever has become of my Daddy, that must be OK.

And what ever is ahead for me, that will be OK, too.

* ** *** ****

The last time I spoke to Daddy, over the phone the evening before his surgery, I asked him, "Daddy, aren't you scared? They are going to open your ribs! Stop your heart!"

"Honey," he said to me, "Where ever I am, I will still be in the Lord's hands!"

I had never heard my Dad say anything like that before, although, as a child, the song I most liked to hear him sing conveyed much the same meaning.

There were ninety and nine that were safely laid
In the shelter of the fold;
But one was lost on the hills away,
Far far from the gates of gold.

Yes, that naughty Little Lost Lamb had gone off against the Shepherd's warnings. Dirty and wounded, calling for help and exhausted, hungry and lonely, he was sorry to have wandered so far from protection and shelter. Did the Shepherd give up? Turn away? Reject the wayward stray? Abandon the stubborn lamb and leave it to the fate it deserved? No! The Shepherd continually reaches towards all the lambs, no matter how determined they are to break away and follow their own erring ways. The Shepherd provides bridges and renewed pathways, signals and coaxing, until at last, a reunion is possible.

I believe that is what has happened for both of the unique individuals who were my parents. I believe that is what every piece of literature and fairy tale and myth and Bible story and Hero's Journey is about. Repentance. Forgiveness. Reconciliation. Homecoming.

Rejoice, for the Lord brings back His own!
Rejoice, for the Lord brings back His own!

REFLECTIONS

Because in spite of everything,
I still believe that people are really good at heart.
—*Anne Frank*

Chapter 4
Wednesday, January 6, 1998
Adopted Dad: Len

No one can go back
and make a brand new start,
anyone can start from now
and make a brand new ending.
—Carl Bard

* ** *** ****

Tuesday, January 6, 1998

He insisted.

He said it was 'The Day of the Kings!' Len said he just had to take us shopping.

So, Nicholas and Toby and I slid into the wide seats of the golden-brown Ford station wagon and off we went.

As we wound our way along the snowy miles down the valley, I couldn't help reviewing the friendship I had unexpectedly found with this little old man.

* ** *** ****

Tuesday, October 7, 1997

The first time I met Len is forever clear in my memory.

It was a sunny October day. Golden birch leaves dappled the mountainside. Gardens, flowers and forest were finished for the season. The school children were still eager for new learning. The Dads not yet anxious about the cold. The Mothers not yet in the rush before Christmas.

It was a golden afternoon and I sat at the library desk, volunteering to be available for the residents of Avola if they wanted to come and visit, check out books, or do a puzzle. I heard the door creak and I looked up, expecting a child or teenager.

With a tip of his brown felt hat, a cheerful nod and a twinkle in his blue eyes, the small, lean, white-haired man with a neatly trimmed white goatee gave a little bow and made his own introduction.

"I hear you are in need of a carpenter." I could see him scan my face, the one-room log schoolhouse, the existing shelves, the stacks of boxes of books and the pile of lumber at the far end of the room. "I am Leonard George Burton. At your service." His formal bow and playful smile instantly tugged at my heart.

"Well!" I had no words. "Thank-you." Now I scanned him. "Yes."

* ** *** ****

The public library had formerly been housed in the third classroom of the Avola elementary school.

In 1983, Kevin and I decided to leave our log cabin lifestyle so far away from town and other children, and move into the town of Avola. The population of less than 200, the three-room school, the 26 students from Kindergarten through Grade 6 and the two creative teachers made the idea very attractive as our children were nearing school age.

But, no sooner were we settled, than the school closed in 1984 and the portable buildings were removed. The Head Librarian came up from Headquarters in Kamloops to scope out the town. The obvious choice was to relocate the library collection into the existing original one-room log schoolhouse. A new electric furnace and updated plumbing were installed. A biannual rotation of books was scheduled. I was one of the three women hired to take three hour turns opening the building on a regular schedule. For ten years, I organized reading challenges for the children, recommended titles, helped with research for school projects, encouraged the homeschooling families, read aloud to the preschoolers, planned seasonal and holiday themes and welcomed newcomers. At the Avola library a fine time was had by young and old.

Then, more cut backs, the population of Avola was too small to authorize the existence of an entire library. From now on we would be served by a Bookmobile, coming from Headquarters in the city two-and-a-half hours away. Open for one hour, every three weeks the bus-like Bookmobile would deliver an interesting assortment of books, but it would just not be the same thing for the social life of our town.

We protested and begged. We rallied and did fund raisers. We focused our efforts to save the sinking ship by selling chocolate bars and used the money to buy cases of books that were out of date which were destined to be discarded. The

Avola Community Recreation Association agreed to keep the log schoolhouse insured and heated so people could still come and socialize. But, with the shelving removed and returned to the city, we only had a pile of boxes of books in a wide, empty room. A donated kitchen table and a few chairs made the room seem bleak where once we had been so well provided for.

By now the children who had participated in all the activities at the library for the past ten years had grown into high school students. The youth had become adults. Two of our own children had left home to attend the Bonnie Hills Church high school in Pennsylvania. There were only eight elementary school aged children left in our whole town! A neighbour and I volunteered to continue to provide a regular time for people to get together.

It was just about that time that Len moved to Avola.

* ** *** ****

I showed Len the donated lumber and told him how much money we had. He could see for himself the stack of boxes of books we needed to shelve. He asked for paper. He had a pencil behind his ear. He stretched out the tape measure he had brought in his brown jacket pocket. Whistling between his teeth he sketched out a proposal.

"Like this?" he grinned.

Len had designed a pair of two-sided shelves for paperback books. Because the room was sometimes used as a community hall, for pot-luck dinners at Thanksgiving, skits for the Christmas Concert, indoor games through the winter months, the whole shelf could easily be moved on rolling castors.

"You read my mind!" I exclaimed.

"It will be easier to see the titles of the books if the shelves are on a slight angle," he pointed out. And so they were. It was a clever design.

"When can I start?" his eagerness was welcome as my ideas had not stimulated any action from the other neighbours.

"I have the key. You can come and go any time you want to. We like to open the library on Tuesday and Wednesday evenings. So, if you could work around our open times, that would be dandy."

"I'll be here tomorrow at 10:00."

"I'll come to help," I was curious about this new character.

"No, thank-you, I prefer to work alone," he was firm.

October, 1997

And so it began.

I came to unlock and offered to carry in his tools. He set up a saw horse and plugged in extension cords. I paused to clarify the limitations of the project and left him to it. I returned in a few hours to sweep up and admire his progress.

I began to ask him questions which became a full interview. His story was so fascinating. I ended up staying for hours at a time.

Len was born in Portsmouth, England, in 1928. His maternal grandparents ran a small grocery store. His Mother was content as three children came along, but ignored a previous agreement with her husband to travel and explore possibilities. Len's Dad felt frustrated. While Len was very young his Dad walked away and ended up in Argentina. Len, his older brother and sister, Mother and miserable grandmother ran the store.

Len was eleven years old when war came.

As I listened, eyes wide, Len described how some of the first bombs of World War II landed in his neighborhood. In the dangerous run to the bomb shelter, Len and his grandmother arrived safely. His mother, brother and sister were crushed. Len was an orphan in grandmother's care.

The relatives swarmed in to pick through the debris and quickly arrange a funeral. They took Len away.

Rationing left him with meager meals. He did not have the security of a person who loved him, nor personal possessions, nor a familiar home.

The moment he was of age (or maybe, with a little white lie, a little younger) he entered the Navy.

Hong Kong, Australia, India, Len showed me his world map marked with places he'd been. He showed me his military records. "Carried out all his duties in a most efficient and capable manner. Conscientious and reliable in all respects. His records show him to be strictly honest, trustworthy and of sober habits."

Sylvia was his sweetheart and he promised that after training in a trade, he would return for her hand. Their portrait is so sweetly bright, so tenderly confident, so looking forward to the future.[21]

Len learned the trade of refrigeration. When he was able to get home, he was grieved to discover that Sylvia had wed. Hopes dashed, he reenlisted, this time he was stationed in Egypt. Unhappy, restless, he looked for ways to find a new life. By chance, he found a Canadian quarter in his pocket and, taking it as a sign, he made plans to emigrate.

Finding work as a photographer, first for the military, then for advertising, he met interesting people and had opportunities to advance. But what life is there taking pictures of soup cans? frozen peas? chicken stuffing mix?

Searching for his father took him to Argentina. Len learned Spanish and worked as a high school soccer coach for awhile. Thinking he was rescuing a moody young woman, he married, and brought his bride to Vancouver. But she longed for her own language, people and traditions and very soon he released her to return to Argentina.

Exactly how or why I did not understand, but he described a black day when he sat on a mountain road in his pickup truck, a loaded gun on the seat beside him, weighing the balance between staying or leaving this earth.

While he worked, he talked. While he talked, I listened. Len made good progress. His shelf design was taking shape.

Most parts of Len's story were hard for me to imagine. But we had one thing in common. As a youth he had played the clarinet. Me, too. Jazz from the Big Band Era was his favourite. Me, too.

November, 1997

In November, when the white paint on the shelves was drying, I brought him to my house to listen to records of Benny Goodman, Glenn Miller, and others. *Licorice Stick* played by Pete Fountain was a favourite.

While he was at my house I showed him what I was working on. It was a richly red, gold and green, handstitched, queen-sized quilt. A Mariner's Compass was in the centre. The border along the sides looped into rings at the four corners. It was nearly finished and looked magnificent. I was especially proud of it because, as a volunteer, without a paying job or any kind of income, I had figured out how to make a significant purchase. "Len, I am making this quilt to trade for my first car!"

Len was dumb struck. He turned to me with appreciation in his eyes, "You made this? You designed this?" I felt like he could see my mind. I felt a wave of confidence and a new experience of a 'Father Figure' who could see the real 'Me' for the first time in my life.

Two years before I met Len, when I was nearly 40 years old, I had taken my driving test and gained my driver's license for the first time. Now I was so excited to be able to own a car!

A few days after I showed him the quilt, I got up my courage. "Len, I have an important question to ask you. When I come home with my first car, will you be my 'Dad'? Will you come outside and inspect it and 'kick the tires' and tell me, 'Well done!' It would be such a good thing to have a Dad on that day!"

Looking directly into my eyes he solemnly pledged, "I most certainly will."

December, 1997

And so, when the shelves and his autobiography were complete, when my quilt and trade for the car was realized, we continued to spend time together.

I invited him for meals, but he was reluctant and embarrassed. He preferred to eat without dentures. But in December, he came to teach me how to make special foods. 'Trifle' was his favourite. With a twinkle in his eye he would add, "And I'm not here to trifle with you!" Len liked puns. Me, too.

Nicholas (10) and Toby (9) watched him unpack the groceries. He began by demonstrating how to cut the pound cake and place long, narrow strips of it along the outer edge and bottom of the glass bowl. Len whistled between his teeth while he puttered at assembling the colourful dessert. "You could use strawberries or blueberries or slices of banana," he suggested while he spooned canned fruit cocktail, allowing the syrup to soak into the pound cake. Next, vanilla pudding, then a second layer of the cake, fruits and pudding again. I whipped the cream and watched in amazement as this beautiful bowl of dessert was finished. Len stayed for dinner that night! My husband and two young sons thought Len was OK after that!

Len told me that he had open heart surgery about twenty years ago. Blood vessels were taken from his legs to replace the blood vessels in his heart. This, combined with his heavy smoking, resulted in a fairly low tolerance for strenuous exercise so he couldn't hike or trample the fields with us. I went to his place to do hand sewing and listen to his music. He came to our house with desserts and kitchen gifts, recommended books and to listen to my music. He had reel to reel and cassette tapes in his collection which I enjoyed. I had records from my Daddy's collection that he enjoyed.

I was in the habit of bringing a plate of Christmas goodies to the elderly in our town. Without extended family close by, it was a way for me to feed my own heart while making others smile, too. But, Len would have nothing to do with Christmas. Not even saying the word. He didn't want music or decorations, not even a card. Certainly not an invitation to join in family fun. I wanted to bring him to our house or at least take over a meal. But he flatly refused. I had never seen his face so downcast. "I never celebrate Christmas. This is the time of year when the bomb dropped. My family was gone." Nearly 60 years had passed and the pain was still so intense. Brooding. Remembering. Silent. Solemn.

January, 1998

But the days passed and the New Year brought a big surprise.

Today, on January 6th he calls me on the telephone, his voice quick and bright. Apparently the custom in England is to celebrate gift giving on the traditional day when the Church of England marks the visit of the Magi bringing gifts to the Baby Lord Jesus.

No longer gloomy, Len's mood has completely turned around! "Let's go shopping. Today is 'The Day of the Kings!' Get ready. I'm coming over." He whistles as he drives the long miles to town. He calls to Nicholas and Toby in the back seat, "Now, I'm taking you to the Dollar Store. You have free reign. I want you to pick out anything and everything you want!"

As they step away from the car I quietly signal, "Make it about $10 each, OK?" It's more than they can afford on the money they earn from doing chores at home.

Carefully, slowly, looking through the whole store, searching high and low, hoping to discover some treasure, both boys choose a space-gun that shoots harmless foam discs, and each boy chooses a few other nifty things.

Len is pleased. The boys are pleased. I am pleased. Next surprise: he takes us to the hotel dining room and orders ice cream! Even the waitress looks surprised. "It's 'The Day of the Kings!' Ice cream all around. No exceptions!" Len announces. I don't think I have ever had ice cream in January, except for my Dad and my brothers' birthday parties. But, Len is the host and he seems to be enjoying the sharing of his wealth a great deal, so there is no resistance from me.

"No, you may not open your space-gun shooters in the car!" is my only governing comment for the day.

When we arrive at Len's home, unload his groceries and start to buckle up in my car, Len accidentally-on-purpose lets his secret out. "That was the best birthday I have ever had!" His grin and twinkly eyes are brighter than I have ever seen. "Yes, indeed! 70 years old today!"

"What? You rascal! You paid for everything today! Now how will I give you a birthday present?" I glance at my watch. I have exactly one hour to go home, make and eat supper, and head back out the open the library tonight. How can I fit in baking a cake and making a card or gift?

"Toby, bring me my penny jar," I command before the car is even parked. "Nicholas, bring me a piece of poster board from the craft room. Blue if we have it." Rapidly, I measure and mix and pour and bake. Meanwhile, I boil water for pasta and heat a jar of spaghetti sauce from the pantry. "Bring me clear tape. Find the markers." The boys recognize my method of moving quickly. In a creative family and sometimes short minutes, obedience without explanation is sometimes necessary. "Now help me!"

Counting out 70 pennies. Marking a big 7 and a big 0 on the poster board. Taping down 70 pennies. "Do we have any balloons? Look in the drawer." I'm watching the clock. We are working as a team. I think we'll make it.

"If you want to come with me, then eat up. We have to be back in the car before 5:50. OK?"

Len is surprised by the knock on the door. Even more surprised by the warm cake still in the pan. And the penny-card and colourful balloons reached a place in his heart that had been long untouched. "Happy Birthday, dear Len!" we sing loudly in the snowy night.

It was a day neither of us would ever forget. It was a moment which changed his role from a little old man who built some shelves, to a little old man who had a place of honour in our family.

* ** *** ****

Because Len had told me so much about how his family died and he showed me how powerful it was to honour their memory on the anniversary of their death, I asked him if I could share what I wrote when my Dad died. And so, as my emotions began to surface, as the second anniversary of my Dad's death approached, I met him to read aloud the words that had poured from my heart when I got home from Toronto. It was a letter I had written and sent to each of my siblings and a few close friends.

I read aloud. He listened so intently.

* ** *** ****

New Seeds From Grief,

by Eleanor Deckert, January 1996

I would like to share my story from my point of view, with my beliefs, insights and feelings.

It is good for people who have shared good times to be together and share the hard times, too. It is good for me to write, to wrestle with words until I make a clear picture. We each feel, notice and struggle with different things. When people care about each other it is good for them to know something of what others are going through. It is a good to compare and contrast my own experiences with others.

So, here is my story. (I welcome yours.) On one level it is just a sequence of events. More importantly, it is also a series of turning points within me as I realize and become aware of many feelings, memories, parts within myself, relationships with others, my history with my father, my personal belief systems. On another level it is about the Lord, and how I see His Authorship as my story unfolds.

~~~~~~~

Already avoiding the issue for three years, my Dad decided to have heart surgery.

I phoned him three times during the week before his surgery. Once for each of my children to talk to him. Once to
~~~~~~~

thank him for the all the music he has given me in my life. And once to say 'Good-bye' before the surgery.

We also exchanged dreams.

He had dreamed about being in Colorado on a beautiful golden day. He was so happy yet also so deeply sad. He woke himself up crying. He said, "It was like the day Kennedy died." I remember how shaken Daddy was the day Kennedy was shot. I felt afraid, "Who will take care of us now?" And I remember nobody ever really knew for sure what had happened.

In my dream I had the same feeling. I was so happy to be in the Church Community in Ontario, but it was so deeply sad. I was looking for someone, a man who was always there, but he wasn't there now! I also saw flowers in precise arrangements. I took seeds from this place to grow when I got home.

At this time I had a very strong premonition of what was going to happen next.

"Daddy, aren't you scared? They are going to open your ribs! Stop your heart!" I was shaking, clutching the phone, trying to keep my voice steady.

"Honey," he said to me, "Where ever I am, I will still be in the Lord's hands!"

I had never heard my Dad say anything like that before. He was always full of theories, 'on the other hand,' perhaps, and 'what if' were almost always part of what ever he was talking about.

Now, he sounded quietly certain, confident, secure.

I said, "Daddy, I feel so strange. I want to be there. I want to hold your hand. If you ever feel alone of afraid, just think of me and I'll be there. I want you to really get this: I love you, Daddy."

He said, "You always have, Dear-Heart."

I cried and said, "I don't want to hang up. I don't want to say Good-bye."

On Wednesday, January 17, he was admitted to the City Hospital. On Thursday morning he had, not the scheduled quadruple by-pass as planned, but five by-passes were made. Before the surgery began a mistake was made which caused his death. By the time the surgery was over and Dad came up out of the drugs, it was discovered that his left side was paralyzed. At this time the call went out to all his children. 'Make plans to come.'

I was told that on Thursday and Friday he responded to touch, voices and instructions.

All day Friday I was on the Greyhound. Overnight I flew on the 'Red Eye.' On Saturday morning, January 20, I arrived at the hospital. I came to his right side and said, "Daddy, I am here. I came to hold your hand!" He was so still. I thought, "Of course, he is still drugged." But I was told, "No, we are no longer giving him drugs as we consider that he is no longer conscious."

Then, with a huge effort of his whole arm – he squeezed my hand!

It was the beginning of the 'so happy yet so sad' feeling from my dream.

And I also thought, "I came to hold your hand, Daddy, but you won't wake up here. You'll wake up in the Spiritual World."

My brother, Andrew, newly married, realized, "When I become a Father I won't be able to learn, to ask, to share my experiences with my own Father." His wife, Lisa, kept the beautiful attitude, "I want to keep learning."

My brother, James, and wife Lily are expecting a baby boy this summer. This will be the first grandchild to have the last name 'Hinkle.' James was very sad to sense that one of the turning points in Dad's decision to have this operation was his strong desire to see this baby!

My sister, Julie, had her nursing baby girl with her. It was so painful and so beautiful to have a baby with us, sparkling and rosy, while a grandfather's body was slowly growing cool and white.

My sister, Carol, is carrying a baby to be born this spring. How we will rejoice and welcome this newcomer to our world! How the newcomers are welcomed and greeted with rejoicing as they leave this world and go to the next!

Uncle Ronald was so shaken. Since he was born, he has looked to his older brother as a role model, a hero, a steady, constant, encouragement. It is so hard to get your bearings when someone who has always been there is suddenly gone.

There was beauty in Shirley's grief. I saw their love and I realized things I hadn't allowed myself to see. Her softness, love, honour and respect for him had changed my Dad. You can see it in his photos. In his eyes you see a sparkle, 'Somebody loves me!'

As for me, well, I learned a lot. Under the terrible sadness, I kept on being glad. Glad that I had worked through a lot of 'ow-y places' with my counsellor so I could talk my childhood memories over with my Dad. Glad that I had told Daddy things, and asked him things, and listened to him, and been heard by him. I felt glad that I had dared to say everything in my heart. I felt glad that I had learned to hear my own deciding inner voice. I was glad I did not feel abandoned. I was glad that I had had the premonition because I was getting ready to travel.

I didn't arrive saying, 'No! No! How can this be?' I arrived saying, 'Be open. Say 'Yes.' Learn. Observe. Feel. Notice. Share. No masks. No 'should haves.' Listen. Pay attention. This is really happening. Remember.'

I was also really glad in my Dad's attitude towards his operation. He knew that death was a possibility no matter what he decided to do. He had closed a number of details, yet he had happy plans to look forward to. His purpose was not selfish, but to be able to travel to see each of us again.

There was a very real sense of submission, noticed not only by me, but by his wife and by our Minister. This is rare and beautiful. Dad always wanted to find alternatives, beat the system, not follow the crowd, fight against what everyone else took as obvious. This sense of submission was, I believe, a spiritual kind of turning point for him, to submit to the indecencies of being an invalid, the humility of not being able to get out of it by being smart, of not being able to argue the point until he won, but to need help and to say 'Yes.'

There is a saying:

> In order to say 'Yes' to life,
> I must be willing to say 'Yes' to my own death.

How sweet, in the sadness, to be with your whole family. The 23rd Psalm becomes very real.

On Saturday evening, January 20, we had all arrived at last. We had the long meeting with the doctors who explained what had happened. By then, we were told, the swelling of the right side of the brain had put pressure on the left brain and down onto the brain stem. In a short while the signals to the heart would stop. We knew he was going to die.

And as we went back into his room and looked with new vision at our brother, husband, father, and realized this really was 'Good-bye.' I said, "It is all right with everyone if we sing?"

So we did. For five hours! Until past midnight!

Singing was wonderful! Daddy used to sing to us at bedtime. Now, memories came flooding in: hymns, poems, silly nonsense, old time spirituals, sea chanties, cowboy ballads, Bach, Handel, Gilbert and Sullivan, Rogers and Hammerstein, Webber and Rice, opera, musicals, National Anthems, lullabies, the Lord's Prayer, Christmas songs. One led to another. We laughed. We cried. We interrupted each other, eager to try to remember all of the verses. We could hardly keep going when the beauty and sadness were too powerful and choked us.

I said, "Daddy loved the sad part." We remembered how he re-told, re-read, re-played, re-recited the sad part, the turning point in plays, poetry, opera, the New Testament, Mark Twain, Shakespeare, the little details, the foreshadowing, the decisions which nobody knew would lead up to the tragedy.

When we realized it was after midnight, now Sunday, January 21, we said, "Six days shalt thou labour and do all thy work, but on the seventh thou shalt rest."

After midnight, different people took turns sleeping on the floor, on coats, on chairs and at his bedside. We had been given a lounge to rest in, but around the corner seemed too far away.

For how much I stay away from gadgets and technology, I was thankful for the heart monitor machine. We would have lost the pulse hours earlier. The straight line finally came. He died just after noon Sunday, January 21.

> We said, "The Lord bless you and keep you.
> The Lord make His face to shine upon you and be gracious unto you.
> The Lord lift up His countenance upon you and give you peace."[22]
> We said, "Lord, now lettest Thou Thy servant depart in peace."[23]
> We said, The Lord's Prayer and "Now I lay me down to sleep."
> We said, "Good-bye, Daddy. Have a good trip. See you there."

After he died, the coroner came and of course we agreed to an autopsy to see if more could be learned.

Phone calls were made and Carol went to the airport to bring her husband, Jeff. As they entered the hospital room and their two little girls turned to the sound of his voice and recognized him, they ran to him calling, "Daddy! Daddy!" He scooped them up for a big, strong hug. It was so special and it hurt so much. I wanted a hug from my Daddy, too! The next time I see him he will be fresh and bright and strong and I will run to him, "Daddy! Daddy!" and I will have the hug I want so much right now.

As I rode away to find food and rest and a new chapter in my life, I was remembering how our Minister had explained death and the life after death. He said, "Imagine a hand in a glove. The glove is what we see. The glove is what we're used to. We touch it and think it is real. But it is the hand that is real. The hand inside the glove is alive. And so it is with the body and the spirit. The body is what we see and touch, but the spirit inside is what is real and alive. When the body dies it is just like the hand coming out of the glove. The glove, like the body is empty. The spirit, the real person, is still alive and goes on to the next world. We are sad and we say, 'Good-bye' to the body, but we are glad to know that we will see the real person again when we, too, lay our body down and our soul goes on to the Spiritual World."

I am thankful for soup and care and sleep. By now I had been awake for four days and I am just so tired of crying.

The Seer states that life after death begins immediately. From the teachings in those 40 books, we believe that the Lord has a place for everyone in His Kingdom. We do not have to be afraid. The body is empty, and the spirit is alive and active and well. We will indeed be reunited.

Someone suggested making something to put in the coffin as a gift. Perhaps a soft blanket. I purchased white linen and asked the women to join me in hand sewing red wool stitches all around the edge. We thought of our love binding us together. We thought of each stitch representing days and nights or years or the people he knew.

As each woman added stitches, I saw how beautiful, how ancient, how satisfying it was to do this with our love. His older sister, Grace, put the first stitches in, his wife, Shirley, the last.

His daughters, his daughters-in-law, my Mother, a niece, and even his sons and his brother added a few.

James said, "In doing these ancient things we are not alone. We join all the other people in all the other cultures who have done this before us."

As I worked alone, Carol's four-year-old daughter, Brenna, came in.

"What are you making?" she asked.

"A good-bye present for Grampsie." I answered.

"He won't see it!" she said firmly.

"I know," I said, "but I still want to say, 'Good-bye' and give love to him this way."

"Brenna," an illustration popped into my mind. "When your Daddy drives away do you sometimes wave and wave and even though you know he's around the corner and you know he can't see you, you still know he's getting the love?"

"Yes," she nodded her curly head and her eyes sparkled.

"And sometimes when you go to bed and your Daddy is still at work do you blow him a kiss? You know he can't really see you, but you know you really are sending him love?"

Again a nod, a smile and now she's sitting down close beside me.

"Well, I know Grampsie can't see this present, but I still want to make it and send him love this way. So? Would you like to sew for awhile, too?"

So she did! It was a golden moment.

On Tuesday evening, January 23, friends and colleagues were invited to gather. Beautiful flowers, cheerful photos, delicious refreshments and familiar faces and voices again combined the 'so happy - so sad' feelings. This is so real and so impossible. It was my Father's wish to be cremated so that his ashes could be scattered in Colorado.

In the evening at the memorial service, the Minister spoke of the Lord leading us at all times and Dad's faith in the reality of the next life.

James shared his thoughts. "Tragedy enlarges the soul, making it deeper, broader, wider, capable of holding more meaning, more emotion, more wisdom, more love. Perhaps the one most transformed by this tragedy was my Father, himself, as he witnessed and as he learned how much we loved him, as we learned how much we loved him, as each of us learned how much the others loved him, and how much he loved us."

I started to cry when James said, "The first songs we ever heard him sing to us as bedtime, were the last songs he ever heard us sing to him at his bedside."

Afterwards, when his colleagues spoke, I realized, 'I knew a giant.' I had a glimmer of the extent of my Father's work, impact and impression on so many people. People sent greetings from New Zealand, Australia, India, Italy, Germany, Great Britain, Ottawa, Washington, D.C., universities and charity groups he had dealings with, organizations he himself formed.

Another wave of hurt came as I stepped into his apartment. Oh, good, now I know where I am. This is familiar. This is real. This is my Daddy's chair, his mug, his boots, his desk. No! These are now empty objects. The master of the house is no longer here! With no owner to make them precious, to fill them, with meaning, the objects have no value.

You have to do something with all that hurt. As we sorted the belongings, I sensed why some people close the door and leave everything as it was...why others withdraw and live in silence, memories crowding the emptiness...why others fill their time with too much busy-ness, their ears with too much noise, and their lives with too many people...why some turn to drink...why others start family feuds and hurtful things are said which echo across generations.

Yet, we went about it very quietly. People had to leave soon. Decisions had to be made. Each person found a treasure, a mug, card, sweater or photo we had given to Dad. Gifts, holding our love for him, which, because he had treasured them, were now holding his love for us. And as we recognized and held them and remembered the golden moment we had shared, the empty hurting place inside us began to heal. We each had an object to look at and touch, to bridge from this world of time and space and empty longing to the world full of love and peace and togetherness which no one could ever take away.

One by one I said, 'Good-bye' to my siblings as they traveled back to their homes. I said, "I feel like we belong to a secret club of people who were together, who were there, who know." Yet, we also join the human race in this mystery: Do things just happen? Or is there A Plan? What lies beyond this life? What does it all mean? What shall I do while I am living here? How shall I prepare for my own death?

I watched the sun rise. I went to church. I visited places where I had played as a child. I walked through the house we lived in. I knew the place on the stairs where I stood when Kevin turned and saw me wearing my wedding dress and the place where we had our wedding. I knew the spot on the driveway where I stepped into our VW van seventeen-and-a-half years ago and left my family, now to be together again.

I remembered my dream: being in the Church Community, being so happy and at the same time deeply sad, not seeing someone who was always there, the flowers arranged in precision and bringing back seeds to grow when I returned home to my family. What seeds? What can grow out of this frozen, January, emptiness, death and loss? The whole earth has shifted. Everything valuable is old and in my past. How can anything new grow?

When I returned to Avola and the husband, children and home I have here, I had new sympathy for Kevin. His heart still hurts on the anniversary of his Father's death, over 25 years ago. I never understood his silent withdrawal from family activities on that day. Now I know.

As I re-entered the everyday world, I was suddenly surprised by other feelings. Jealous. Angry. Fearful. I wonder. When will it be my turn? Will I be ready? Will my children be grown? Death seems all around me. Some days I feel foggy and dull and nothing in everyday activities has any meaning. Only memories and my private inner world seem important. What I see with my eyes is like a mirage. What I see in my memory is solid and clear. I wonder what will my life be like if I don't have Daddy woven into the pattern.

Is it real to have peace? To say in every second, in every place, in every circumstance, 'Thy will be done'? Were the details governed by an unseen Hand? Or is it real to make war? To go rampaging against the people who, in that one second turning point made a human decision and an act of human hands that could have been different?

When I told my story to a friend, she gave me a single red rose bud. My eyes saw only the rose bud I placed on my father's casket...the last moment I ever had with him in this world.

Now, I watch it begin to open. I feel like screaming, "No! Stay the way you are! Don't change!" I feel like gluing it, or putting an elastic band around it, or wrapping it with lots and lots of tape to keep it the way it is now!

But, I have decided to watch, to let it open. And as it does, it teaches me that I must do the same. It is OK to change. It is OK to open. It is OK to be young and love and beautiful and then to pass through change until you are old and withered and parts stop working. It is even OK to die.

The love is what's real. The love is what lasts. The love is still there. The gift is gone but the love inside the gift is the real treasure.

Holding on, staying the same, is worse than death. It is better to change and go forward accepting death – having lived!

So, this is one of the seeds I have to plant: That love is real.

Daddy loved music and he passed that on to me.

I love passing that on to others.

Daddy loved reading, reciting and telling stories.

I love passing that on to my children.

Daddy loved his family and going on outings.

I am going to rededicate myself to these things.

He loved the Lord and as Fathers have done since Old Testament times, he told the next generation.

I love to do this, too.

So, this is my story. On one level a series of events, on another level a sequence of turning points within me, on another level it is about the Lord as I see His Hand and Authorship as this story unfolds.

My purpose in telling is it this: if any thought, feeling, belief, or insight from my experience is helpful to you as you Journey, it is a gift.

These are the seeds I brought back.

* ** *** ****

Len was completely silent when I stopped reading.

"You must publish this," were his only words, and again, after a moment of silence, almost a whisper, "You must publish this."

I have never in my life had an audience like Len. No corrections. No one-up-man-ship. No 'that's pretty good for a girl.' No pontificating. No changing the subject. No stealing my thunder.

Attentive listening. Appreciative focus. Stating the obvious.

"You are a writer," he said. And, coming from a reader, that is high praise!

* ** *** ****

During these months of getting to know Len, listening to his memories, helping him work, sharing music and books and recipes and learning from each other, something was happening inside my heart. It was hard to find words.

I kept my husband up-to-date on the things we talked about and how we had so many of the same interests and the little jokes Len said to make me laugh.

"It's strange," I told my husband. "It's like I have a new Dad. He doesn't expect me to do work or clean or cook or look after him because he's old. He doesn't flirt with me of say or do anything fresh. He listens when I talk. He thinks I have valid things to say. It's hard to describe."

I fumble for an illustration. "Here's a contrasting example. Imagine my Dad sitting reading the newspaper. Then I bring him my report card to read and sign. He would peek around the side of the newspaper, glance at it absent mindedly and sign it. Or else I'd protest, 'Daddy! You didn't really look! See all of the 'A' and 'A+' grades? I got a lot of high marks! Then he'd say, 'That's just fine, Dear,' or 'We Hinkle's are pretty bright' like he was the one getting the 'A'. He and all of his family were good at academics, so it came as no surprise to him that I was good in school, too. But then, if I excelled at something he wasn't good at, say gymnastics or playing the guitar, he would barely acknowledge that my effort was important or that my skill was valid."

Kevin knows my family. He can imagine the scene. "Remember?" I continue, "When we had the big dream to 'go out west and build a log cabin and go homesteading,' he just poo-pooed the idea. He never said, 'Good for you' about any of it." It always makes my heart really hurt to remember this part of my life.

"With Len," I continue, "I feel like whatever I do is OK. Whatever I say is OK. Whatever I like or don't like is OK. It is new for me to want to expand and be bold and take up space and achieve. I don't have to earn his praise. I already have worth!"

"I think the word you are looking for is 'Mentor.' He respects you," Kevin adds. My husband is not jealous. He values this connection because it enriches and somehow heals hurt inside me. "Your Dad kind of patted you on the head. Len sees you for who you are. He's the Dad you never had. He has a special place in your life." I stepped into Kevin's warm hug, tears forming. "It's not a small thing."

* ** *** ****

"We are 'simpático.' It's Spanish," Len said. "It means we are compatible, we get along, things are pleasant between us. We have a companionship."

I certainly felt an unusual friendship with this kindly, sympathetic old man.

"I was married once for a few months. But when she came to Canada she missed her family in Argentina so much, I let her go. I have had two sons, neither of whom I raised. My parents and siblings are dead. My sweetheart married another. I have never had a daughter," he mused.

When I got home that day, my heart pounding, I used a pair of blank certificate pages, decorated with a border, to write out adoption papers. To make it seem more formal, I mailed them to him to sign. When I went to his house he was so happy. He showed me a secret drawer he had built into his table. "If my house is on fire, these are the only things I need to take with me: wallet, glasses, papers, banking...and this." He held up the adoption paper.

Certificate of Adoption
Application has been made
and a thorough search has been conducted
to adequately match:
a fatherly Mentor and Friend in need of companionship with
a Simpática Daughter in need of extended family.

Such a match was made effective by a mutual
verbal agreement January 17, 1998 and is recognized officially with this document.

Date: January 27, 1998
name of adoptive daughter____________
name of adopted Father, Mentor, Friend______________

I signed his copy. He signed mine.

March, 1998

You are my sunshine, my only sunshine.
You make me happy when skies are gray...

It was Len! Singing! To me! It took me a minute to recognize his voice over the phone first thing in the morning. But it didn't take too long for this greeting to become a daily habit.

May, 1998

When springtime came, Kevin had to be away for a few days to take a required railroad safety course in the city. Len insisted that I punch in his phone number on my cordless phone so that, in an emergency, I would only have to hit the 'redial' button and I would have immediate contact with him. Speed dial was a new feature at that time.

He missed calling me at the usual time the next morning. I waited awhile, then phoned him.

"Good Morning, Len, how are you today?" was my cheery greeting.

"Terrible," was his grumpy answer.

"Oh, Len, what is it?" The problem with having a friendship with an elderly man is that one of these days, something bad might happen to him. My mind imagined the worst.

"I hardly slept at all last night!" He grumbled, his voice was so heavy and tired sounding.

"Why, Len? What's wrong? Are you OK now?" I was getting worried. It wasn't far. I could be there in a minute. "I'm coming over right now." I hung up, grabbed a coat and my keys, called to the boys, "Do your chores," and dashed out of the driveway.

When he answered the door, I could see that his wrinkled face, disheveled hair and untucked shirt showed that indeed, he was not his usual, tidy, cheerful self.

"I slept with my clothes on, with my shoes on, on top of the covers. I had my machete in my hand all night," he explained. "I wanted to be ready in case you needed me."

"O, Len!" I was sad for his discomfort, but astonished at his loyalty. He was ready all night to come rescue me, fend off any foe, whether a wild animal or a human invader!

June, 1998

Meanwhile, I was working on my speech! I had been invited by the President of the Bonnie Hills Church high school to give the parent's address for Elise's graduating class! Len offered to coach me. I read it aloud to him three times, marking places to pause ("They're going to laugh," he'd say), places to control my tone of voice ("Be careful to convey the emotion to the audience without bringing your own tears," he observed), places to use clear diction ("No 'ums!' No 'ahs!' No muttering!" he insisted).

It had been a big decision to send our daughter, Elise, away to school. Although I had struggled with some of the teachings in The Seer's 40 books, walked away and formed some of my own beliefs, still, when my Dad died, I realized that the education I had been given and our children might gain through the Seer-Church was part of their heritage. It seemed important to allow the next generation to go, learn and form their own conclusions.

And she did well. Elise found the challenges and opportunities stimulating. After two years in the high school. It was time for graduation. Kevin and I flew to Philadelphia for the ceremonies.

* ** *** ****

June 1998, Bonnie Hills, Pennsylvania

For the graduating class 'Roots and Wings' by, Eleanor Deckert

We join in celebration to congratulate and recognize the graduating class of 1998.

And what could be said which would underline the importance of the accomplishments of these scholars, would honour and respect their teachers, would thank family and friends for their love and support, and which would ease the joy and pain tugging at the heart of each parent as their precious children cross this threshold?

I have a message for each of you. It is the same message, yet, each of you stand in a different place and each receive it in a different way.

> There are two lasting bequests we can give our children.
>
> One is roots.
>
> The other is wings.[24]

Roots means we are a physical being. Wings means we are a spiritual being. Roots means how things have been. Wings means how things could be.

Roots means we are connected, to the past, to each other, to the Earth, to the Lord. Wings means we are individuals, we hope for the future. We dance together, yet keep our own identity. As birds in the sky, our ideas flash and soar. We dream, imagine and rise to higher things.

Roots means we have been made by the Lord and are part of His creation. Wings means we have been called by the Lord and we respond in action.

Roots means we are hungry, curious, seeking. We reach deeper and broader for something new. We search for and find valuable resources. We continue to learn. We keep growing. Wings means we are hungry, curious, seeking. We stretch higher and farther for something new. We seek out a glimpse of further horizons. We continue to discover. We keep growing.

The purpose of roots is to go deeper, to tap nourishment, to go broader, to support, to store up resources and to hold fast and resist change, to gather together and unify, to be able to reproduce. The purpose of wings is to rise higher, to be able to gain perspective of the big picture, to elevate so as to see far and wide, to let go and be spontaneous and try new creative things, to experience the thrill of adventure and seek the unknown, also to go away from and return to the nest, to provide for and protect the young.

Parents, like you, I remember bursting with thanksgiving, praise and love to the Lord when the newborn gift He had given me was placed in my arms. I promised Him then that I would care for her and do my best to return this child to Him. We have exposed our children to as much of this world as we can, and introduced them to what we can know of the Spiritual World. In this way we have been providing for their roots, giving them both strength and depth.

Today we shift our emphasis. Today we allow them to open their wings. The purpose, after all, of each new thing they learn is so that these young people are no longer dependent on us, but have their own inner strength, can make decisions and act in their own freedom.

It seems so drastic and hurts so much to let them go. And yet, we have had practice with separations. Many times they have moved away from us. Many times we have felt the flutter, the lift, the joy of them being on their own.

How long ago it was big news: your little one could take the first steps, cross the street, tie their own shoes, tell time, ride a bike.

Although it hurts to let them go, the alternative is to hold on too tightly to our children. Sometimes in an effort to protect them from any and all harm, I am tempted to keep my children as Rapunzel was kept, high in a tower, far from the world of troubles. Yet, she had neither roots nor wings. She did not know where she came from. She had no hope for the future.

Graduates, I invite you to think about this.

> What you are is God's gift to you. What you make of yourself your gift to God.[24]

Everything your parents, teachers and friends have ever tried to give you up until today – your roots – has been a gift from the Lord. Everything you do from now on – your wings – will be your gift to the Lord.

The places you've live.
The teachers you've had.
The places your parents have taken you.
The music which you enjoyed in your home.
The special foods and customs for each holiday.
The books which were read to you.
The movies you watched together.
The lessons and after school activities you participated in.
Your family's pets, neighbours, relatives, guests.
The games you played.
The songs and jokes you shared.
Causes your family gave support to.
Ways you volunteered in your community.
Changes and moves, births and deaths.
How you start the New Year.
How you say good-bye to each other.
How decisions are made and carried out.
How disagreements are expressed and resolved.
How money is earned and saved, given and spent.
Stories you've heard about your ancestors.
Stories you've heard about your parents as youngsters.
Stories you've heard about your-
self as a baby or adorable tot.

All of these strands braid together to form your roots. The Lord has given you these resources to draw on. Now, as each of you set out on this new part of the your Journey, He will be there to guide you.

Honoured guests, thank-you for joining us today, the parents as we look back and ahead, the students as they venture forth, the staff as they finish their work for another year.

You have had a place in the life Journey of these graduates. In each of our stories there have been days when we felt like giving up. We couldn't keep going even one more step. On those days – your hug, your letter, or phone call, a care package, or an ice cream cone gave us a boost so we could carry on.

You have known these young people since they were babies. You have watched as a child draws upon past experiences - roots - to be able to try something new - wings. And you have cheered them on.

Today is graduation day.

Why are we doing this? Why is every high school in North America participating in a similar ritual?

Sometimes ceremonies and rituals seem hollow and meaningless. Sometimes details, timing or personal problems dampen and darken our joy. It is hard to enter into the festivities. I believe that this and all other ceremonies and customs are containers. By themselves they are empty, but there is something invisible inside. Love, satisfaction in a job completed, pride, joy, and pain, and the realization that each of you now stand with all those who stood here before you.

Graduates, as you go forward, may you find a balance: a balance between roots and wings, between old and new, between holding on and letting go, between connection to others and being your self. Move back and forth within the balance. Feel the need for both. Continue in your own growth for the purpose of doing what you were made to so. Believe in what is invisible.

> Hold fast to your dreams, for if dreams die,
> life is a broken winged bird that cannot fly.[25]

Teachers, may you renew your calling to nurture yet another classroom of individuals and delight as they experience and experiment with their own self discovery. Hold this banner high:

> If you can imagine it, you can achieve it.
> If you dream it, you can become it.[26]

> Friends cherish one another's hopes,
> are kind to one another's dreams.[27]

Parents, it is time to enjoy the fruits of our labours. A new kind of love will flood into our hearts. Not the nesting love of the infant, not the protective love of the toddler, not the instructing love of the child, not the tough love of the teenager, but the 'step back and let go' love of the artist, the teacher, painter, inventor who is eager to share what s/he has been working on, now ready to share with all the world.

> There are two lasting bequests we can give our children.
> One is roots.
> The other is wings.

* ** *** ****

I wore the bracelet Len braided for me. He marked on his calendar the exact time (accounting for the three times zones) when I would step to the podium. He made me promise to phone him as soon as I could to let him know how the speech went.

It was exciting to travel 'all expenses paid!' It was exciting to see Elise in her long, white gown with all the other graduates. It was exciting to be back on campus and see my classmates.

It was exciting to walk in with the formal procession, to step up to the podium, to face a room of over 700 people. It was exciting to hear the audience sigh, laugh and applaud. It was exciting to learn afterwards that I was the first female to speak at the graduation ceremony since the beginning of the Bonnie Hills Church School, 125 years ago!

There was another exciting experience waiting for me when I got back to Avola. I brought home a recording of the ceremony. As Len watched the video tape, his knees close to the TV screen, his eyes never wavering, focused, encouraging, he suddenly burst out, "Who is that fellow sitting behind you on the stage? He keeps rustling his papers and looking away!"

"The man wearing the red robe? That's the Bishop!" He held the highest position in the Seer-Church.

"He's not paying any attention to your message!" Len was outraged. He championed me. He felt that my effort was significant. It was a wonderful feeling to have a Protector!

There is a place in a girl's heart that is only for a 'Father.' Confidence and trust, quiet strength and steady encouragement, he can see who she really is. There is no need to dress up or act, no need for her to try to impress, she already has a place in his heart. She doesn't have to earn it. She can't pay for it. There is no explanation for it. But, she can rest with inexpressible comfort.

That is what was happening in my heart as I experienced this rare friendship with Len.

January, 1999

That summer and autumn, we invited Len on family outings, had him over for dinner, and of course, met at the library every week.

When winter snows covered the slopes and early darkness made travel less likely, driving slowed down. There have to be several reasons to make the trip to town, and if a neighbour asks if you need anything when he or she makes a trip to town for a few groceries, that is an offer that is always accepted. One clear winter day, I took my boys to town in my car to do the payday grocery shopping. Len asked for two items that were easy enough to include on my to-do list.

Although the one hour drive to town was fine, the weather closed in by afternoon. I knew it was not safe to attempt the trip home.

"Kevin," I was phoning long-distance, "the boys and I will be staying at Amy's place tonight, the snow is really coming down here. Could you please phone Len so he won't worry? I don't want to add more to Amy's phone bill. Thanks, see you tomorrow." It was not uncommon for me to stay overnight. And, since Kevin was a First Responder for the ambulance, he was highly in favour of me choosing the safest option. He knew how serious a car accident could be.

In the morning, when the plow trucks had been through, the storm was over and the visibility was clear, we continued home, stopping at Len's place to deliver his groceries.

He was outside, carrying in firewood for the day. "Good Morning!" I called in a bright, cheery voice, "Boys, you can hop out. Toby, help him stack that wood. Nicholas, grab the shovel. Let's get his driveway cleared. I'll carry in the groceries." I told them in a quiet voice. "Hey, Len, how are you today?"

But, he wouldn't look at me.

He turned away. His face was down. I never saw such an expression on anyone's face. Angry? Sad? Disappointed?

"Len, what's wrong? Why won't you talk to me?" I was so anxious now. "I'm sorry your groceries are later than you expected. We stayed overnight in Clearwater because of the snow storm. I asked Kevin to phone you. Did you get the message?"

Turning to me suddenly, eyes fiery, face hard, mouth pressed tightly shut, he suddenly burst out, "I thought you were dead!" My heart felt the echo of his pain. "The phone rang and I was afraid to answer it! You didn't come! The roads were so bad! You are a new driver!"

We went inside and I put the kettle on. I could not just drop off the groceries and go straight home. I quickly phoned Kevin to let him know that we had arrived and sent the boys to walk the rest of the way home. When the tea was ready I sat down across the room from Len who was leaning way back in his favourite recliner.

Quietly, the mixture of emotions on his face impossible to interpret, he said to me, "You've ruined my life."

Gasping, I was unable to comprehend, not ever wanting to damage this old man's heart. He had seen enough loss. Not ever wanting to end this once-in-a-lifetime friendship. I had been isolated for so long. Holding back my voice and struggling to keep my face composed, I whispered, "Len, what is it? Tell me what you're thinking?"

"I moved here to sit in my chair and read my book and listen to Mozart and wait to die. You've ruined my life. I didn't want to care about anybody anymore."

1999 - 2003

Our bond continued for several years, although, to pay less rent, he moved about 20 miles away to live in a tiny one-room log cabin on a sheep ranch. Now I could only phone or drop in every two weeks before or after my payday trip to town. He no longer came to our house.

But the companionship continued. Through his encouragement I often wrote articles for the newspaper. He clipped them and saved them, bragging to his other visitors. He always had a cup of tea for me and a bag of fancy cookies for the boys. He enjoyed the rancher's children and made visitors feel welcome. He loaned me cassette tapes of classical music. I brought him news from Avola.

My eyes followed his mannerisms. How he put the kettle on the same burner every time. How he mourned my request for weak tea. "What a waste of a tea bag!" he moaned. Looking over his shoulder at me with a big grin, he would always say, "I like to pound out every last morsel of flavour!" He stirred and pressed the tea bag against the side of his customary mug. "Would you like three grains or four?" he teased me. I didn't want very much sugar, either.

If he was making me a sandwich, first he tore off a precise amount of waxed paper to lay on the counter top to keep the food clean. While he listened to music he leaned his head back, conducted reverently, whistled a little, savoured the rise and fall of each phrase.

His collection of radio plays and ridiculous comedy sketches were preserved on cassette tapes. English comedy team, Flanders and Swann, combined rapid-fire rhythmic rhymes with punctuation and flourishes on the piano. 'At the Drop of Another Hat' featured the song *The Gas Man Cometh.*

Oh, it all makes work for the working man to do.
On Saturday and Sunday they do no work at all,
So it was on the Monday morning that
the gasman came to call.[28]

Gerard Hoffung[29] recited the 'Bricklayers Lament' with carefully timed pauses, making the listeners wait for the expected repetition as the ropes and pulleys and weight of the bricks keep raising and lowering against the weight of the workman trying to finish the repair safely.

I didn't realize how much music from the 1930's and 40's and 50's I already knew! My Mother and Daddy must have been singing in the car or while they worked or at bedtime. Len and I even had songs from World War I and II in common!

K-K-K-Katy, my beautiful Katy,
You're the only g-g-g-girl that I adore.
When the m-moon shines over the cowshed
I'll be waiting at the k-k-k-kitchen door.[30]

And we both loved the Andrews Sisters *Boogie Woogie Bugle Boy of Company B.*[31] It was so much fun to sing together, scrambling for the quick, witty words.

July, 2003

By now, both Elise and Michael were living away at school.

At this time, I was developing my seminars[34]: 'Seven Predictable Patterns®' for parents, teachers, homeschoolers and others who work or volunteer with children. I had earned my Adult Instructor's Diploma. I wanted to go places! I planned a train trip east, but, first, Nicholas, Toby and I needed to touch up our wardrobes. Somebody needed shoes. Both boys needed a new outfit. I had ordered business clothes embroidered with my logo. I had seminars scheduled in seven cities. It would be my first time on a business trip. It would be a home-schooling field trip for the boys! We would take the train to Ontario, visit relatives and volunteer on an educational farm for the first month. Train across the border and visit relatives in New York City, and attend the Bonnie Hills Church School near Philadelphia for another month. Then a 30-day pass on Amtrak would take us to Chicago, St. Paul, Colorado Springs, Los Angeles, Tuscon, and Seattle before heading home, north of Vancouver. We were leaving early in September and would be home in mid-December!

Then came a dreadful day: July 30, 2003. How could one cigarette butt, dropped 90 miles away change history for so many people?

On that day, the boys and I had planned our shopping trip to Kamloops, two-and-a-half hours away from home. We had a fine time together and the new clothes made everyone feel confident and prepared. But, on the way home, we were stopped by a huge line-up of traffic. A tiny fire started by a cigarette in dry grass that morning had expanded to hillsides and forest. No vehicles were allowed to use the highway. The town of Barriere was ordered to evacuate.

Turning back, we retraced our route and tried to go north again along a dirt road across the river. Billows of dust from oncoming vehicles showed us that traffic was moving. Billows of smoke were making the sunset an orangey-gray glow. Then the flow of traffic stopped. Everyone was turned back. The fire had lept across the North Thompson River! Dry grass and tall ponderosa pine trees grew along the steep unpopulated slopes. Rapidly, huge areas of land were engulfed by the roaring flames. Plenty of fuel. No barriers. A forest fire is a hungry beast, devouring everything in its path.

By now it was nearly 10:00pm. We would have to stay in Kamloops overnight. I knew where to go and ask one of Kevin's Amateur Radio friends for a place to stay. Telephone wires and electric lines had been destroyed by the fire. I talked to Kevin on the Ham radio. The next day he told me to go 200 miles around by Highway 97 and 24 to get back into our valley at Little Fort.

The fire had destroyed electric wires and telephone lines. No credit and debit cards would work, nor the pumps at gas stations, unless a generator could be found. In the morning we skirted the danger zone and re-entered the valley 40 miles north of the fire. I decided to stop in at the emergency headquarters in Clearwater, gain facts and deliver messages to other villages up the valley. It was a very scary time. The numbers describing the size of the fire kept getting bigger.

Then I stopped in to see Len.

I wanted to convince him to come home with me and stay at our house until the fire was out. I tried to describe the huge, charred landscape, the power lines and telephone lines would be out for miles and would not be repaired for days. The hospital in Clearwater was preparing to evacuate. If any new fires start, or the wind picks up, it would be possible for the fire to reach his location, and there would be very limited ways to communicate and only one escape route. "It would be better for you to come with me. Now." I tried to balance blunt urgency with coaxing welcome. Unsuccessfully.

He wouldn't budge.

That night, just as I was serving supper, Len's car pulled in. At the same time, Kevin's truck arrived. I hadn't seen my husband for two stressful days. We had much information to convey. Kevin's radio skills and training as an emergency volunteer meant our home was the hub for our tiny town. He described the devastation he had seen, the friends who had lost or still had houses, his responsibilities on the railroad, his understanding of the fire fighting force, the importance of his radio communication with emergency personnel. Len was in the background. The boys got him supper and a made place for him to sleep.

During the long summer daylight, I stayed up late and nervously packed to evacuate. It was strange to go carefully through the house gathering photos, papers and mementos, baby clothes, wedding and baptism clothes, recordings of children's voices. How could I decide what was irreplaceable in the event of an evacuation?

"Your husband doesn't want me here." Len told me in the morning. He did not have a clear understanding of the clipped, focused, information exchange between Kevin and I. We were not extending our usual hospitality. He felt unwelcome.

"Let's take a drive down to your house, Len. We need to clean out the refrigerator," I tried to persuade him. "The electricity won't be on again, maybe for weeks. Your food will all go bad."

"I just went shopping. My milk is fresh," he contradicted. He didn't seem to comprehend the situation at all. I knew the food would be rotten and smelly in a few more hot summer days. I wanted to take care of it before something else went wrong. I was anxious with the smoke in the air and the crunchy, dry grass underfoot reminding me that the entire forest was just as dangerously dry. I was anxious about the amount of time it would take to go, do the work and come back. I would be away from my boys.

Eventually, Len agreed to go. When we arrived, I made quick decisions and actions to sort out what to keep and what to throw away. Len was upset. When we got home he went over to the neighbours to stay.

I walked over to try to invite him back to our house.

He pushed me away. I had triggered his childhood memory of when the bomb dropped in England. The aunts and grandmother came to empty the house and make a quick exit and took Len away. He had harboured resentment for 60 years! In his mind, now I was one of the 'Bad Guys!'

He stayed with the neighbours. For three days I walked over to apologize for the hurry and tensions of that first day. Each time I approached, he got up and walked away. He refused to speak to me. I still felt the life-altering affection and loyalty of the 'Father-Daughter' bond. In his confusion, he rejected me. Entirely.

At home, I sobbed. Devastated.

August, 2003

It took three weeks for the fire to die down.

September-December, 2003

Nicholas and Toby and I left on the train trip for nearly four months.

January, 2004

When I got back, he didn't remember me at all. He didn't remember anything good about our friendship. If I called, he hung up the phone. If I knocked on the door, he wouldn't answer. He was upset if I came near, so I stayed away.

Len had dementia.

2003-2007

It didn't take long for him to end up in the hospital. The neighbours got to visit, look after him, check with the nurses. Not me.

I confided in one of the nurses, "We adopted each other. I am his Daughter. He is my Dad!" She conveyed tiny pieces of information.

Three-and-a-half years went by. Every so often I would hear that Len was in the hospital or back home. He went in, by ambulance. He walked out, confused. I saw him in the grocery store once but he didn't recognize me. I ached for the friendship we had enjoyed.

And yet, I was spared from the agony of observing the deterioration. I could treasure the bright memories without having to endure the dark reality.

April 13, 2007

Then, I got a call from the nurse at the hospital. Len died.

I drove to see him. My Friend. My Mentor. My Protector. Silent.

As he wished, his cremains were allowed to travel in the river. The family from the ranch invited the neighbours and I. They didn't know that Len had assigned me, his adopted and only daughter, the place of honour.

I could hardly bear for my eyes to see the gray ashes swirling in the clear water. For a moment: Here. In a moment: Gone.

I stood on the river shore. Comfortless.

I have some photos. I have his atlas. I have his brown jacket. I have his cassette tapes. I have his favourite autumn-plaid shirt. But, I don't have my adopted Dad. The whole planet feels barren.

April 13, 2007

The only good thing that happened after that day was when an envelope came from Ottawa. The day Len died was the same day that my first copyright was registered.

And so, I felt a final blessing from my adopted Dad: Len. "You are a writer," he said. "You must publish this!"

REFLECTIONS

We must believe
that we are gifted for something,
and that this thing,
at whatever cost,
must be attained.
—*Marie Curie*

Chapter 5
Friday and Saturday, December 31, 1999 - January 1, 2000
Youngest Son: Toby the Inventor

No matter what happens, keep on beginning... and failing.
Each time you fail, start all over again, and you will grow stronger
until you find that you have accomplished a purpose,
not the one you began with, perhaps,
but one that you will be glad to remember.
—Anne Sullivan (Helen Keller's teacher)

* ** *** ****

1999

I decided to save, just in case.

The cedar chest Kevin built for me twenty years ago when we lived in the cabin, is full to the brim with non-perishable food. Flour, sugar, milk powder, rice, pasta, beans, canned tomatoes, jam, tuna. It looks about like our pantry, but, it is in addition to the usual winter storage for our family of six.

I don't want to be full of fear. Will the world come to an end because the computers aren't prepared for the 2000 date? Y2K.[32] I have no way to evaluate the media hoopla that trumpets terrifying scenarios about the collapse of the western world.

For over twenty years Kevin and I and the children have worked as a team to fill the wood shed to heat our home. I have a propane stove, or I can cook on the wood stove. I have gravity feed water, or I can carry buckets of water from the river if necessary. I have candles, flashlights and batteries, or even a kerosene lamp. I have already learned how to live without electricity. We did it for five years in the cabin. I know we will be OK... for the short term.

I am reminded of 'Chicken Little' hollering, 'The sky is falling!' In Medieval times people feared comets and meteors and other celestial warnings, thinking they signalled the 'End of the World.'

Still, banks and bills and deliveries and education and telephones and news and every kind of commerce and technology are all linked to computers now. So, if there really is a problem, the dominoes would fall and the catastrophe would blackout cities, airports, generators, water, food, transportation, medical equipment.

It was a dreadful thought.

As December 31, 1999, approached, I kept quiet and waited to see how things would play out. Kevin didn't appear to be worried. Surely 'they' have figured out what to do. Surely 'the media' is sending a fearful alarmist message just to keep the viewers tuned in?

In Avola, neighbours traditionally buy small fireworks to set off in their yard. Others make a bonfire. Our family custom is to bang pots and pans at midnight. This year, Kevin plans to fire his muzzle loader at midnight. I decide to invite Nicholas and Toby to stay up all night and watch the special BBC program[33] sharing scenes of celebration as New Year comes in all around the world.

"Let's get cozy," I suggest as we often do for a TV movie night. Since we live 120 miles from a movie theatre, we have to make our own family entertainment and customs. Grandparents send video tapes for birthdays or we can borrow video tapes from the Bookmobile and we have one movie channel.

"Toby, you open the fold-out couch, then get your pillows and blankets. You are the 'Prince of Pillows.' You can build us a nest!"

"Nicholas, let's brainstorm for meals and snacks for the day and night. Just think! It will be a 24-hour marathon!"

Nicholas and Toby are in public school this year: Grade 7 and 5. It is only the second year they have gone to school. The rest of the time we have been homeshcooling.[34]

"I'll make popcorn later," Kevin offers.

Nicholas has taken inventory. "We have all the usual goodies for a New Year's platter: sausage, pickles, olives, an assortment of cheeses and crackers."

"I was thinking that we could have turkey sandwiches for supper while we watch the show," I want to get some nourishment into tummies besides all the goodies.

Toby pulls open the folding couch and arranges the cushions across the back.

"I like making the veggie plate," Nicholas offers "We have carrots and celery, baby tomatoes as well as broccoli and cauliflower. Can I open a jar of the beet pickles you made?"

"Of course," I answer, "and look in the pantry for that jar of fancy mixed sweet pickles from the store."

Toby is tossing pillows and rolling quilts down the stairs. "Mom! Can I make one of my 'Invention Snacks'? You know, when I melt chocolate chips with peanut butter and other secret ingredients and pour it over popcorn or Cheerios?"

"O, goodie," I smile at him. "Your inventions are always so tasty. Sticky! But yummy! And at midnight we'll have our traditional root beer floats!"

It is the second Christmas and New Year celebration we have had without Elise. She graduated from high school in 1998 and stayed on at the Church College. It feels empty to have fun without her. I miss her helping hands, creative ideas and the fun way she teases with her brothers. Kevin misses her, too. They have a special Father-Daughter bond. But we know the family she is staying with. She phoned on Christmas Day to describe it all to us. "They celebrate Christmas the same way we do. On Christmas Eve they had family worship with everyone taking turns reading parts of Luke and Matthew, choosing hymns and of course the Nativity figures set up and lots of candles. On Christmas morning they have the same sequence: first stockings, then breakfast, then slowly enjoying the gifts." So, although my heart feels sad to be without her, I also feel glad that she is having a good experience away from home. The time has come. Our children are growing up and leaving the nest!

It is the first Christmas and New Year celebration we have had without Michael. This year he will graduate from his final year of studies at the Bonnie Hills Church School and will most likely stay on for college. It feels empty to have fun without him.

I miss his good ideas and help with meals, the way he respects Kevin and encourages his brothers to cooperate with me. But, opportunities lie ahead and I did not insist on his return. Kevin is relieved from the pressure of driving nine hours to the Seattle airport over winter mountains, first to pick Michael up, then again to bring him back.

And, so, this is the first time we have been a family of four for the holidays.

"I saved some Christmas cut-out cookies for tonight," I add. We always bake and decorate gingerbread cookies in the shapes of bells and stockings, candy canes and Christmas trees, doves, stars and hearts. When the cookie dough is almost used up, I cut diamond shapes. When the cookies are all decorated with coloured icing and pinches of shredded coconut, sprinkles, gum drops, silver beads and other delights, then each person can feast on the diamonds with mountains of leftover icing piled high.

"We're going to have a feast tonight!" Toby announces. He has piled up the pillows and cushions, layered quilts and gone back for a load of stuffed animals to invite to the show. "Mom! Where's the globe?" Toby wants to follow along as the program moves from east to west, through all of the time zones, all the way around the world. What a splendid program! BBC has arranged for newscasters to share both prerecorded and live footage from 60 countries over a 28 hour marathon. It is the largest world-wide broadcast ever. I don't want to miss a minute. Since 1984, when my husband and I decided to settle in the tiny town of Avola, I have had very few opportunities to share world culture with our four children. Christmas specials on television were our only connection to ballet, symphony, theatre, figure skating, world-class musicians. We made a point of watching the Olympic events for days, especially the gymnastic, diving and equestrian competitions. I taught the children the names of instruments in the orchestra, informed them of celebrity performers, and watched the Royal Family. We also used the television and documentary videos borrowed from the Bookmobile to explore cities and ecosystems, oceans and deserts, delving into the past with archaeologists and anthropologists.

Tonight will be like icing on the cake: a World Tour!

And so, on 1999-2000 New Year's Eve, we are armchair travellers to: Hong Kong, India, Sydney, Greece, Rome, Egypt, Sweden, Paris, London, Iceland, the Caribbean, New York, Niagara Falls, the Arctic, Vancouver, Hawaii. One after another the camera brings us glimpses of fireworks and ice sculptures, camels and reindeer, grass skirts and fur coats, skyscrapers and yurts, bright lights and candles, crowded cities and remote islands. It is fascinating. It is a stretch for the mind. It is heartwarming.

"I wish I could go there," Toby tells me at almost every new scene.

"Look at Len's Atlas," I reach for another teaching tool. "See? He has been to Hong Kong, Australia, Egypt, Argentina and of course, England and Canada. Grandma D went to Hawaii. Grampa Hinkle and Shirley went to Italy and Greece. Elise took a trip to France. We have friends from India and family in New York City. They did it. You can do it!"

Toby had a remarkable focus throughout the program. As they appeared on the TV screen, we found all the places on the globe. He recognized the Sydney Opera House, the Eiffel Tower, Big Ben, the Parthenon, the Pyramids, Niagara Falls, CN Tower and the Statue of Liberty. Not bad for a youngster living in the woods! Maybe I was doing OK as a homeschooling Mom!

But, alongside this technological wonder of communication, I was simultaneously aware of the little boy nestled up against me.

"Mom! Don't let me fall asleep," he said as the others drifted off. Toby recognized geographic features, located cities on the globe, remembered details from our studies and asked curious questions about each place. This experience was becoming embedded in his mind. With wide eyes, he had a realization that we are all connected. He was mentally tallying up the places he'd like to see.

The world was experiencing the New Millennium. As with every New Year's Eve, I felt heightened awareness of the passage of time. And, since my two eldest children were already launched, my heart felt the sweetness and sadness of knowing the reality that these other two younger children would also grow up all too soon and leave home. How to store up these precious fleeting moments? How to hold on while letting go? That is my on-going dilemma.

So, while the Earth rotated, millions celebrated and the thousands of technicians brought the world streaming into our little log house in the woods, my family shared a Golden Moment. I allowed my memory to bring me pictures of this Lad. Toby would turn twelve this summer. He was not a little boy anymore. Not yet a young man. It was a precious time to pause and recall his early years.

1988

"Mr. Gibson wants to sell us his house," Kevin announced as he walked through the kitchen door.

My eyes popped open. My jaw dropped open. My head was dizzy. "Not funny! No way! Don't even say it!" I spluttered. The beautiful riverside property featured rich, black garden soil, fruit trees, a lovely old house, out buildings, forest and field. It was just over two acres and was a dream come true for the

'Back-to-the-Land' lifestyle we had been developing since our wedding in 1978.

Kevin stepped back, astonished at my reaction. He thought he had found the 'Pot of Gold' at the end of the rainbow!

"NO! That property is between the river and the train tracks! I don't want dead babies!" My terror washed away any potential positive view of the situation.

Kevin went back to tell Mr. Gibson, then returned to me with another message. "They only want $7,000."

"Get a pen!" I said, "Where do we sign!"

In October, we helped with the good-bye party for Mr. and Mrs. Gibson, both well past 80 years old. The Old Timers, friends and relatives loaded eleven pickup trucks to help move out. I spent several days scrubbing walls and floors and cupboards and then we moved in. I didn't know then that I was already carrying Baby #4. But I soon felt the familiar nausea, hunger, sleepiness and other physical signals that I was pregnant.

Gladness and disappointment crashed in my heart together. Hurrah for new life! How marvelous that my body is healthy and our family is eager for new members. How exhausting to have a nursing six-month-old and a growing embryo within me.

How much I was looking forward to hard work on our new land: digging fence post holes, cutting down trees, dragging branches, piling up bonfires to clear the land, preparing the garden, stacking firewood, renovating the house. With a Baby and a Belly, and later with two babies and then two toddlers, I just can't see how I will be of much help. Elise and Michael are homeschooling, there is the garden, housework, volunteering and now two little ones. There will be enough to do just to make it through the days! (and the nights!)

I delayed reporting the pregnancy to my neighbours and even my parents. In fact, with the recent trend to have 2.6 children as a way of 'helping' with the 'population explosion' I was already getting raised eyebrows when the third child arrived. "Four? What are you thinking?" people seemed to signal. Kevin and I believed the Lord would give us as many children as we could raise while ever mindful of the healthy nurturing of their heart, soul, mind and body.

One voice of encouragement came. Father Emil Sasges, a travelling Catholic priest, had recently brought me some colourful children's books to include in my Sunday School resources. His ready smile and bright eyes signalled a warm welcome and wonder. "A Gift!" he announced when I told him we were expecting. "A Gift!" His confidence and perspective were reassuring and inspiring.

"It's like he has words for what we already believe," I said to Kevin.

"Affirming," Kevin said. "In this world of so many people rejecting and reconstructing and rebelling against conventional 'religion' and experimenting with so many various beliefs, it is a comfort to have someone to talk with about life decisions based on a firm foundation and trusted traditions."

In July, my Mother (who asked not to be called 'Grandma' but wanted us to call her 'Dearma') came from Florida to stay with the older children. The due date came and went. The Doctor sent me to the city to be induced. I was pretty scared of all the technology. Why interfere with Nature and what ever God had planned? But, the experience was not as difficult as I had anticipated, and soon I held a healthy son in my arms.

We named him Thomas Benjamin. 'Thomas' for the bold declaration of faith after doubt. 'Benjamin' for the youngest son.[35] But almost immediately we all called him 'Toby' which reminded me of the story of the little boy who ran away to join the circus.[36] Which turned out to be rather prophetic. Toby always had 'good ideas' which were different from everybody else. Maybe someday he'll be rich and famous?

Because the baby was born two weeks later than expected, Dearma already had her airline tickets and had to leave soon, I asked to go home from the hospital on the second day. Kevin brought a car seat. The homecoming was sweet. Little Nicholas was in his highchair eating strawberries. When Dearma held the new brother for him to see, 15-month-old Nicholas, with a big grin, offered to share the juicy, ripe strawberry he had in his chubby hand.

Elise was eight and very capable. Michael was six-and-a-half and was learning many household tasks. I came to rely on both of them to answer the phone, make their own lunch, hang up laundry, fold and put away towels, take out the compost.

* ** *** ****

When do you become who you are?

I have always wondered about this.

'Nature – Nurture' the popular psychology books say.

I deliberately observe the 'First Face' of each of my children.

Newly-born I watch each of my babies stretch and open up after living in such a tight space, surprised by the light, sound and gravity, rubbed dry, wrapped tightly. I eagerly search the face, feel the deeply warm weight, cradle my baby in my arms. I speak soothingly, "Let everything that breathes praise the Lord."[37] Then I wait for the miracle. How does a Baby know how to make eye contact? How do the muscles of the face know how to form an expression? Sleepy, discomfort, smile, raise or lower eye brows, puzzled, curious, alarmed, each of these signals I have seen, yet, I am amazed that a person so small, with no previous experience can communicate so much.

First-born-daughter: frowning brow, puckered face, she seemed to be asking, "Not too comfortable here. Can you make this loud, bright bombardment slow down and let me relax?" It took her several hours to trust and soften and begin to believe that life on Planet Earth was OK.

First-born-son: cocked his head, raised an eyebrow, looked me straight in the eye. He seemed to be challenging me, "So? You think you're the boss? We'll see!"

Third child, a son: The doctor passed him to Dearma, he arched his back and twisted, hearing and recognizing my voice. His eyes seemed to shout, "So *you're* my Mother! How do you do?"

Fourth, another son: lifted his head, searched for my eyes, seemed to say, "OK. Maybe. Maybe not. There's probably another way. What's around the corner?"

That is how I interpreted those first contacts. I believed they were already 'real people' and that it was my task to nourish heart, soul, mind and body, provide as many varied experiences as possible, steer them away from hazards, protect while allowing exploration, be a Tour Guide of the Planet.

And, yes, I learned over the years that the 'First Face' was a fairly accurate indication of 'who' each child already was. A daughter who seems a little out of place and would rather observe than dive in, a son who challenges authority and comes up with alternative ideas, another son who notices how others are feeling, and now I have another a young lad to raise. This one is an Inventor and Explorer.

* ** *** ****

Each generation tries to make improvements over the previous generation. New parents look back at their own parents and try to solve problems, prevent difficulties, try new methods of child-rearing, provide security for their children.

On my Mother's side: Opa's father was so physically violent at home, that when Opa was only twelve years old he left to sleep in a neighbour's barn. Opa lived in Europe during World War I and experienced poverty and hunger. He emigrated to the USA and provided a better life for his eight children than he ever had. But his strict discipline prompted his children to leave home as soon as possible, the girls through marriage, the boys into the military. My Mother made huge improvements to her parenting style with creative play, music, cultural outings and lots of books. Yet, she had delivered a fair share of spanking to my siblings and I, too. Now it's my turn to look at what to keep and what to improve about how I was raised and how I want to raise our children. In an attempt to relieve the pressure of strict discipline, I am trying to offer options and guidance as opposed to forced obedience.

On my Father's side: 'The Depression' was not a good time for Grammie and Grampa to be raising five children. When their first child died at age four, and employment options kept crumbling, it was the beginning of frequent moving from place to place. Daddy gave his children a much stronger sense of stability with continuous progress on his career path and providing us with comfortable homes, travel, education and a sense of loyalty to family, Church and nation. But, Daddy was a theorist. Dinnertime conversation was peppered with 'Maybe this and maybe that.' Politics were a shambles. The history of the Christian Church was layered with heresy. The economy was teetering. The scientific and medical world was built on shifting theories. It was very confusing for me, as a child and teenager, to make any sense of the world. Now it's my turn to provide stability and attempt to offer a less tumbled world view.

Yet, doubtless, my children will look back at what I am doing now and see ways I let them down. They will have their own decisions to make about how to shape their families.

1989

'There is Probably an Alternative' would be a good title for Toby's memoir. For his first birthday, he somehow managed to drag the brand new little four wheeled bike up onto the back of the couch, straddle it and ride it all the way down!

I sent Elise and Michael to school that year. I knew I could not juggle the responsibility of homeschooling a first and third grader while simultaneously dealing with all the interruptions and needs of two mischievous, curious, nonstop toddlers!

Kevin was night patrolman on nine miles of train track. He was also volunteering to build a water reservoir. As a First Responder he answered radio call outs for highway accidents. He was gone a lot. I was proud of his accomplishments. He was proud of mine.

We were a parade on the way to the school bus stop. I carried Baby Toby in a front carrier and later a backpack. I pushed Nicholas in an old fashioned metal stroller, bumping over the potholes in the gravel road. Elise and Michael carried their lunch in their backpacks (Care Bears and Garfield) sent by Grandma D.

At home, my day was naps and food and laundry and interruptions. "Come with me." I encouraged little Nicholas to tag along and 'help' load the laundry from the washer to the dryer, stand on a bench beside me while I kneaded the bread, cut the vegetables, grated cheese. "Come with me." I brought him toddling along out to the garden to pull beets, dig potatoes, pick blackberries. "Come with me." I coaxed as I raked the lawn, carried firewood, pushed the wheelbarrow.

I carried Toby everywhere I went: grocery shopping on payday once every two weeks, in the kitchen, in the garden and walking to the post office. If I put him down in his highchair, even with the seat belt latched, he squirmed out! If I put him in the playpen, he managed to make an escape. He did stay strapped in his car seat, thank goodness.

I planned my day around the needs of the two little boys. And it was wonderful to watch their interest, understand their first attempts at words, provide safe ways to interact with new experiences: water, snow, pets, climbing, tastes, sounds, new people, storybooks.

"Put your head down." I spoke soothingly. Maybe both Nicholas and Toby would take a nap at the same time and I would be able to sleep for awhile, too. We had a 'Family Bed' with two double bed mattresses side by side on the floor. I had stacks of cloth diapers on the go. The laundry and dishes were never caught up.

But, everyone was always learning. It was a sweet time and I knew it would pass in a flash. So, I tried to focus, taking pictures to send to the grandparents, phoning them often to tell little family stories, making family customs, trying to remember events to someday write in my 'Memoir.'

Grandma D came for Christmas!

Kevin picked his Mom up at the Kamloops airport on December 9th. She was such a help! Until then, I simply could not get away from Nicholas and Toby long enough to get even one Christmas task started, no less finished!

Grandma D fed the children while I climbed up to the attic for the decorations. She watched them while I got a few cards ready for the mail. She held the fort while Kevin and I dragged in a tree. She cooked and washed up while I made more messes with fancy cookies and German Stollen and melted chocolate. We even teamed up to sew fifteen meters of red flannel into matching PJs and nightgowns for all four children and their dolls and teddy bears!

1990

Dearma came for the summer. It was Toby's second birthday. She rented a little yellow cottage in Avola. I carried Toby in the backpack to walk over every day. I pushed three-year-old Nicholas in the stroller. Elise and Michael were our escort on their bikes. Through the vegetable garden, up the road, beside the river, across the train tracks, up the hill, past the playground, and into her little yellow two-room house we made the daily trek.

She helped in the garden. She blanched the garden greens and helped fill the freezer. She bent to pick wild blueberries. She stirred the boiling jam. She came on our firewood cutting days. She made supper while I kept stacking the wood shed rows. She hung out the laundry. She read aloud at bedtime. She borrowed my sewing machine and made a quilt for Elise and PJs for the boys. Her presence gave me confidence that I was doing OK as a mother. It was wonderful to be a three-generation family for the whole summer.

We had Christmas in July that year. We brought her a tiny tree, paper chains and tinfoil stars, decorated cookies and wrapped homemade gifts.

That was the year that Kevin started to work on track maintenance in the day time. He drove 25 miles north to Blue River to start at 7:00am and head home at 3:00pm. He had Friday and Saturday off.

This gave me a Golden Opportunity. Every Sunday I could pack the kids up for the day, walk to the highway and flag the Greyhound bus at 9:00am. We could go to the Blue River Christian church! We could go to Sunday School! We could be in their Christmas Eve Pageant! I could sing! I made Elise a red velvet dress with a wide white lace collar. The three boys had white dress shirts, blue pants, red sweater vests and bow ties.

Somehow, that Christmas made up for that first lonely Christmas in the cabin twelve years ago. Our dreams were indeed becoming reality!

1991

Another harvest, another winter, another spring, another summer, another grandparent came. This time, Grampa Hinkle flew to Kamloops, rented a van, came north to pick us up and drove us to southeastern Washington for the wedding of my cousin, Claire. While Elise and Michael entertained themselves with books, word games and looking for the alphabet on license plates and signs, Nicholas and Toby and I watched for horses, cows, sheep, bridges and played singing games.

Toby had a ukulele with no strings, which was a pretty good arrangement for six people in a confined space for over ten hours. I kept the songs coming. *Eesny-weensy Spider, Ponto lost his tail, Twinkle-twinkle, little star.* I had a long and varied repertoire which my children were familiar with. But, Toby's favorite songs were from Sunday School, and the educational TV shows: 'Mr. Dressup' and 'Sharon, Lois and Bram.'

Sometimes Toby was eating. Sometimes Toby was drinking. Sometimes Toby was sleeping. A lot of the time Toby was singing... accompanied by his stringless ukulele.

I just keep trusting my Lord as I walk along.
I just keep trusting my Lord as I sing this song.
Though the storm clouds darken the sky or the Heavenly Trail
I just keep trusting my Lord, He will never fail![38]

Maybe he'll grow up to be a cowboy?

Ridin' along, singin' a cowboy song,
Ridin' along, singin' a song.
O-lee-o-lee, O-lee-o-lee, O-lee-o-lay, O-lee-o-lay.
O-lee-o-lay.[39]

As the wedding guests gathered, cousins and aunts and uncles swarmed around, my children were not used to that kind of attention. Toby stayed snug in my arms. He was three years old and getting heavy. I wanted my dress to be unwrinkled but he was so shy and stayed tightly attached.

And then he saw the bride!

Claire seemed to be floating in her full-length, hoopskirt, ivory lace gown. Her auburn hair hung in long ringlets. Her matching ivory earrings and necklace set off her pale complexion. Her quiet voice and charming mannerisms spoke straight to Toby's little heart. He was smitten. In a room full of moving people, music, decorations, and a feast, he had eyes only for her. He called her 'The Beautiful Lady.'

Before the ceremony, Elise lit the candles. At the reception, Michael tied a dozen blue helium balloons to his belt in an attempt to become airborne. Nicholas caused a disturbance in Aunt Grace's garden when he thought the tulips were cups and poured his milk into one. But, Toby stayed close to me with eyes soaking in the loveliness of 'The Beautiful Lady.'

1992

So much happens during these early years. 'Mr. Dressup' and other children's educators and entertainers spend their entire career writing, performing, singing, and demonstrating interesting things to four-year-old children.

And Toby absorbed so much so quickly.

I have been a babysitter, nanny, tutor, volunteer teacher, Brownie and Cub Scout leader, Sunday School teacher, librarian, and brought skits and experiments and crafts and educational projects to hundreds of children by this time in my life, but, I have never seen anyone do the things that Toby could do.

The summer that Toby turned four, we renovated the old Gibson house. We tore down the old frame living room part of our house and added a much larger log addition. The barn roof made rooms for the children upstairs. The downstairs was one big space for whatever creative activity family members might enjoy.

Homeschooling projects, crafts, sewing, roller skates, dance, fitness, jump rope, tricky tricks and an aquarium as well as a computer desk and a 30 foot long book shelf filled the sunny space.

Toby wanted privacy. He made a fort under the table. I peeked in to see why he was so quiet. He was writing squiggly attempts to print letters in the boxes of the order forms he found in a magazine.

Toby wanted to read like his older brothers and sister. He started by searching for letters he recognized in the Bible.

Toby wanted to write. He typed long pages of random letters pounding on my Dad's old typewriter, then brought them to me to read aloud. I circled any combinations that were actually words.

Cnapetyt a vanmfgporunhe ja dhshdogt rtr bocupcucu
shfog sppegthegnsalalaplncancbeatbaudfiogvb
gajigsvatdtoeje fvwppquienfaju dhata foof
goodjfa akkdf a fygugyrollwanmtw

It was a challenge to read and a celebration to find treasure.

Toby wanted to learn how to use the sewing machine. I cut strips of fabric, sat him on my lap, I pressed the foot pedal and he guided the cloth. He designed and sewed his own quilt at age four!

Toby had a little two inch high fuzzy white teddy bear. He saved toilet paper tubes. He had scissors, tape and a cereal box. He made a slide for the teddy to come down and around the chute and pop out at the bottom. I don't know how he did it. I don't even know how he thought of it. But he did.

Toby had a sense of fashion. He loved family trips to the Thrift Store because I said, 'Yes' to wild alphabets, bright colours, giant Pjs, a leather jacket, cats on coveralls, backpacks and shoulder bags and fanny packs, hats and sunglasses and suspenders, boots and belts and wristbands. Toby had a style all his own.

Toby was quick to get into mischief, though, and I carried him a lot, asked him to come and 'help' and made sure I knew where he was and what he was doing...unless I wanted a big mess to clean up later!

1993

Winter included another trip with Grampa Hinkle. We arranged to travel by Greyhound and meet him in Canmore, Alberta. This time to ski!

In the springtime, I took all four children to Florida to see where Dearma lived. Elise and Michael stayed for two weeks. Dearma took them to the seashore, to Busch Gardens, to craft lessons, to church and to her Nanny job. The family she worked for had a swimming pool!

Meanwhile, Nicholas, Toby and I went to Ontario to see Grandma D in Kitchener and Grampa Hinkle and Shirley in Toronto.

Grandma D still lived in the house that Kevin grew up in, so I told them stories about when he was a boy. Growing up in such a tightly packed part of the city, they could see that Kevin had a very different childhood. His Dad worked in a nearby factory and had a model train set up in the basement. His Mom ran a store at the front of the house. She knew everybody. Kevin's brother left home at age 16. Kevin was only six. He looked after himself from a very young age. The family rented a farmhouse in the country. Kevin had experiences working on farms, roaming the fields, gopher hunting, camping out and learning mechanics. But, other people brought beer and girlfriends and loud music and fast cars to the farm. Kevin stayed away from the party groups. He'd much rather be on his own.

Grampa Hinkle and Shirley had a nice apartment on the nineteenth floor! We could see eleven lanes of traffic down below! "Daddy, I just realized something funny," I observed. "When we lived near the university and went to visit your parents on the farm, I got to pump water, use the outhouse, pick berries, gather eggs, shuck corn. Now, I bring my mountain children to your city home and they get to ride the elevator, use the computer, swim in our pool, order pizza delivery, and go up CN Tower!"

I noticed another big difference, too. Dad and Shirley were much more compatible than my Mother and Dad had been. When decisions were being made, there was dialogue. When it was time to get some task done, there was cooperation. When differences of opinion came up, there was respectful listening. When Dad told his oft-repeated jokes, Shirley thought he was charming. When Shirley had a story to tell, he admired her. I could hardly believe what I was seeing and hearing. Comfortable companionship. Teamwork. Pleasant voices. Calm interactions. No tension.

Toby carried his own backpack full of necessities: Lego. Yes, all of our sons found Lego to be the most satisfying toy. Rockets and castles, villages and planets, machinery and inventions of all kinds were proudly displayed, saved for awhile, then taken apart when a new idea burst forth.

It's never fun to say, 'Good-bye.' Dad took us to the airport. After the usual hugs and thanks, I suddenly turned back, a look of anxiety and a wave of unexpected emotion came over me. "Daddy!" I stepped into his arms, clinging to his shoulders, gripping his woolen coat in my fists. "Daddy!" I was choked up and couldn't speak.

"Honey, what is it?" his eyes met mine.

"It's so far! When will I see you again?" I didn't know it then, but it was the last time I would see my Father until the dreadful day when he lay dying in the hospital. I felt dizzy. Like it was the first time I saw him as a person. Like it was the first time he saw me as a person. Airplanes, tickets, clocks, and miles pulled us apart. But, for that moment, we had been together: Father-Daughter.

1994

When he turned six, 'The Lion King' video tape from Grampa Hinkle was the best present. Toby's room got painted deep green along the bottom half and deep red along the top half separated with a border of African-style geometric patterns. I made him another quilt with camouflage fabric and pictures of lions, giraffes, elephants and rhinoceros. Toby saved up and bought a stuffed lion, decorated his room with nets and reflective tape and geometric patterns.

Last year, for Halloween, Toby dressed up to be a robber. This year he made a bat costume for himself: black pants, black sweater, black face mask and cardboard strapped to his arms, covered with a black garbage bag, cut with points for wings. He used the cloth drawstring robber-bag again for trick-or-treat. He hid some of his own wrapped candy in his bedroom: behind the furniture, deep in a drawer, under some books. "That way, on Saturday, when it's Room Cleaning Day, I will find a treat to reward myself!" he told me. Such a clever boy!

That robber-bag got him into trouble, though. "I'm going up to my 'Secret Tree', Mom," he would let me know when he headed outside after homeschooling lessons were finished for the day. Elise and Michael were gone on the school bus attending high school in Clearwater. Each of the children had forts here and there on our property: underground, up in trees, behind a fallen fence, sheltered by bushes, lean-to over a log. Toby climbed up to his 'Secret Tree' on an upside-down metal garbage can, reached up to the stubs of cut off branches, built a platform with some plywood and had a private haven in the evergreen boughs for his boyhood imaginings.

However, over time, Michael and Elise reported some of their most prized possessions seemed to be missing. A walkie-talkie, a camera, a pocket knife, a watch, a whistle, mostly gifts from grandparents, definitely the kinds of things a person keeps safely in a certain place, not haphazardly mislaid. I decided to pay more attention to sounds from the upstairs when Toby was alone. Sure enough, I heard rustlings in rooms he had no business in. I climbed the tree and discovered, laid out neatly, each of the items the others had reported missing.

A little overwhelmed at the deliberate repetition needed to accomplish this, I had to think clearly how to deal with it. 'Let the punishment fit the crime' was a line from the 'Mikado' that Daddy used to sing to me. I have been a Mother for fourteen years now. I have smacked little hands that reached for the dog food, slop-water bucket or hot wood stove. Like my own Mother, I have made good the warning to 'wash your mouth out with soap if I hear that word again!' I have smacked a sassy mouth. I have withheld privileges. I have spanked naughty boys. I have sent people to their rooms. I have made charts to record the ratio of cooperative and deliberately non-compliant behaviour. But, I have never been the mother of a thief!

Once, just before Elise turned three, she decorated her hands and face with indelible black magic marker... just a few days before our flight to visit grandparents. I quietly lifted her, carried her outside to where Kevin was working and said, "I don't know what to do about this." He had a gentle lanolin based cleanser which removed the ink completely.

Once, after several empty candy wrappers were discovered where I sent Michael for canned goods in the root cellar, I put ten chocolate chips in a sandwich bag in his pocket to carry all day without eating them. "It is possible to control your appetite. It is important not to take what is not yours. 'Can you stop yourself?' That is the question."

Lots of times, when the summertime daylight makes it hard for children to go to sleep, I have stomped up the stairs to send mischievous children back to bed, half laughing, half serious, "Fee-Fi-Foe-Fum, here comes the mean old Mum!" Books quickly inserted into PJ pants have protected little bottoms from the possibility of a wooden spoon reminder like my Mother used to say, "Do you need a special invitation?" to prompt reluctant children to do as they were told.

Table manners, chores, school work, pet care, little lies, toilet training, hazards of the river, highway, train tracks, using a knife, matches, tools... all of these things have had their own forms of instruction and guidance backed up with a punishment if deliberately disregarded. Some things are social customs. Some are life-and-death. Some are inconvenient. Some are moral or ethical intangibles which are harder to pin-point, yet, need to be corrected.

'Thou shalt not steal' is rather urgent. And it is not an optional item with alternatives for the creative child to discover. "Toby, go to your room. I need to think about this." I opened my Bible to the concordance and found a helpful verse.

"Do not men despise a thief...? And, if he is caught, he will pay sevenfold. He will give all the goods of his house." Proverbs 6: 30-31

After I explained things calmly to Toby, we spent the afternoon making piles of seven items that belonged to him to pay back for each item he had removed from his brother's and sister's rooms. I made sure he put thought into each group, sacrificed things he valued, kept an accurate tally. I coached the older siblings to accept this in seriousness, even if the items they gained had no special value to them. It was a lesson with weight.

That was also the year that Toby invented 'The Candy Graph.' At the Community Hall Christmas Concert every year, the children in Avola plan entertainment, the adults organize a visit from Santa, gifts and refreshments. Santa gives each child a candy bag. Toby sorted out his wrapped candy into piles: butterscotch, lemon, raspberry, cinnamon, peppermint, toffee, orange, lime. Then he taped rows of each colour to a board. He could see how much of each kind he had. He could plan what order to eat the candy so he wouldn't run out of the kind he liked best. He wanted his own Christmas tree in his own bedroom. I said, "No." But Santa said, "Yes."

1995

Playing chess was a family favourite at this time. But the usual rules were not challenging enough for Toby. We made agreements to set up the pieces in different ways. Diagonally was interesting. With the pawns on the back row and the more powerful pieces up front didn't work too well. We played until all the pieces were gone. We tried 'suicide' chess where you deliberately put your piece where your opponent will have to take it.

Most popular was 'Three Second Chess.' I was learning to drive. I needed to look, decide and move without long pauses and hesitation. Michael and Toby were worthy opponents. Multiple rounds of 'Three Second Chess' helped me procrastinate less and become more determined in my own decisions and actions.

When we went to a mountain chalet every summer, 'Scrabble' was a favourite game. But, we changed those rules, too. "If you can pronounce it, and give a definition for it, then it's a word." The words were long. The scores were high. The definitions were hilarious.

I pulled seven letters: s-o-t-m-e-j-n-v. I made a word: 'stogemntv.' The definition: "This is a genre of TV show, like murder mystery, romance, western. It is slang for 'heist' movies... a short form for "stole gems on TV." And since I have the 'V' over the double letter square, I will get a bonus addition to my score!"

The team spirit in our family was strong.

1996

In January, 1996, when my Dad died, I came home from Toronto with a new appreciation for what he had given me. Not material possessions, but education. Not only 'book learning' but trips and family outings, music and theatre, curiosity and the teachings of the Seer-Church.

Those 40 books that were written back in the 1700s held amazing doctrine. The Seer, also called a Mystic, claimed to have had contact with the Spiritual World every day for 26 years. Heaven, Hell and the World of Spirits were all described in great detail. The inner symbolic meaning of large parts of the Bible were explained. The vision of Nebuchadnezzar's dream in the book of Daniel was the key. The previous 'Churches' had been represented by the golden (Most Ancient Church), silver (Ancient Church), bronze (Hebrew Church), iron (Christian Church) and iron mixed with clay (the fallen Christian era). The Great Rock was the new 'Church' which would crush the others, grow and expand to fill the world. The Seer declared that our 'Church' was that glorious finale. Although I had some misgivings myself, it still seemed important that I pass these teachings along to my own children.

The best way to do that was to send them to Bonnie Hills Church School in Pennsylvania. Elise was already old enough to go away for school. In June, Elise, Nicholas, Toby and I travelled for four days on the train to Pennsylvania to visit the campus and see if she was agreeable. In late August, our whole family drove to the Seattle airport to see her off. Toby was only eight years old and our family members were already branching off, each to go their separate ways.

Eight years old. I always feel especially aware when each of my children turn eight. So many significant things happened, impressions were made, interests began to shape my life when I was eight years old.

Toby quite clearly had a character which sought out alternatives. Taking things apart. Putting things together. Substituting. "He breaks all the rules!" I held a conference with my husband.

"Well, we might as well accept his curiosity and encourage him to explore, and give him guidelines for safety sake," Kevin replied.

I observed myself saying "No." Sometimes 'No' was a 'life-and-death' emergency. Sometimes 'No' was a time delay because I was too tired to think. Sometimes 'No' meant, 'I need more information' or 'Ask me again later.' Sometimes 'No' was a barricade I put up, like damming a trickle of water along the roadside, to redirect the activity because I wanted things to go another way. Sometimes 'No' was cultural, good manners, civilized standards. Sometimes 'No' meant we needed to have a heart-to-heart talk about ethics, morals, taboos.

And, I had to pay attention when Toby said 'No' to me! It was not automatically disobedience. Sometimes he had good ideas or another way to solve a problem. Sometimes he wanted to redirect a homeschooling project to go in an equally valid different direction.

I had no doubt that I was attempting a different parenting style for this youngest son than I did for the first. Michael was sure to notice. "Mom! You would *never* have let me do that!"

1997

Toby turned nine at a picnic on a mountain in Colorado. Our whole family took the train, rented a van, met the relatives, saw my childhood home. A photo album records people, places, sequences and events. We each kept a journal.

Michael: age 15, July 1 and 2, 1997. Activities.
There is lots to do here. On July 1st, Uncle Ronald and I got dropped off at the top of the Rampart Range Road and ran down the trail to our cabin. It was three miles. When we drive to the top of Pikes Peak next week, he wants to run down that trail, too. On July 2nd we went swimming in the Green Mountain Falls pool. Mom learned to swim there. I helped my younger brothers learn to back float. I helped them get to the deep end of the pool and back. Dad is going to take us to the Cheyenne Mountain Zoo tomorrow. Mom wants to show us the church and school and places she played when she was a child.

Eleanor: The Mom, July 3, 1997. Remembering my Childhood. I sure like travelling by train. It worked out great for each person to rotate and take turns to be in charge of a meal or a snack each day. I'm 'Home!' The children recognize so much from my descriptions. But, I miss my Dad. Where ever I go I feel, "Thank-you, thank-you, thank-you!"... for the hikes, for the property, for appreciating art and music and theatre and literature, for the cabin and the house, for lessons and experiences. Yet, some places we went on outings also have memories of fear. But, since I've been to counselling and kept a journal and now that I am a parent and have an adult perspective, I can see it all more clearly. The place where I got stuck on the cliff? The rocks really are crumbly there, like ball bearings! Today, I climbed to the top of Bald Mountain to make a rock cairn using one rock for each member of our family tree.

Elise: age 17. 4th of July.
We went to the Rampart Range Road reservoir for a quadruple birthday picnic with Aunt Esther, Uncle Doug and Mom's two cousins. The boys went fishing and rock climbing and Toby had a birthday kite. Aunt Esther had a white cake with purple flowers. Toby had a carrot cake. Mine was chocolate fudge and the 'Uncle Sam' cake for the 4th of July was red, white and blue. Dad took Michael and I to the movies to see 'Men in Black.' Mom gave me a T-shirt she got at the zoo. Mom is American. She waved a USA flag and was singing all the national anthems. We watched 4th of July fireworks from the Rampart Range Road. We could see them from the top of Pikes Peak and three towns: Green Mountain Falls, Chipita Park and Woodland Park. They lasted from 9:00-10:00pm.

Toby: age 9, July 5, 1997. Aunt Charlotte.
I like Aunt Charlotte. She is cool. She has cool music. We went for a hike together. I climbed rocks. She carried my water bottle. We saw Rampart Range Road from the Crags. We had pizza delivered for supper. I ate six pieces and ice cream with butterscotch syrup and a cookie.

Kevin: Mountain Dad, July 6, 1997. Molly Kathleen Mine.
While my wife went with her aunt to enjoy memories and visit her dance teacher, I took the four children on a drive. We went to Cripple Creek, famous for the Colorado Gold Rush as well as the abundance of silver and platinum. We looked at abandoned machinery at 'Eagle Vista' mine. Then we took a lift 1000 feet underground to tour the 'Molly Kathleen Mine.' We drove back by way of the Phantom Canyon.

Nicholas: age 10, July 7, 1997. Pikes Peak.
Pikes Peak, elevation 14,110 feet. We didn't take the cog railway because Mom was too scared when she was a kid. We drove. Dad is an excellent, safe driver. We went to the top. Mom started to sing. We threw snow balls. Michael brought hacky-sacks and started to juggle. Mom took a picture of me pointing to our house down below. Toby and I went to the gift store and bought patches to sew on our Cub Scout blankets. On the way down, Elise helped get the picnic ready.

> *O beautiful, for spacious skies, for amber waves of grain,*
> *for purple mountains majesty above the fruited plain.*
> *America, America God shed His grace on thee,*
> *And crown thy good with brotherhood*
> *from sea to shinning sea.*[8]

1998

This summer, my siblings, their spouses and children met at our property in Colorado. Daddy left it to all five of us in his Will. But, how can five people, each living entirely different life-styles, share one piece of property? There is much to discuss. There is much to decide. There is work to be done: paperwork and physical work.

Kevin, Elise and Michael stayed home this time. Nicholas, Toby and I took the train again. It is familiar now: times and distances, stations and supplies, maps and tickets, always the same, always variations.

Hiking and swimming, scrubbing and sweeping, painting and playgrounds, we pack a lot into a few days.

Nicholas and Toby keep journals again. I take pictures and keep a calendar. The boys know some of their cousins and meet the rest. Suddenly I realize, "We need to take a picture!" Reluctant to follow instructions from their bossy older sister, somehow I arrange the set up. "Look, we can match each of us with a little niece or nephew who is the exact age we were when we moved away!"

I was ten years old, and so is Nicholas. James and Andrew were nine years old, and so is Toby. Julie was seven years old, and so is Carol's eldest daughter, Brenna. Little Carol was not quite three, and so is her youngest daughter, Katy.

We take more group photos before people start to leave. There are fourteen people in all. A neighbour drops in. She holds all the cameras.

It is disorienting to be in Daddy's house without him here. So many memories flood my mind and heart. My siblings and I laugh and recall episodes, compare points of view, share details with our spouses and children. This land has seen four generations of our family!

Nobody really wants to do the honours. Grieving is both a personal and a collective experience. Carol's husband, Jeff, and I arrange for a short memorial service. Julie suggested we plant a tree near the house. Jeff read aloud Psalm 1:1-3.

"Blessed is the man that walketh not in the counsel of the ungodly, nor standeth in the way of sinners, nor sitteth in the seat of the scornful. But his delight is in the law of the Lord; and in his law he doth meditate day and night. And he shall be like a tree panted by the rivers of water, that bringeth forth his fruit in his season; his leaf also shall not wither; and whatsoever he doeth shall prosper."

James read from Deuteronomy 6: 4-7.

"Hear, O Israel: The Lord our God is one Lord: And thou shalt love the Lord thy God with all thy heart, and with all thy soul, and with all thy might. And these words, which I command you this day, shall be in thy heart: And thou shalt teach them diligently unto thy children, and shalt talk of them when thou sittest in thine house, and when thou walkest by the way, and when thou liest down and when thou risest up."

I played the guitar so we could sing *Dona Nobis Pacem* as a round and one of Daddy's favourite bedtime hymns, *This is my Father's World.*[40]

James' wife, Lily, spoke of the 'new heaven and the new earth,'[41] and lead us in the Lord's Prayer. Andrew spoke quietly, emotionally about Dad's influence on his early life. Julie told about her sense of adventure and the way he encouraged her independence. She was allowed to climb Bald Mountain alone because Daddy could see her flash a mirror as an 'all is well' signal. Uncle Ronald recited lines from Robert Blair's poem, 'The Grave.' Carole felt too overcome with emotion to attempt to make a speech. We planted the tree, each placed a rock, quietly went away.

I walked with my Daddy to scatter his mother's ashes. Now my siblings and children are here to scatter Daddy's ashes. Will my remains be returned to this place? Will my sons and daughter shoulder this duty?

1999

It was a little gray, fluffy kitten, and somehow, she decided to be Toby's kitten. Which was fine. Elise and Michael have left for boarding school. Nicholas has had a turn with a pet. Now Toby gets the fun of that bond and trust that children form with young animals.

He slept on the top bunk, so he brought the kitten up at bedtime. Since we homeschool, it's OK for bedtime to unfold slowly. In fact, although we start to bed on time every night with after supper chores and routines of baths, toothbrush, good-night greetings to Daddy... still... questions, songs, memories and back rubs can fill another cozy hour together.

The kitten became part of a unique bedtime ritual.

Toby told his kitten the story of her grand-ancestors, beginning with the dawn of time.

"Little Kitty, do you wonder where you came from? How you got to be here? I will tell you everything.

"First, there was nothing. Nothing at all. Black, empty space for infinity. Which would be bad for a Kitty, because what would you eat? Where would you sleep? Who would love you? There would be nothing to play with or climb or explore. So, Kitties had to wait to become Kitties. The world was not ready yet.

"After awhile, God, who also didn't have anyone to love or play with, began to get things ready. First He made light, so He could see, and dark, so He could sleep. And then He felt thirsty, so He made water next. He knew that Kitties and other things

He had in mind would need more things, so He made the land, mountains and good farm soil and beaches of sand, all kinds of pretty rocks, too, like diamonds and rubies and emeralds and sapphires. After He had fun with that, He was still lonely, but He couldn't make Kitties yet, because first He had to make plants. I know you aren't too interested in eating fruits and grains and vegetables. But, the birds and mice need them, so He had to make them first.

"I guess He realized that the plants would die unless He made the sun, so that was next and the moon and stars added a few lights for the night time. Now that's important to you. Just wait until you find out about your relatives. They love to prowl around at night.

"Now we get to the tasty part: birds and fish. Ooo, you're listening now aren't you Kitty? I can show you pictures of all the kinds of birds and fish. Some large fluffy birds can't even fly! Jungle birds have bright colours and strange beaks. Hunting birds with sharp claws and keen eyesight and wide-spread wings keep soaring above the fields looking for mice and rabbits. Wading birds find fish in shallow waters. Hummingbirds dart about licking the sweet juices in each flower.

"And the fish! Weird deep-sea creatures would give you nightmares. Star fish live along the beach. Swarms of thousands of fish swirl in spirals in the water. Tuna and salmon end up in cans just for you to feast on.

"So, He started making animals: huge ones like elephants and hippos, fast ones like deer and horses, tame ones like cows and goats, and hunters like wolves and (are you ready?) cats!

"You have so many relatives: striped tigers in Asia, lions with manes in Africa, jaguars in South America, cougars in North America."

Toby paused to ask me, "Mom, what other kids of cats are there?"

I had to think fast to add to his story. "Leopards have spots and Cheetah run fast. Lynx have a stubby tail and Bobcats are quite small. Ocelot have markings in patches. Some people have different names for the same thing: Puma, Mountain Lion and Cougar are all the same kind of cat."

Toby continued. "God had a fun time thinking up all of those amazing varieties. But, He still didn't feel like He had anyone to play with."

"Sweetheart," I interrupted. "I think your Kitty has had enough of a lesson for one night, so let her sleep now."

But Toby's mind was full of information he wanted to pass on to his new Kitty. The next night the story continued.

"OK, Listen, Kitty, here is more of your family history.

"Most of the animals were either wild or tame, but you cats could be both. Mom told me about the 'Cat that Walked by Itself' and also 'How the Leopard Got its Spots.'[42] I can ask her to tell you those stories another time.

"So, when God made people, they named all of the animals and got to walk among all of them because everything was peaceful and calm in this beautiful garden where everyone had plenty and no one had to fight.

"But, after that tricky snake and the first fight between the two first brothers, a lot of bad things started to happen. The animals got dangerous, too, and no one was friends anymore. Claws tore. Talons pierced. Teeth bit. Fangs slashed. Tusks and antlers and horns did battle. It was a very scary time.

"Finally God got an idea to start everything over again. So He told this one guy to build a boat and bring a boy and a girl of each kind of animal on the boat to save them from the flood. So, that's where your family continued. On the Ark. The first Kitty in the garden led to the first Kitty on the Ark. And all the Kitties in the world come from your great-great-great-grandma and grampa Kitty who rode on the Ark!

"After everyone unloaded the boat, all the animals and all the people started to spread around. The cats and their kittens did, too. Some liked the dry lands and some liked the rain forests. Some liked the mountains and snow. Some needed the heat. Some allowed themselves to become tame.

"In Egypt, people made statues and paintings and head dresses that looked like cats.

"Then people started inventing things and began to explore and travel to see what it was like in far off places.

"Cats were very valuable on ships because they kept hunting the nasty mice and rats. Your great-great-grandma Kitty and great-great-grampa Kitty came to this part of the world on a ship, too. It was dark and rainy and chilly and crowded, but they were brave sea-cats and they made it to Canada. They had lots of work to do here. The people made cabins. The mice got in through the cracks. But the Kitties hunted them so the people were glad.

"Canada was a really nice place. More people came on boats. Plus, the people and the cats had lots of children. When farms got crowded into towns and towns got crowded into cities, some of the people decided to build wagons and see if there was any place with more room so they could spread out.

"Wagons weren't very good places for cats! They were hot and dry and bounced along. Your great-grandma and great-grampa Kitty had to stay in a cage so they wouldn't run away from the bumpy wagons. But they were happy when they got to see the prairies and the mountains. The people decided to build a train track so everyone could travel without the bumps. Grandma and Grampa Kitty liked that much better."

"I think you have told enough of the story now, Toby," I was watching the clock.

"But, Mom, I'm just about done," he replied, giving me those asking brown eyes, that little pout and melting my heart with his creativity.

"So, when my Mom and Dad came driving to the mountains in their VW van, built their cabin, had their babies, moved to the town and finally built this house, they asked and looked and searched for a kitten to make their family complete. That's *you*, Little Kitty. We had a pretty nice family before, but now we are complete." And so, snuggling down, content and oriented in the 'Grand Scheme of Things,' Toby went off to sleep with a fluffy gray kitten purring in his arms.

* ** *** ****

2000

We tried so hard to stay awake all day and all night to watch every piece of the BBC program to celebrate the arrival of the New Millennium! Kevin went to bed. I'm sure I dozed. Nicholas might have napped. Toby briefly snoozed. I think I heard a snore.

As each time zone passed, mid-night, I relaxed. It looks like there won't be any computer 'glitches'! No shocking collapse of civilization. Telephones and email bring greetings from my siblings.

Life is grand. The day is new. We begin again.

Toby will be 12 this year, and Nicholas will soon turn 13. No little children are left!

Michael will graduate and turn 18 this year. Big decisions lie ahead.

Elise will turn 20! That is the age Kevin and I were when we got married, loaded up the VW van and headed for the mountains. What choices will she make out in the world?

Moms
by: Toby, Grade 6

Moms can be very nice.
Good work.
Nice job.
Have a good day at school.
Moms can help you on the ice.

Moms can be very strict.
Go to bed!
Come here now!
Be quiet!
What was that you just flicked?

Moms can be both sometimes.
Nice job, now go to bed.

But, I guess Moms are what they are,
And no one can change that!

REFLECTIONS

All life is an experiment.
The more experiments you make the better.
—Ralph Waldo Emerson

Chapter 6
Wednesday, January 12, 2000
First Son: Mighty Michael

Great intelligence, vigour, and strength of will, however marvelous,
produce nothing unless they are harnessed and given direction.
Harnessing means restraint. And restraint means obedience.
And obedience means respect, perhaps love
for something other than one's self.
—Robert Russell

* ** *** ****

Seventeen years old

The phone rings.

Possibilities, like popcorn popping, appear in my mind as I stop what I'm doing and walk towards the telephone.

If the phone rings in the morning, I have to stop washing dishes, dry my hands on my apron.

If the phone rings in the afternoon, I have to struggle awake from the nap I often take at the same time as our small children.

If the phone rings at suppertime, I have to check the pots and pans to be sure nothing will boil over or burn while I am distracted for the minutes I am talking while I cannot reach the stove.

But now, it is evening. In fact, I was just coming down the stairs, finished putting the children to bed.

Who could it be? Not a business call, or an appointment confirmation, or a catalog order arrived, or a library book that's in. It's way after businesses hours. Not a relative. It's too late in the evening. All of my relatives live in times zones to the east and would not be up this late. Not our son or daughter who are attending the Church high school and college back in Pennsylvania. It's 8:00pm here so it's 11:00pm there.

It might be a friend. Someone local. Someone with a story to tell of some cute thing their little one did, or a homeschooling Mom who would like an encouraging word, or a granny with an invitation to tea.

"Hello?" My ears are eager to guess who it might be from the first sound of the voice.

"Hello, Mrs. Deckert?" It's the Principal of the Bonnie Hills Church School. I glance at the clock again. It's 11:00pm in Pennsylvania! This is not a social phone call, or some kind of poll, or an announcement, or invitation, or minor update.

"Yes?" I am already a little weak in the knees. Or maybe stronger. Bracing myself for the incoming message.

"This is Mr. Downs, the principal of Bonnie Hills Church School. Is your husband home, too? May I speak with both of you together?"

I spoke with the principal only ten days ago. In the excitement of the New Millennium, our son, Michael, couldn't resist pulling a prank on campus. He had climbed onto the roof of the Dining Hall with a friend. The police and fire rescue crew had to come because the girl was unable to get up her courage to climb back down.

Mr. Downs had spoken with a clear warning. "Because Michael's action was during the Christmas-New Year holiday and he was not staying in the dormitory at the time, it was not, strictly speaking, a school matter. So we are not going to expel him. But, I thought you should know. This is not the kind of behavior we can tolerate here with so many youth living away from home." He was straightforward. I was grateful.

Yes, I knew that Michael was a bit of a prankster. He felt safe and confident in his own ability, but his idea of fun did not always coincide with what field trip supervisors, or school bus drivers, or teachers, or librarians and especially principals considered standard behaviors.

So, while I waited for my husband to pick up the other telephone, I got ready to hear another surprising event, and felt sure that I would not be all that surprised.

"Your son has been in a car accident. I have just come from the hospital. He has a broken leg." His voice was steady, well prepared, quickly conveying the primary information without allowing for alarm to begin to escalate through his tone of voice.

My mind is forming images rapidly with every scrap of new information. Car accident? Where? Injuries? What part of his body? How badly is he hurt? How sure are the doctors? Have they done every test? Will there be more news? Worse news? Is there something dreadful he is holding back to tell me after I have adjusted to knowing this much?

I battle my imagination to stop conjuring up pictures of wheel-chairs, spinal cord injuries, twisted limbs, mangled body, bloody bandages, permanent damage.

"He has no critical injuries, only a few scrapes."

Now fireworks are going off, thankful. Release the balloons. Worst anxieties begin to quiet.

"They want to keep him in overnight to observe and monitor him. Your insurance has been informed. The House Master went in the ambulance with him. He is in excellent care."

Beginning to understand, not wanting to allow emotions to flood, grasping for more facts I ask, "Can we talk to him? Is there a telephone in his room? Can we talk with the doctor?"

"You won't be able to speak with him for a few hours. Here is the House Master. He can tell you more."

Pictures are flashing so rapidly in my mind. Every flicker of memory from the past is right before my eyes. My son! My baby! My adorable tot! My rascally boy! This handsome, smart, creative young man! Potential and untapped opportunities are spread out into the future. Or are they suddenly to be clipped short, snuffed, smothered, crushed?

"The car actually hit him while he was crossing the street. The x-ray of his leg led to the decision to surgically pin the bone. He is in surgery now. The break is right above the knee joint. Miraculously the joint itself was not damaged. Although there is no sign of internal injuries, his blood work caused the doctors concern so they want to keep him for 24 hours and more tests."

"What were the circumstances? How could he cross the street and not see the car?" My mind is trying hard to comprehend. I need facts. My imagination will concoct a wild and frightening story if I do not have facts to build on.

"He had just finished a sporting event in the Field House on campus this afternoon. It was getting dark, chilly, rainy, foggy. He left the competition with a friend and they were still in their uniforms, eager to cross quickly and get showered and to the Dining Hall on time. The friend said that they looked both ways and started across, but there had been a second, unseen car closely following behind the first one. Quick and alert from the sporting event, the friend was astonished when he saw Michael vault with his hands on the hood of the car, break the driver's window, roll across the roof of the car. He was flung forward into the ditch. He was not unconscious. As you know, the ambulance shed is close by. He received immediate care."

There doesn't seem to be anything else to say.

"Thank-you for your explanation."

"I will call you again as soon as we have the test results. Your son is a very strong lad. He is expected to make a fine recovery."

Now bedtime seems out of the question. I cling to my husband, gasping in his arms. The sound of the phone ringing, the tone of voice, the information pierces my heart. "Your son has been in an accident. He was hit by a car. We don't know, until the test results are in, how badly he has been hurt."

"I want to rush to be with him," I look into my husband's eyes. But it takes two whole days to travel! I would not have any news. Bus, taxi, airport, arranging to be picked up. I can't think of all the details to arrange! Besides, by the time I get there he will be released and everything will be fine.

Unless there is some unforeseen further injury. I struggle to hold my mind from nightmarish distortions, disfigurement, disabilities. "They said he was conscious. They said he could speak." I remind myself over and over again.

I sit by the phone. How long until additional news? Until I hear my son's voice?

Pushing the heavy, sloth-like minute hand, wanting, but dreading the news. Agony, knowing his body is bruised and bleeding, wounds I cannot soothe, blood I cannot wash away, suffering I can do nothing to prevent. MY SON! Each beat of the second hand seems delayed. Time is drawn out. Extended. My heart is tortured on the rack.

* ** *** ****

What do Mothers do when their children suffer? What thought can I hold on to? What face? What voice? What courage can I borrow to keep me from falling to pieces?

Mary. A picture of Mary[43] comes clearly into my mind. She knows. She is a mother. She watched, helpless as her Son was bruised, bleeding, painfully gasping for breath. Mary stood at the foot of the Cross. Agony as she watched, waited, powerless. What will happen next? John stood beside her, helped her home.

Yes, I can hold onto the idea of Mary, the example of Mary, the endurance of Mary, the unwavering trust within Mary.

During the night time hours of sleeplessness, fearful, anxious, without any action I can take to hurry towards more information, I will not be alone. Treasuring my own precious memories, I can better see how she and I are the same: Mothers.

Like Mary, my heart lifted to hear the glad tidings, "You are with child!"

Like Mary who ran to tell Elisabeth, I confided in an older friend. I felt encouraged as I heard others tell their own birth story, entered the woman's role of pregnancy, birth, nursing, infant care. She adored His precious face. I savoured that first eye contact with my son.

And so, I recall soothing memories during the long hours of night. Tomorrow is always unknown. Today is too difficult. If I collect images from yesterday then I will feel security and calm.

Before you were born

The summer of 1981 was an exciting time for Kevin and I. Baby Elise and I had spent the winter months with my Mother in

Ontario. The cabin Kevin and I had built when we first arrived in British Columbia was too cold for a baby. We would soon be moving out of the one room log cabin we had built that first summer of 1978. No more frigid winters. The new stackwall house was also small, but the one-foot thick walls would keep out the chill. Little Elise had her first birthday. My brother, James, and a young friend named Matthew, came to help Kevin finish the building. Last summer, we had almost finished the walls. This summer, we needed the upstairs floor joists, roof beams, tin roof, insulation and windows.

I kept the food coming, feeding little Elise, three working men, while eating extra myself while nursing a tot. I kept the wood stove going to bake granola, muffins, bread, casseroles, cookies and pies. But I couldn't seem to keep myself satisfied. I always wanted more food. In fact, sometimes I felt dizzy and needed to put my head down until I could think of what I could eat right away. And, no matter how much I ate and drank, I didn't seem to be making enough milk for Elise.

"You're pregnant," Cheryl bluntly stated the obvious when I confided in her during a visit to Avola.

How could I possibly eat enough for three people? From then on, I never went a day without having fresh baked muffins available. Molasses or cinnamon, or coconut, or peanut butter, or raisins, or dates, or bananas, or apples, or wild blueberries, or grated zucchini, always made with bran and whole wheat flour, that is what this baby will be made of! Although summertime baking on a wood stove makes the cabin loft very hot, we live 45 miles away from a store, so making my own food is imperative.

We moved into the stackwall house just before Christmas! A new wood heater as well as the wood cook stove meant that we were cozy and warm while upstairs sleeping under the barn style roof complete with skylights. At first we had no furniture at all, only the mattress from the cabin loft which we wrestled up the stairs.

Washing the dishes was awkward. Without a table or counter, I put the dishpan and a clean towel on the floor. I knelt on the floor, my big belly leaning forward over the dishpan. Little Elise wanted to paddle in the water. One by one I washed the dishes, poured hot water from a jug to rinse them and laid the clean dishes on the towel. I was exceedingly happy a few days later when Kevin came home with a kitchen table. He built a bench. Elise had a highchair, sent from Kevin's Mom and a rocking chair which was a gift from from my parents. I covered a piece of foam mattress to make the cedar chest into a comfortable place to sit. The kitchen hutch was moved from the cabin to the new house. Soon Kevin built a work counter and another counter for the kitchen sink. It was starting to be a civilized place to live.

The baby inside me was growing well. Every three days Kevin brought home a gallon jar of fresh milk from a neighbor with a cow. I skimmed off the cream and shook it in a glass jar to try to make butter. But I never shook it long enough. I made whipped cream, on the oatmeal, on the cream of wheat, on peanut butter toast, on soup, or a bowl of apple sauce, or piece of cake. I had to use it up. We had more cream coming in another three days!

Contractions started in January, one month before the due date! They weren't strong or making progress, but I was not willing to stay out in the woods with no telephone, or neighbours, or vehicle while Kevin went to work. He was gone over ten hours patrolling all night on the train tracks through the rock cuts beside the icy river in the dark. It was winter. It was stressful.

So, we packed up and asked Fran and Archie[44] if we could stay with them again. Jim and Cheryl and all of the brothers had moved out of the farmhouse and Fran and Archie had room in their attic eves. Kevin and I whispered names. Boy names. Girl names. Middle names. Names from the family tree. Names from the Bible. Hippy names. Classic names. Combinations of names.

Elise was 21 months old, learning rapidly and beginning to talk rather well. Although I didn't lift or romp with her with my huge belly, I played singing games with her on my lap and taught her lots of traditional English nursery rhymes. Grammie used to take me on her lap, bounce her knees and give me a pony ride. Elise also enjoyed the contrast of the steady trot and the big bounces as the pony jumped.

Trot, trot, trot, trot my pony, trot.
Over grass and over gravel,
Oh what fun it is to travel.
Never, never stop! Trot, my pony, trot!

I enjoyed watching her face as she anticipated the exciting climax of this old Nursery Rhyme.

This is the way the Farmer rides:
Hobble-dee-hoy, hobble-dee-hoy.

The day you were born

In February, Kevin went to the city and brought back a gift for me. It was a funny book called 'David, we're pregnant!' by Canadian cartoonist, Lynne Johnson. I burst into tears and asked him, sniffling, "Do you love me? Do you really love me?" I felt miserable, swollen, tired, clumsy, always hungry, always sleepy. Then I remembered that I had been all teary and emotional just before I went into labour the first time. Here it was,

Kevin's birthday, and he gave me a present. Here I was feeling sorry for myself, without a present to give him. I felt blue. Fran made a lovely supper and a cake. Then she put curlers in my hair.

In the middle of winter, in the middle of the night, I tip-toed down the stairs to the bathroom and realized that the birth sequence had started. I chuckled while I took the rollers out of my hair. My curly head looked like Raggedy Anne!

I was a little more nervous to go into labour the second time. The first time I had been trusting in the forces of Nature which all women experience. I had prepared by reading books and listening to other ladies tell their stories. I believed that good information and a good attitude would give me a good experience. But now I knew that giving birth was a long, hard day and not all parts of the experience were easy to work through.

Kevin was there. Cheryl came to coach. "Use your breath, Eleanor. You can do this." That baby was big. All of that fresh milk made for a baby weighing nearly ten pounds! He looked like a three-month-old! The sleeves of the newborn sized nightgown were too short. The tiny diapers were too small. The doctor cautioned me not to lift more than ten pounds.

A boy! Part of me was terrified. Popular psychology at the time frequently blamed 'The Mother' for any misbehaviour of her son. Not only through childhood and school yard pranks, but right up until adulthood this was the explanation for the crimes of the son: arson, rape, theft, addiction, domestic violence, molesting children, homosexuality. Make a list! It was all 'The Mother' who was to blame! How 'The Mother' raised her 'son' was the main reason the kid was in jail.

How would I do any better? What were these mysterious cruelties 'mothers' were delivering to boys? My blood felt cold in my veins. Who was this stranger? How could I govern and instruct, guide and prevent, nourish and protect this Little Man?

I don't think anyone handed me an Owner's Manual?

Good thing my Mother arrived just then. Dearma flew up from Florida all slim and trim and tan. She got right to work shaking the cream, baking the muffins, looking after Elise and carrying my baby up and down the stairs.

When you were a baby

Elise loved her brother from the first moment. As they grew, their bond became stronger. Her language skills meant that she could negotiate options for lunch (Would you like your sandwiches cut in squares or triangles?) and story time (Shall we read the same book again or try something new?). Michael's physical skills meant that he could climb to reach (a ball or toy or book) and entertain (with jumps, tricks and dramatic poses).

I took lots of pictures with my Instamatic camera. On payday we stopped at the pharmacy in Clearwater to drop off the film. In two weeks, on the next payday, we went back to town to pick up the double prints when they were developed. Grandmothers enjoyed getting a letter with photos of birthday cakes (Garfield), dress-up clothes (Super Man, magician, Prince), outings (waterfalls, huge cedar stumps and logging machinery), holidays (July 1st parade, Halloween costumes, Jack-o-lantern, kids on Santa's knee), working together (kitchen, garden, firewood).

I also took pictures of Michael when he was asleep. All of his nonstop activity and my scolding, the Lego and toys all across the floor, the curious questions and noisy romping, the messy meals and soggy towels were finished for the day. Sweet cherub lips, chubby rosy cheeks, darling toddler hands, adorable little boy. Still. Silent. He is in dreamland.

One year old

Michael took his very first steps just as I aimed the camera to take a picture of him on his first birthday!

They say a one-year-old is more active than an Olympic athlete in training. I got tired just watching Michael's antics.

Are girls different from boys? Oh, yes they are! When Elise was one year old, she posed in front of the mirror with a hat or scarf. She said, "Hat on" when she stacked blocks. She was cooperative and easily understood my words. She enjoyed mimicking my sweeping, washing, feeding the animals. She wanted to write and made an 'X' and 'O' on the letters I wrote home. She wanted to read and held her doll to see the pictures while she retold stories from the books I read to her. I thought I was a 'Good Mother' because little Elise was such a 'Good Girl.'

Are boys different from girls? Oh, yes they are! When Michael turned one year old, he would rather crash the blocks than stack them. He said no words until much later. If I called him to come, he ran the other way, looking back over his shoulder with mischief in his eye. He was forever climbing, making truck noises, and had little interest in books. I thought I was a 'Bad Mother' because little Michael was so uncooperative and rebellious.

Two years old

When Michael was two years old, Kevin was on the Search and Rescue Team. He was learning First Aide, steep embankment rescue, auto extraction techniques and how to track missing persons. He showed us Sign and we became very observant. My sister, Julie, was intrigued with Michael's world view. She took him for a walk and he picked up a stick that had no bark on it. "Beaver did it," he pronounced, because we lived near a beaver pond and such findings were quite common. Next he noticed a squashed pine cone on the road. "Truck did it," he explained. After awhile he looked up at the crescent moon in the morning sky. Familiar with the cut-away tree stumps where we live, he quite accurately deduced from the missing chunk of the no longer round moon, "Chain-saw did it," which Aunt Julie will never forget to chuckle about.

All of life is an interesting experiment when you raise a son! How naughty can one little scamp be in a day? I was bewildered. As a babysitter, I had so many successful experiences with small children. I thought I would be able to breeze right through these early years with my own children. I had never, ever delivered a spanking. In all my years of child care, there was always a fun distraction or compromise or clever way to solve a problem.

Why was being a 'Mother' so different?

All I ever seemed to say to this little boy was, "No!" or "Get down!" or "Stop!" I was raised, like most people at the time, with spanking. Other families had a belt, wooden spoon or 'Board of Education.' The Principal at school could administer the strap. Disobedience had a physically painful consequence. In the 1980s, the generation Elise and Michael were a part of, the idea of 'hitting' your own child was starting to be discouraged. Parenting courses, self-help books and stylized forms of communication were being encouraged.

"Three times is a spanking," Cheryl coached me. "More than that is hitting. You don't want to do it because you have lost your temper. Some kids don't learn with words and explanations."

Three years old

Michael didn't talk much, but he sure had opinions. Sometimes I thought that he was in charge and I was the one taking orders. I wanted my children to have choices, but I also wanted them to obey. When Michael was three years old, I was getting exhausted by the weight of lifting him and the strength it took to get him to 'stop' and 'go' when I needed him to cooperate. In order to demonstrate my superior authority without shouting or spanking, I decided to invite him to have daily wrestling matches.

We cleared the floor, faced each other diagonally across the room, palms together, bowing formally, we pledged these words in unison. "I promise I won't really hurt you. No hitting. No kicking. No pulling hair. No biting. No grabbing Mom's glasses. But... I *am* going to wrestle you down!"

I did not 'let him win.' The object of the game was for me to convince him that I was the 'Alpha' here. When I gave him instructions, I wanted him to obey! Again and again, laughing so hard, pushing and grunting, twisting away and grabbing the shoulders, I held him down for the count of ten. I knew that he would one day grow to be stronger than me and I wanted him to know who was the 'Boss.'

But, there are so many interactions every day, climbing to dangerous heights, opening the lids of spice jars, dumping water out of the bathtub, pestering the cat, refusing to come, or stop, or wait, or be quiet, or bring me what I asked for. Spanks were still part of some days. Elise didn't seem to ever disobey. But Michael could look me in the eye and defiantly act directly in opposition to my instructions.

Four years old

One golden September day when Michael was four years old, while we were harvesting the garden I suddenly had an idea. Since we cut and chop and stack the wood so we have enough for the whole winter and also make jam and save the food from the garden in the freezer so we have enough for the whole winter and we dig the potatoes and save them in baskets so we have enough for the whole winter... if only there was a way that I could store up a supply of "No!" and "Stop!" and "Don't!" so that I wouldn't have to say it anymore until springtime!

Four-year-olds love to learn. Michael was continually eager and curious. That winter, when it was pitch dark at 4:30 in the afternoon, he made binoculars with toilet paper tubes, bundled up in winter gear and went outside to study the stars. I gave him a black piece of paper and white chalk. He went out on the front porch to look up at the constellations, then came back inside to plot the stars on his map.

Mayonnaise jars in summertime held a zoo of bugs. Tadpoles matured in an aquarium we bought at the Thrift Store. Rocks and seeds, feathers and driftwood, sea shells from Florida and postcards from cities were all collected.

And what was in his pockets? I was afraid to put my fingers in! Flattened bottle caps, a rusty nail, rocks with shiny mica, dried up worms, a muddy penny, broken brown glass, a bent key.

Never a dull moment!

Five years old

I decided to homeschool. It just seemed to me that the natural rhythms of the day and night, physical activity and following his own interests were more important for Michael than alarm clocks and bus rides. I couldn't imagine him indoors, sitting down, waiting his turn. There is so much stylized behaviour. Typically, school work focuses on learning from books and writing answers to tests. At home I could allow for more movement, less writing, more oral interactions, and plenty of hands-on learning.

When he was five years old and again when he was six, baby brothers arrived. First Nicholas, and a little over a year later, Thomas Benjamin (who we always called 'Toby').

Michael's famous response to the news of another sibling on the way was the same both times. "I hope it's a boy and I'll take him behind the couch and teach him to be bad!" It kind of summed up his world view at the time.

But, he didn't teach them how to be bad. Indeed, Michael proved to be an excellent big brother. Tender with the babies, energetic with the tots, a reliable example for the preschoolers, he seemed to have a keen interest in the younger ones and a knack for leadership and teaching.

Since my own brothers were twins, they had a kind of closed system. They competed and cooperated with each other and that was enough. I noticed Michael's 'Big Brother' behaviour and tried to observe it developing naturally without interfering as much as possible.

Six years old

> Now that I'm six, I'm as clever as clever,
> So, I think I'll stay six now for ever and ever.
> —*A.A. Milne*[45]

Pirates! That was an interesting homeschooling topic! Michael was kindergarten age and was learning to use the globe, aware of resources around the world, willing to spend time with books about ships and weapons, gold, pearls, silk and fur. Elise was interested in royalty. The books she chose from the Bookmobile showed gowns and crowns, wigs and tiaras. And, to my surprise, it turned out that the queens got their jewels and finery from the loot the pirates brought them! My Dad sent a pirate flag for Michael's sixth birthday. I made a treasure map for him to search for his gifts and cake.

"But, there aren't any pirates now, are there, Mom?" he asked, wide-eyed at bedtime.

"No, darling. We are safe, there are no pirates now," I soothed his imagination so he would sleep soundly.

But, as I went downstairs, I realized: there was plenty of violence associated with the drug trade.

Having time to spend with my children at bedtime is one of the most important advantages about the homeschooling schedule. If questions arise, there is no pressure to 'Be quiet and go to sleep.'

Another night time question caught my attention. "Mom, why do we call Jesus the Lamb and the Good Shepherd?"[46] I had no answer, but I was astonished to hear such amazing insight from one so young!

Michael liked to play, 'Not touch the floor.' Pillows and benches, ropes and belts were arranged so that he could travel through the house. Michael liked to collect unusual toys. He wanted to buy a rubber snake. I asked him to promise not to scare anyone, not even grownups. I asked him to tell me three ways he could play with the snake that would do good not harm. "It could reach down to someone who needs to be rescued. It could bring supplies to people who are hungry. It could eat harmful bugs, mice and weeds in the garden." Michael likes to make mazes. For his birthday, I gave him a huge ball of string. He looped and tied it to make a web across the whole room.

Seven years old

The next winter Elise and Michael went to school. I knew I couldn't manage Grade 3 and Grade 1 lessons with them at home while the two little brothers were scrambling underfoot. Every morning I walked with Elise and Michael to the school bus. Michael was always bigger and stronger than the other children his age. I saw the other children playing on the high snowbanks, pushing and sliding down and climbing back up was fun. But, I was afraid that Michael didn't know his own strength. Instead of going to school that day, I took him back home. We were going to make a chart.

Throwing, hitting, kicking, pushing. We measured Michael's strength for each of these activities. We recorded the data on a graph paper chart. I used a tape measure to mark how far he could throw. I let him use a broom to whack the snowy branches of spruce trees. We weighed a laundry basket full of blankets, then books, then firewood to indicate how forceful his kicking could be. A bathroom scale could measure pressure when held it up against his shoulder while he pushed heavy furniture. I needed him to understand that he could generate enough force to really hurt the smaller children.

After each demonstration, I asked him to think. I wrote down his answers. "Tell me three times when you would get a prize for throwing? People would cheer! You would be famous!"

"If I was playing football and scored a goal, or basket ball, or if I was in the Olympics and threw a javelin the furthest." Excellent answers!

"Now tell me three times when you would be in big trouble for throwing something. Maybe even go to jail. Maybe even kill someone." I really wanted him to consider the consequences of thoughtless action.

"If I threw something in a museum and broke something valuable. If I threw something and broke a window in a car or house. If I threw a knife or sword." All serious.

We continued with each of the physical tasks. "Your muscles are strong. You can use them for good or for harm. Your muscles are a healthy part of your body. They can do work or damage. You get to drive your body. You can make things happen. My brain is not attached to your body. I cannot make you 'stop' or 'go.' I will not always be watching to see what you do. You will have to decide for yourself, even if no one can see you." I was very aware that he was his own self, that I had a limited time to instruct, share values, allow for development and try to help him avoid mistakes.

"Three harmful things," Michael was catching on to the pattern. "I could push an old lady, or scare someone in a wheel chair, or push something breakable over the edge. Three helpful things: I could help you push the furniture when you're cleaning, or push the grocery cart, or push my baby brother in a laundry basket and make him laugh!"

'Tell me three times when' became a regular and frequently used feature of my parenting style.

Eight years old

Big Brother Michael was an excellent example to the younger boys in so many ways.

He pulled them on sleds, pushed them on swings, made snacks in the kitchen, learned to work in the garden, looked after the chickens, helped his brothers find books at the Bookmobile, coached bicycle riding, and most valuable of all, taught them how to build with Lego.

Space ships and towers, weapons and explorations, kingdoms and factories, wizards and dragons, ambulance attendants and cowboys were all assembled, became the focus for several days, and morphed into a new story or civilization.

Lego was the centrepiece for our Palm Sunday[46] celebration. The tiny colourful townsfolk lined the streets waving palm branches from the tropical Lego set. I cut tiny cloth robes for them to lay on the path ahead of the donkey (we had to substitute with a horse). 'Jesus' was a bearded Lego man dressed all in white. The Medieval soldiers played the role of the Roman soldiers, looking very threatening. The Lego wizard became the High Priest near the Lego temple. As the boys set it up, and Elise read the story aloud, I could sense conflicting forces at work much more clearly than I had ever been aware of before. The disciples were just beginning to glimpse the prophesies fulfilled. The temple officials huddled, whispering, alarmed at the sudden rise in the wandering preacher's popularity. Armed soldiers stood rigid, at the ready, trained to obey whatever the command. The peasants gathered, cheering, voicing their hope that this miracle worker would soon be their King and military leader, crush the oppressors with a single mighty blow. Jesus, quiet, calm, is the only one who was not surprised by all the commotion. Was He entirely aware of the way this scene would play out?

My Dad gave me money. I bought an electric keyboard. I showed Elise and Michael how to play *Chopsticks* and *Doe a Deer*. Michael composed a little tune using only the black keys.

Foggy mists arising early in the morning.

And another one.

Christmas bells merrily ring
for the Saviour Christ the King!

Eight years old always seemed very significant to me. I remembered the turning points in my own life. I believed that a child can begin to make decisions and strengthen self-discipline and be trustworthy. Kevin and I agreed that 'eight' was the age to present the birthday child with a pocket knife.

"A knife is a tool," Kevin brought his philosophy to his son. "You can use it for harm or for helping. You are the driver. You decide on your own actions. This knife will be taken away if you demonstrate unsafe activities."

And he did. So it was.

About the same time that the knife was confiscated, I was alarmed to find a piece of paper in Michael's bedroom that had burn holes scorched through it. He had used his magnifying glass to focus the sun's rays and singe the paper. Living in a wooden house with no local fire department, this was not a joke! To mimic the severity of loosing all of our possessions in a house fire, I insisted that Michael sleep on a mattress on the floor without access to any of his possessions for as many days as there were holes in the paper.

* ** *** ****

"Get in the truck," Kevin announced when he got home one hot day. "We're going to see eagles. The salmon are running!"

That was the summer when Dearma came to stay in the little yellow cottage. As we drove to the place Kevin wanted to show us, he spoke to her. "We live here," Kevin said, "This is our 'back yard.' This is where our children learn and grow."

Astonishing to see over 30 bald eagles perched high along the river for miles. Astonishing to see the water whipped by the fish thrashing their tails. The females belly-scrape the gravel to make a basin for their nest. They are so weak from the 400 mile fight upstream to the original creek they themselves were hatched in. After they release hundreds of eggs, it won't be long before they drift, dying, downstream. The males come and spray their cloud of sperm to fertilize the whole nest of eggs. The eagles get an easy feed. Bears know it is time. Nature's cycles are powerful.

The salmon were so big, so strong, so many, so close together.

I stayed on the shore with Toby in the backpack and kept Nicholas safely on dry land. Dearma went to a shallow place to watch more closely. Elise waded near her. Michael went chest-deep into the frothing creek with the fish, focused on their life-supporting task, were oblivious to his presence. Kevin had the camera.

Later, I added to Michael's previous instruction. Like my Mother, I had taught him the facts of human reproduction within the context of the commitment of marriage, the purpose of stability for raising children in the family and God's Providence. Now I wanted to emphasize the value of consent and self-control. "While we were watching the fish today, I realized how far they have come and how difficult their journey is from the ocean to get here. The whole reason they did that was for the females to make their eggs and the males to fertilize them so there would be more baby salmon next year. That is how powerful the force to mate is in fish and birds, animals and even people. The difference with people is that we are careful to choose who we will marry and have babies with. We decide with our minds and hearts before we take action with our bodies. You will someday feel that force in your body. It is very strong. You will need to learn how to strengthen your self-control, how to wait, how to choose a wife and ask for her to marry you, how to recognize this special gift from the Lord and only participate in these strong feelings when your heart and mind and spirit as well as your body are giving this special gift to your wife. We don't grab each other like some animals do.

We don't change partners like some animals do. We don't mate and die like the fish do. The Lord gave us more than He gave the animals. He made people so they could stay married and learn to love each other. The two halves seek to make a whole."

Nine years old

I don't remember why. I don't remember when. Exhausted by interrupted sleep, the responsibility of the family, isolated from supportive extended family, stressed by stretched finances, I lost my usual level-headed, creative, deliberate parenting skills. I spanked Michael. More than the count of three. In fact, I felt like I was thumping the dust out a rug. He met my eyes, alarmed. Realizing I had moved past logic, I stepped back, my face surprised. "Go to your room! Right now!"

I had always wondered how it could happen. Now I had done it. "I am so sorry" doesn't erase the action. There is no 'rewind' button.

Would this one incident overshadow our otherwise wholesome family dynamics?

From that time on I governed with the use of charts. You can't argue with a chart. You can't talk back. It was simple. You did or did not do what was expected. So, you did or did not get the anticipated benefit.

Like my own Mother, I expected some chores to be done as part of responsible family life. Make your bed. Clean off your place at the table. Bring your laundry to the basket. Some daily chores had a regular payment which, if completed as assigned, would add up to a comfortable amount of spending money in time for payday. Rotating duties at the end of each week ensured that each child was learning valuable skills. Food preparation and kitchen cleanup, caring for the animals and garden, seasonal work like lawn and snow, housekeeping duties and laundry.

The advantage of using charts was immediately evident. There was much less conflict between Michael and I. "Obey me now!" was not my primary message, with mounting anger when he did not. Instead, I simply said, "Go. Look at the chart."

"You may watch the TV show if you have read this number of pages before the show starts."

"You may go outside when you have finished today's school work assignment."

"You will be paid 10¢ when the job is finished."

"I will read to you when you have finished the three bedtime routines."

I made revolving charts. Charts with arrows. Bar graph charts. Pie charts. Tally charts.[34] I used graph paper and coloured paper and drew little stick men brushing their teeth, putting their laundry in the basket, feeding the dog.

I remembered peppy songs my Mother used to sing to encourage cooperation. I used them when I had the play-school and Sunday School at our house. Now, although Elise and Michael were a little too old for this kind of prompting, Nicholas and Toby were exactly the right age.

This one helped to start the day.

Wake up in the morning cheerful and bright.
Hop out of bed to start the day right.
Put socks on your toes and polish your nose.
Before you forget, hang up your night clothes.

This one made cleanup before supper run smoothly.

Helping hands, helping hands.
My hands will be helping hands.

Helping Mom. Helping Dad.
My hands will make others glad.

Hang up clothes. Pick up toys.
Help the other girls and boys.
I'm so glad God gave me
Hands that can be helping hands.[47]

And of course lullabies brought the day to a peaceful close. Many familiar songs came from musical movies we were familiar with: 'Mary Poppins' or 'Cinderella' or 'The Sound of Music' or 'The Wizard of Oz.'

Because I was so bombarded with taking care of the two younger children, the two older ones were becoming more and more capable of taking care of themselves and I had less time to closely monitor their behaviour. I needed to emphasize 'self-control.' "I cannot always be with you to tell you 'yes' or 'no.' You have to begin to think for yourself and make healthy choices."

A book borrowed from the library became a very helpful tool. Written for children it introduced '+, 0, - Ethics.' Examples from daily life illustrated '+' plus ethics as an action with positive motive and results. 'Helping an old lady across the street' is the classic example. A neutral '0' ethical act might be returning your library books. It is expected and you did it, but it wasn't a significant bonus to anyone. The negative '-' minus ethics would be any action that would be harmful to another person or yourself.

I could see that I was already thinking this way. 'Tell me three times when...' was bringing a way for the children to think through the effect of their actions.

Now I added another phrase to encourage our children to stop and think about what they were doing and how it would influence others. It started with the days when Elise and

Michael made their own lunch. Did I have to grant permission for each item they suggested? Or could I help them see the categories so they could make decisions on their own? I gave them a framework to sort out the options: 'Is it Growing Food, Treat Food or Garbage'[34]? I asked and let them see for themselves. 'Growing Food' is anything that your body actually needs to grow and thrive: vitamins, minerals, protein. There are various sources. You can choose. 'Treat Food' is primarily for taste and variety: ketchup, pop, candy and party foods. They won't help you grow, but they're fun to enjoy. 'Garbage' will actually harm you: poisons, allergens, tobacco, alcohol, drugs.

After they had practice making decisions within these categories, I realized we could talk about other topics. Movies and advertisements and peers are constantly tugging at young people to 'Come try this!' How will they know if it is a healthy choice? With a little practice we could talk about jokes and slang words, music lyrics and TV, fashion and even decisions about boy-girl touching. They can be looked at as 'Growing Food, Treat Food or Garbage.' After all, I don't want my children to copy me, or cling to me, or be limited by my choices in life. I want them to think for themselves, but not just grab what ever is entertaining. Rather, be informed, deliberate and self-governing.

The ability to examine yourself, stop, change course, begin again, is, I believe, the most valuable skill of all.

Ten years old

Sometimes homeschooled, sometimes attending public school, Michael's research skills grew strong. He was the quickest to learn on the computer my Dad gave us. He retained facts that he absorbed while our family travelled to meet relatives and see different geographical regions. He learned from television shows, listened to our elderly friends, from Kevin's guidance working with tools and machinery. He recalled interesting details in class to bring a kind of maturity to discussions that the teachers didn't expect.

I needed to concentrate on teaching the two younger children their ABCs. Elise and Michael attended Grade 7 and 5 at the Blue River school 25 miles to the north. There were only enough students in seven grades for two classrooms.

"I am hoping Michael will improve in spelling and writing. We do so much of our lessons orally at home," I stated during a parent-teacher interview. "We haven't done much with French, nor can I teach him computer skills, and of course, Michael has very little practice with team sports."

However, through the year, there was a range of disappointments. It was difficult to resolve problems and reach understandings. Since I did not have a driver's license, it was almost impossible to stay in communication with the school. First, the spelling list stayed the same week after week. To 'build self-esteem' the teacher decided to give the whole class the same list until everyone got all of the words spelled correctly. Second, the students made rude remarks on the computer and those privileges were taken away. Next, the French teacher got upset at the silly pranks which happened behind her back, so that class was cancelled. Also, with so few classmates, Michael still had to slow down during team sports to be careful playing near the other children.

Making decisions as a parent is never easy.

Eleven years old

Students living in Avola found that getting to school took a bit of an effort: hurried early morning routines, bundled up to walk uphill to the school bus stop, half hour ride north in the winter darkness to Blue River to attend elementary school. Or, when it was time to attend high school, the school bus ride was nearly one-and-a-half hours long in the opposite direction. So, when Elise began high school 45 miles to the south, I just couldn't put Michael on a bus headed 25 miles to the north. I decided to homeschool Michael for one more year: Grade 6.

I knew I would have to give him challenging assignments. He was like a strong horse I needed to keep reigned in. One Math project was on-going. I asked him to keep a chart and calculate the dollar value of the food we brought in from the garden, chickens, raising rabbits and a pig, as well as the venison and bear which Kevin brought in from hunting. Michael weighed the vegetables every time we brought them in. He tallied up the weight of the raspberries, blackberries, wild blueberries and Saskatoon berries. When we bought cases of ripe tomatoes and cucumbers, peaches, apricots and apples to process into canning jars, pickles, jam, pies and to fill the freezer, the task became more complex. He had to keep track of the store-bought ingredients we used, too. Were we really saving money to preserve all of that food?

Even home baking became part of his Math assignment. Which is more cost effective: oil, butter, margarine, or shortening? What about the cost of the various forms of chocolate: baker's chocolate, dry cocoa powder, chocolate chips or blocks of chocolate in the bulk food bins? What is the savings to buy in bulk: ketchup, flour, sugar, oatmeal, rice?

In the end, the efforts of the whole family had filled two full-sized chest freezers with meat and vegetables, I had 150 jars of pickles, jam and fruit in the pantry, three laundry baskets of potatoes, as well as onions, carrots and six boxes of apples, and baking supplies for the winter feasts. The total dollar value of the food we had stored up was $7000!

Twelve years old

In late summer, 1994, when Michael was twelve years old, a phone call and a few seconds brought a life-changing event.

"Mom! I never get to answer the phone," Michael ran to get there first. "Hello? Yes. OK. Sure. Just a minute, I'll ask my Mom." His voice showed that is was someone he knew. His face showed eagerness that I would agree to whatever had been asked.

"Mom! It's the Bookmobile guy! He wants me to come and work for him. He said he would pay me 50 bucks! He wants me to come and meet up with him. Can I go?" Michael was holding his hand over the mouthpiece. But, $50 is a lot of money. What ever could the guy want to hire a child for? I wondered. Besides, the Bookmobile came through yesterday. It had no reason to be here overnight. I took the phone.

"Hello?" Silence. "This is Eleanor." Click. The phone went dead. My blood ran cold. I had heard of luring children. 'Come see my puppy.' or 'Would you like some candy?' or 'Your Mom said I should come and pick you up and take you home.' or 'Come and help me with my yard work.'

"But, I wouldn't go unless you let me," Michael's logic helped a little to calm my jangling nerves.

"You could have been kidnapped! If he had said a smaller amount of money, I might have let you go!" I was shaking. I called my children to me. I got on the phone. I called every home in Avola. Either no one was home, or an adult had answered and the person who called hung up! I was terrified.

Just then Kevin walked past the window. I jumped, thinking the kidnapper was already here!

Rapidly relaying the information, I told Kevin, "Go to the gas station. Go to the pub. Go to the motel. Go where the pay-phones are. Ask if anyone saw anything!"

I kept my children with me. I phoned the police. I phoned the library headquarters. Of course, it was not the real Bookmobile guy. It was a fraud. I was in a panic.

How easily our family could have been ripped apart!

I kept my children with me. They had to sleep on the floor of my bedroom. They walked with me to the post office. They came with me to the garden. We were scheduled to go to a church camp for the weekend. As we drove along the highway, I realized that every time I saw a parked car, my imagination was immediately invaded with pictures of gory murders. I couldn't eat or sleep.

"Kevin," I spoke to him privately, "You will have to make all of the decisions this weekend. My answer for everything will be 'No' so you'll have to give permission for the children to swim, go with a friend, visit someone else's tent or go on a boat ride. I can't make up my mind about anything!"

When we got home, I phoned the medical clinic. "If there is a mental health person here, I need an appointment."

Fear had eclipsed every other thought and feeling. Counselling was very helpful. I was able to examine my whole life, revisit 'The Doll in the Oven' and 'The Day on the Cliff,' come to a better understanding of my family of origin, my marriage, and my beliefs and decision making process. I read. I journalled. I talked things over with my husband. I slowed down and took pressure off of myself. I began to make clearer choices as a parent. I started to take better care of my Self.

Thirteen years old

All too soon, Michael joined Elise in the Clearwater high school for one year. He found the wood and mechanic shop irresistible, the challenges to build and invent were a satisfying match to his interests. Sports and the challenge of competition as well as the benefits of team work were quite a new experience. Michael's abilities could really expand.

For one year brother and sister attended the same school. That was the year my Father died. In the sorrow, I realized how deeply important it was in my life to have had the religious upbringing and education Dad had provided, so we made plans to send Elise there for Grade 11 that autumn.

Fourteen years old

After Elise left, for one year, Michael made the trip to high school on the bus every day. He read Tolkien's 'Lord of the Rings Trilogy' all the way to Clearwater. Wrapped in a blanket during the winter months. Unable to participate in after school activities. Packing a lunch. Working on homework. The routine carried him through while I built a creative homeschooling program for the younger brothers.

After only two weeks on the Bonnie Hills campus, Elise phoned home to say, "Please, let Michael come next year. There are so many interesting people and opportunities and activities."

From February on we were filling out papers, arranging transportation, medical insurance, applying for grants, budgeting for tuition, choosing courses, anticipating his departure, and together, Michael and I designed and constructed a denim quilt for his dormitory room.

Fifteen years old

Leaving home at 15 years old? Was that a wise parental decision? How would Michael cope with the rules of this more formal atmosphere? The pressures of a higher standard of education? The close quarters of dormitory life? The institutional food? The requirement for a chaperon at every boy-girl event? The realization that parents are nowhere nearby to check up on him?

He got a perfect attendance award in Grade 10! I thought that was a pretty clear indication that this remarkable young lad could self-govern so well. He participated in so many activities that I knew we had done the right thing to send him so far away.

Sixteen years old

When he came home for the summer, he had the responsibility to earn enough money to pay for his own text books, clothing and personal expenses. It took a lot of penny-pinching and my own small earnings to cover the tuition, and room and board after the generous grants we were given. The first summer Michael cleaned rooms at the Avola Motel. The second summer he took the 'Food Safe' course so he could do kitchen jobs. Since I had to drive him to the course, I decided to take it, too.

Suddenly a misfortune and an opportunity landed at the same time.

A lightening strike directly across the river from our house started a forest fire. Nicholas and Toby actually saw the strike, smoke and first flame. Kevin phoned it in.

Forest fires are given an identification number. Other codes indicate the intensity, size, growth, wind, dryness, type of fuel, distance from water, risk to infrastructure, populations.

The summer of 1998 saw a high number of fires, several started at the same time. Our fire was relatively unimportant. There was no risk to dwelling places or infrastructure, the wind was low and the fire was heading away from the highway. It was dramatic to watch. The steep mountainside was a perfect place for rising flames to find more fuel. The dry evergreen trees lit from the lower branches, quickly, loudly, crackling as the sap ignited, orange flames 'candling' up and up to the top-most branches, gradually one tree is consumed, but the wind carried exploded sparks or chunks of bark to ignite the next tree. When the rush of flame reached the top of the mountain, the burning debris on the forest floor rolled down. Four-way expansion was happening: candling, rushing to the heights, wind pressing, and tumbling fireballs.

Part of me was fascinated by the spectacle. The wide river lay between our property and the blaze. The wind was pressing the fire further and further away from our location. Smoke billowed black all day and glowed orange when darkness came. The crackle and pop, the rushing roar when a new tree caught fire, the helicopters overhead as the fire command began to send help were exciting. But it was the smell of fire that triggered alarm within my instinctual 'Mother' mind and heart. The ancient fear could not be ignored. I had to get my children away from this ever-expanding danger.

I loaded the car up with irreplaceable items: my hand-stitched quilts, the Nativity set I had painted, my jewelry box full of mementos, photographs and an antique chair from my great-grandmother. Nicholas and Toby could do nothing to help, so I delivered them and the cargo to Clearwater. "You should sign up to work in the fire camp," a friend recommended. "They're short on help now with so many fires in the region."

"Michael, get packed! We're both on the kitchen crew," I announced. Elise stayed home to man the radios, keep the garden and animals and help Kevin after his long, hot days on the railroad.

The fire camp was in Blue River. When we hired on that afternoon, it was expected to be a 60-man crew. By morning it grew to 160 and jumped to 300! I did whatever I was told to do. Count. Measure. Pour. Fetch. My first job every morning was to crack and beat dozens and dozens of eggs. My last job before leaving was to prepare a huge bin of sliced fruit, melons, oranges, grapes. Another cook came in to bake all night and wrap sandwiches for the men going out on the mountain the next day.

Michael got all the 'Cinderella' jobs. As I ran up and down the stairs, I saw him hunched over the stainless steel sink, scrubbing a tall pot. As I scurried back and forth to the cooler, I saw him hunched over a bucket, pealing a whole case of potatoes. When I was finished serving porridge, or soup, or gravy I brought him another giant pot to wash. The dishes were all disposable. The water came in hoses from the town water supply. The kitchen was a trailer brought in by truck. The refrigerator was a second trailer. Tents with cots were set up for the fire-crew. Fortunately, we got motel rooms.

We worked fast and hard for ten days of twelve-hour shifts. Michael earned enough money for his needs for the whole school year.

When we took him to the airport, my heart was aching: This was his last summer holiday. Next year he's in college. He can get a summer job on campus. He will never live at home again.

Seventeen years old

It is exciting for parents to anticipate their son or daughter's completion of school. Graduation in the year 2000! That is a pretty exciting thing for everyone! The graduating class has so many traditions: a trip to Washington DC, volunteering, the Prom, and the school play. Michael has a part in Shakespeare's 'Much Ado About Nothing.'

And now, tonight: this phone call. Every parent's nightmare. Future? What future?

What if...?

* ** *** ****

It is a long night. If the House Master's reassuring message that "The doctor's think that he's going to be fine" is actually true, I still can't help wondering if his injuries will block him from participating in the final months of activities.

But, no Mother can ever see her child's future. Again my mind turns to Mary. Even for her, there were wisps of foreknowledge, faint murmurings of ancient prophecies, glimmering reassurances, and yet, an ominous dread. What did she know for certain? What did she fear?

It was not until I became a Mother myself that I first started to think about Mary as a real person.

When I was bursting with joy and thanksgiving at the news that I carried a new life within me... I suddenly thought of Mary hurrying to tell Elizabeth.

When I first held my precious newborn, warm, tiny baby, wrapped and safe... I realized anew that she held Him in the darkness of the barn.

When neighbours came to see and bring gifts... I thought of the shepherds, wise men, gold.

And when my child sleeps, breathing softly, I look, my heart filled. No words can contain my feelings of commitment, love, sacrifice, joy, pain, past, present, future, all sculpted into a sleeping child.

Mary knows these feelings. Mary tucked the covers in and stood watch over Him. Smiling at His sweetness, new words, silly games, questions, adventures.

Like all Mothers, I wonder how the days turn into years so quickly? How can it be that my child is taller, stronger, running faster than me? And what is this schoolwork about? I can't even read it? What a strange, disorienting feeling for my 'baby' to launch past me academically!

Ahh, yes, this is a part of Mary's story, too. Jesus in the Temple, both listening and asking them questions! He's moving away from her. Just as my son is moving away from me.

The Seer wrote that the core task that Jesus accomplished while living on Earth was this: "Putting off the human from the mother." ... But, no, I do not want my son to 'put off' what I have given him. I want him to remember and treasure, to weave his own creed from the values I have introduced, to store up customs and skills and travels and music and use them to sculpt his own family, choose between options, build a masterpiece.

That is what happens with each thing I teach my son: first steps, ride a bike, answer the phone, open a bank account, read, write, butter toast. Every single thing I teach him is a gift to cherish so that he can move away from me, be himself, live his own life. I hope he will develop and use what I have given him, not reject it!

Today I stand in a place near Mary. Suffering is a place I had hoped I would not ever have to share. It is hard to control my own anxiety while I wait for the test results and the brightness of morning.

Mary watched her Son, slowly, painfully, breathe His last. Will that day come for me?

* ** *** ****

Morning comes.

"Your son will be fine," at last the Doctor's voice reassures me. It's true! I breathe again, and tears flow in thanksgiving! "The surgery went well. The tests we were concerned about showed unusual counts because of the sporting event and Michael's physical exertion of the previous hours. Everything reads 'normal' now. He will be released today. His quick thinking and vault up onto the car saved his leg from shattering and irreparable damage. He is one lucky guy!"

Now, overjoyed, I experience a tiny sample of Mary's gladness on Easter morning. The women return from the seplecure, their faces a-light! John runs back with happy news, "He is a-risen!"

I grasp the telephone so tightly my knuckles are white when I finally hear Michael's voice on the phone. "Mom! I'm OK! As soon as I learn how to use these crutches they'll let me go back to the dorm. Don't worry, Mom. In the play my character is a soldier returning from battle. The crutches will make it more realistic! And all the girls want to write on my cast," he sounds energetic, looking ahead, not afraid, aware of the privilege and good fortune and relatively minimal injuries.

"Oh, Michael, I am so happy to hear your voice! I want to climb through the telephone and pop out beside you!" I can hardly contain my gladness and sense of relief.

"The Housemaster rode in the ambulance with me to the hospital. He asked me 'Would you like me to call your parents?' and I said 'No way, I'll call them from my room after I get splinted up and settled in.' I thought that way I could say 'Hey parents, just calling to let you know that I was injured but I'm fine' then give you the details. I knew you'd worry, Mom. I tried to prevent that long wait. So, after I had the surgery and I heard that the Principal had already called to say 'Your son was hit by a car, we don't know how bad it is' I was super pissed for just leaving you hanging with no good info."

"Oh, Michael!" I could hardly imagine the sense of compassion he had for me even while his own painful ordeal was unfolding.

* ** *** ****

This much I have learned:
Mary was a real person. Her Son was a real person.
I am a real person. My son is a real person.
And the relationship between a Mother and a Son is of profound significance.
For both of them.
A son does not 'put off' what he gained from his Mother.
His concern for his Mother and her concern for
him is part of what makes him healthy within
himself and also the interactions he has in all
other relationships throughout his lifetime.

REFLECTIONS

> Undertake difficult tasks
> by approaching what is easy in them.
> Do great deeds
> by focusing on their minute aspects.
> —*Tao*

Chapter 7
Saturday, January 5, 2008
Twin Brothers: Companions

Every person born into the world represents something new,
something that never existed before,
something original and unique...
If there had been someone like this in the world,
there would have been no need for this person to be born.
—*Martin Buber*

* ** *** ****

"Happy Birthday, my Brother!"

It's 9:00am where I am and 12:00noon where he lives. "I hope this is an OK time to phone? I figured you'd break for lunch?"

"Well, Hello there, Sister. How nice of you to call!"

"How does one celebrate such things in New York City?" I can tell by Andrew's voice that he's smiling. He can tell by my voice that I am smiling, too.

* ** *** ****

Andrew's life experiences are so different from mine. He cycled from Ontario to Pennsylvania and later up through Vermont. He attended three colleges and universities. He got a scholarship and travelled to Europe. His career path to be an architect led him to New York City. From his apartment window, he watched the Twin Towers crumble and fall. Although he was the photographer for our wedding, I wasn't able to travel to Vermont at the time of his wedding.

I have been to visit my brother several times. The level of trust, the fun times, the turning of the seasons, the experience of big city life in New York City made a big impression on me. I liked it. And, during those visits, we developed a very strong bond.

It was exciting to see the excellence he had developed in his career as an architect. I did not feel one single twinge of jealousy. He did what he set out to do. I have accomplished what I set out to do. Very different, and yet, at the core, precisely the same.

Maybe you have to be nearing 50 years old to be able to see your own Life Path clearly.

* ** *** ****

"How is your family?" we both asked each other at the very same moment.

I burst out with my big news. "Kevin is only four years from early retirement!"

"And my career is just peaking," Andrew said a little wistfully. "You have to be an architect for quite awhile before you get publicity in magazines." And he is getting publicity! During my most recent visit, Andrew took me to see some of his work. His designs are crisp and clear, straight and clean, no ornamentation, only peace and quiet for the eyes. One home had a smooth, oval, black stone sink. A bedroom wall rotated to open to the den. A beautiful wooden kitchen wall was actually cupboard doors which would spring open with a gentle touch. Spiral staircase, glass staircase, floating staircase, special lighting were design features in different projects. Tiny windows framed postcard perfect views of the New York City skyline. Andrew had projects in Japan and Texas, Europe and in his own home.

* ** *** ****

I eagerly listen while Andrew brings me up-to-date with the current adventures of his family, career opportunities, creative endeavours, and new projects.

"Well, you let me know if you'd like me to come again," I hinted. I just loved learning how to use the subway, take in museums and parks, get to know friends of the family.

* ** *** ****

I have a photo album preserving snapshots of our time together. Andrew took a half-day off to come to the Brooklyn Botanical Gardens. The cherry blossoms were frilly pink parasols. A heron waded in the pond. The orange spotted fish swarmed and the turtles were on the rocks in the sunshine in the Japanese garden. We watched a family play together on the wide, smooth grass, a rowdy game of tag complete with flips and romping, blind-folds and laughter, rolling and jumping made it a memorable outing.

Other memories are preserved in a sketch tablet I kept as a daily journal while I lived with the family.

What fun we had on April Fool's Day! Andrew and I remembered the pranks we used to play that were not harmful, wasteful or mean. Little Andrew giggled with rascally glee while he switched pillows and cushions from the formal living room to the bedrooms to the family room, while James slid books into pillows in each bedroom, stuffed crumpled balls of newspaper into shoes and coat sleeves. Mommy used to make Sunday brunch with green food colouring in the scrambled eggs and the toast cut into funny shapes.

When we were kids, we built a tent in the family room with cushions, chairs and sheets. Mommy let us sleep in our tents. We could also remember life in the cabin in Colorado, even having baths in the kitchen sink!

Remember when we planned a 'restaurant'? We made a menu, listing all the left over possibilities that were easily reheated. We had choices of beverages, salad, main dish, vegetables and desserts. Daddy was greeted at the door by James, wrapped in an apron, "Right this way, Sir, your reservation is ready." His eyes were wide with surprise, but he quickly caught on to the theme of the evening.

"Here is our finest menu," Andrew explained. "We will bring you anything you'd like." The boys had to relay messages to me, the cook, and then carry the plate to serve their Daddy with formal manners and polite conversation.

On rainy days, we would gather our abundant collection of toys in their large bedroom. We built a town with an airport and railroad, museum, fire hall, school, store and nearby farm yard. In Colorado, we never had opportunities within walking distance: playground, movie theatre, music lessons, soccer field, museum, library, art gallery, children's science museum with hands-on activities, puppet plays, parades, church and picnic grounds. We went sledding in the snow. We stomped in the puddles. We ate Jello powder sprinkled in a bowl of clean snow.

I remember one day in Florida, Mommy took us to the ocean to go swimming. It was a long ride in the car. We had a lot to carry. The wind and waves and sunshine and sand was a stimulating outdoor experience. As we packed up the picnic, towels and toys, the walk back over the shifting sand to the distant boardwalk looked like an endurance test. "I'm too tired," James and Andrew began to complain. Mommy was already carrying little Carol, encouraging Julie. I had a load in both hands. How could we ever get home without a meltdown? That's when the 'The Grumpy Camel' was invented!

"You sound just like the Grumpy Camel!" Mommy demonstrated exaggerated sighs and moans, grumbling and muttering. They couldn't help it. The boys started to smile. Mommy launched into a story to distract the little ones from their problems. "Yup, 'I'm too tired' that's what he always says!" She had everyone's attention now. Making her voice sound as dramatic as possible, she began to describe the character of the Grumpy Camel.

"After a fun day hiking, or swimming, or sailing, or at the beach, or in the mountains, the Grumpy Camel always complains on the way home. Even though just a minute ago he was having lots of fun running all around, whenever he has to help carry stuff and walk back home, he moans, and groans, and whines, and bellyaches. 'I'm too tired!' and 'Do I have to?' and 'How come I am the one who has to do it?' and 'When are we going to get there?' and 'My feet hurt!' He feels just like how we feel right now, but he is so much better at moaning and groaning than you are!"

So, we practiced moaning and groaning and complaining (and laughing) while we walked over the hot sand, climbed up the steep sand bank to the car, unpacked our heavy loads and headed upstairs for a soothing bath before supper.

* ** *** ****

"Any chance we get to see you out here any time soon?" I continue the birthday phone call. It is unlikely. Both Andrew and his wife have demanding careers. When the whole family does have holidays together, they enjoy a Vermont retreat to a family farm.

"Well, it is something we talk about," he sounds nostalgic, realizing that I continue to live in the mountains as we did in our childhood.

I like to describe my wilderness mountain home in Canada, I would love to show him our house, our dog, Max, and for him to come and experience the changing seasons where we live. In the wintertime, we have to carry firewood into the house to burn in the stove. We have shelves full of jars of jam from the berries in our garden. We have baskets full of potatoes to last the whole winter. We have to shovel the snow from our driveway before we go to town when it's payday, every two weeks. In the springtime, we plant the garden and in the summer we gather up the vegetables to put in the freezer for the winter. In the autumn, when the crab apples are ripe, I hear Max barking because a bear comes to eat the crab apples. I bang pots and pans and shout to chase the bear away! When it starts to snow, I get busy making Christmas cards to mail to the aunts and uncles and grandparents.

"It would indeed be splendid!" I eagerly reply. "And I hope you have a very Happy Birthday, Brother!"

"Thank-you for calling, Sister!" So warm. So welcome. The miles don't seem to separate us.

* ** *** ****

What a pleasant surprise! My husband stops in at home. It is the middle of his wintery railroad workday. We have a few minutes to share the day's news. I tell him all about my Birthday Brother conversation. "I love talking with Andrew. He listens so carefully. He appreciates little details. He can sense the feelings and significance of what I am saying. He is so grateful for the time I have spent with his family. I am so in awe of the way he and Lisa are raising the boys and balancing the work--home responsibilities. It's nice to be comfortable together."

"I'm glad you went to help out. Those boys will grow up fast and not need you any more," Kevin replied. "But I'm even more glad that you are safely home now. I will always need you," he smiles and holds me close.

* ** *** ****

"Happy Birthday, My Brother!"

I have to do double duty every January 5 with twin brothers!

It's 12:00 noon where I am and 8:00 at night where he lives. It's the best time of day to phone. Everyone is home. Supper is over. It is not bedtime yet.

"Well, Hello there, Sister, thank-you very much! I did indeed have a happy day."

"How does one celebrate such things in Jolly Olde England?" I can tell by James' voice that he's smiling. He can tell by my voice that I am, too.

"Oh, the usual: breakfast pancakes, Lily and the girls went to their dance classes, Jay and I stayed home to do homework and grade papers, a special menu for dinner, little packages from the children, an especially chosen card from my wife. I am feeling bitter-sweet this year, just knowing that I am approaching the age that Dad was when he died. It kind of makes me grateful for each and every day." My brother is a professor of philosophy, so his pondering is always especially thought-provoking.

"I know what you mean," I sigh. "I feel it, too. One never knows, but I do count it out every year. What if I only have fifteen more years to live? It's silly, but it keeps me motivated to stay on task if there are things I want to accomplish."

"Agreed." There is a moment of silence. As if we are side-by-side, although a continent and an ocean separate us, we can both see the sequence of events surrounding Daddy's death, although they happened twelve years ago.

"Next year are you turning 50?" It is hard to fathom. My younger brother has lived for half a century? How old does that make me?

"Yes, it's hard to believe. Gray hair and all. But, of course, it gives me a more authoritative look when I make my presentations," he has a little swagger in his voice.

I interrupt. "Speaking of 'getting older,' you know how I have been talking about 'I am going to write a book' for my whole life. Well, I have made a start! I only have four or five pages for each chapter, but, it's more than nothing!"

James chuckles. For a moment it feels like I have a 'Big Brother' looking out for me, proud of my accomplishments, admiring my enthusiasm. "Well!" he exclaims. An author himself, working in the world of medieval texts, painstaking research, careful translations, speaking in front of an audience of experts, writing to defend a specific point of view, and publishing for the academic elite, James knows more about the process than I do.

"Since my book is about the first ten days we lived in the cabin during the dead of winter, it helps for me to focus on writing at this time of year. The cold. The dark. I don't have to imagine it. It's really here! I have absolutely no idea how to go about publishing, but at least I am highly motivated to write! It feels great to be making my dream a reality!" I feel like bursting, I am so eager to make a good impression on my scholarly younger brother.

"That is fine! Another family member with their name on the spine of a book!" James sounds genuinely pleased.

* ** *** ****

James has entered a world I will never understand: History, Philosophy, Religion, Europe, the Holy Roman Empire, languages no longer used, handwritten letters over 500 years old. Then there is the academic hierarchy. In which institution did you study for your degree? Who was your Professor? Which institution has hired you? What position do you hold? What grants have you successfully applied for? What have you published? Who wrote your review? Where have you been invited to lecture?

To be successful, he not only has to master his subject, he also must conform to a seriously detailed social environment. Carefully moderated behaviour, gestures, tone of voice, facial expressions. Carefully modest clothing, grooming, every hair in place. Proper attention to the ladies present. Respectful focus when a superior is speaking. A ready reply if interviewed. The annual cycle of the school year. Competition with neighbouring schools. Status.

Yet, for all the contrasts between his formal 'British university campus' world and my remote 'log cabin in the Canadian wilderness' world, James has a great deal of respect for my accomplishments, too.

Homeschooling is no small feat, and our four children have stepped from the tiny town of Avola to reach for their own academic and career achievements.

* ** *** ****

It seems to me that the roots of my talents and creativity in educational settings begins way back in early childhood. In fact, James and Andrew were my first pupils. I taught them about Mary, Joseph and Little Baby Jesus. From there, my love of teaching Sunday School has grown. My love of directing skits and plays first found expression when the two cousins came to live with us. I found costumes for Peter Pan (Andrew), Captain Hook (James), the Lost Boys (Little cousin Daniel and little sister Julie), Wendy (played by Mommy), Tinker Belle (cousin Janet), and I had a minor role, Tiger Lily, because mostly I was busy narrating.

My current interest in volunteering to prepare skits for Christmas festivities, Brownies, Cub Scouts and Sunday School is also rooted in early happy experiences with my brothers and sisters. That fort we built with the branches of the Christmas tree way back in Colorado stimulated creative dramatic play for weeks. The shelter became a pirates lair, the prison cell where the kidnapped victim was locked away until the ransom was collected, a lone covered wagon separated from the wagon train where the orphans had to survive the winter, a tribal tepee, the Swiss Family Robinson's jungle tree house, a castle dungeon, a hut where runaway slaves hid from the bounty hunters, all of these imaginings stretched my storytelling skills.

My brothers and I helped our two younger sisters plan a circus for Daddy when he came home from a trip and later we made a Mother's Day talent show for Mommy. We invented a percussion band and begged a neighbour to take us in his pickup truck in the annual summer parade, much to the annoyance of those who were riding horses.

Then there was the three-line play we put on for our parents one winter afternoon. Elaborate regal costumes were required for the three sisters. Hair was ornately decorated with bows and veils, hats and scarves, flowers and silver clips. Gloves and cushions, hand mirrors and embroidery indicated the delicate position of these splendid ladies in their finery. James, in a belted plaid bathrobe, and Andrew, similarly dressed, were both armed with long handled wooden spoon-swords. One was The Guard. One was The Invader.

"I vish to zee da maidens!" the suspicious looking character approached speaking in a thick German accent.

"Vat do you vish vit da maidens?" the Guardian replied.

"I vish to keeel the maidens!" the Bandit shouted, brandishing his sword.

After which a lot of screaming and running and hiding ended the not too complex plot.

Later, when we were in our early teens, we teamed up to provide a formal dinner and entertainment to celebrate our parents' twentieth wedding anniversary. Julie and I cooked a Sunday Dinner style meal: ham, sweet potatoes, green beans, tossed salad. Andrew printed a menu in fancy script with stars indicating 'Today's Special' (which of course was the only available option). James made a cardboard violin, dressed with a white shirt and red sash, and found a recording of a string quartet to play to serenade them while they dined. Carol was the waitress in an apron and cap. We sent a written invitation in advance so our parents could dress. I dialed the kitchen telephone and hung up to make the upstairs extension ring. "Your reservation is ready," I announced in a French accent, rolling my 'r's.

The table was set in the living room with a white table cloth, the best china and silver, long-stem glasses and a floral centerpiece. Mother wore a smooth fitted royal blue dress with her sparkly blue necklace and earrings. Daddy's suit and tie, shiny shoes and slicked back hair indicated that he was taking our efforts seriously. Staying in their roles, their manners were formal, yet, kind as they ordered dinner, enjoyed a beverage, exclaimed over the lovely arrangements and had polite conversation while eating. The violin music was rich and sweet, the service helpful and the fresh fruit salad dessert especially tasty.

"Did you like it? Were you surprised?" We eagerly gathered around them for hugs and kisses when the façade came down and we returned to our familiar family roles.

* ** *** ****

"Oh, James," I continue our birthday telephone conversation, "Every year on our wedding anniversary, when I look at the photos that Andrew took, I am again thankful for the music you composed for our wedding day. And I am so glad you came out west to see the log cabin Kevin built. You stayed that summer to dig the garden, build the shower house and fence. You've hiked our mountains! You've eaten summertime berries! Was it ten years ago when you brought your wife and little son? You've seen where we live now, how our lives have unfolded!" When you add up all the good times we have had, the distance in miles and years doesn't seem so large. "I hope from time to time you know that I love you, Brother," I sigh longingly.

"Well, I most certainly have a visual reminder of exactly that!" he responds. "The magnificent hand-stitched quilt you so generously designed for our wedding is an ever-present message of our sibling affection and attachment." Underneath the fancy vocabulary, I think he just said, "I love you, too."

My wedding in 1978, Carol's wedding in 1989, Daddy's funeral in 1996, the Colorado gathering to scatter Daddy's ashes in 1998: those are the only times we siblings have all been together.

"Now, I need to ask you a very important question," James begins a new line of thought. "You might need to consider options or weigh variables before you respond."

Now I'm curious.

"But first," he interrupted his train of thought, "let me ask about your family members. Your children are young adults now, while mine are still so small."

"Well, Kevin and I recently had our second Christmas with just the two of us. We are getting used to this 'empty nest' phase of life. It has been a huge adjustment, but it is also kind of fun. Kevin has four years left on the railroad until he takes early retirement! He continues instructing at training events for Trackers in law enforcement, Search and Rescue, First Aide and Ham Radio." James has a high regard for Kevin's activities.

"Now that I have a driver's license and my own car, I have all sorts of new activities. I have a job! Can you believe it? I am teaching young parents nursery rhymes to encourage them to have face-to-face playtime with their little children. I also volunteer one day a week at the elementary school and after school as a Brownie leader. I'm in the interdenominational Christmas choir and I've joined a quilting club. Whoppee! What a life!" It all seems small compared to him, but grand compared to the isolation of my earlier years.

"Elise and her husband live near the Bonnie Hills school where she is a teacher now," I continue. "Michael and his wife live in Colorado where he is part of the research team for a pharmaceutical company. Nicholas lives near Vancouver and has a promising career at a lumber supply company. Toby is planning to live in Atlanta while he is studying to be an architect." A lot has happened in the last few years.

"But, enough about me. What was it you were going to ask me about?" I am eager to discover my brother's question.

"We will be in-between Nannies for our three children this summer. Andrew spoke so highly of your skills when you came to help out with his children two years ago. I wondered if we might be able to persuade you to consider a voyage across the Atlantic to extend your British Brother the same service?"

"Oh, James! How exciting! I have never dreamed of travelling to England!" How can I ever manage it? I wondered.

"Of course we will pay your airfare. It works out to be roughly the same amount we would pay a full time Nanny for the six weeks of summer that the children will be home from school. We are especially hopeful that your experience with special needs children might benefit our little Sarah. Her language development needs to be coached through the summer." James outlines the duties and expectations. "Of course you are more than welcome to stay longer as our guest and tour the area in September after the children return to school."

My mind is swirling with the possibilities.

Buckingham Palace! Big Ben! Hyde Park! Lady Diana's Fountain! And further away I might get to see stone circles, Land's End, horses, castles, cathedrals, double-decker buses, punting on the Thames, Botanical Gardens, museums, art galleries, music, theatre. I was getting dizzy.

Shakespeare! Queen Victoria! Tolkein! Louis Carroll! Mary Poppins! The Railway Children! Peter Pan! I wonder if I could go to see Beatrix Potter's house? I know there are places more grand, but I have been reading aloud and admiring her stories and drawings and paintings for so many years.

I am certain I can do the domestic work James will be expecting. I am certain the educational songs and games I know will benefit the children and that I can be a reliable child care provider while both parents are at work. I wonder how I will react to the eight hour time zone change, the culture of the British, the words, foods, customs and attitudes we experience differently in North America, the currency and driving on the opposite side of the road?

But it only takes an instant for me to accept.

"Of course I will do it, James! How exciting!" Now I want to know more about their house (a row house on the corner near the park), their yard (a tiny walled enclosure), and most importantly the children (Jay is twelve, a reader who will be away sometimes for tennis lessons), Sarah (who's health issues require special diligence) and Francine (a creative, china-doll six-year-old). James' wife, Lily, has finished writing her book. Some of the time she will be home, but must focus to proofread the manuscript before it goes to press. James will be a short distance away meeting with his graduate students over the summer. Both of them need to schedule office hours, but both will be available if I need anything.

James describes outings in their town, attending Mass with his wife, places I might find fitness or dance classes. The library and grocery store are near by. A shuttle bus will bring me from the airport to the right town and from there it will be a short taxi ride to their house. There are details to arrange, but I am definitely going to go forward with this opportunity.

My imagination is already listing possible activities. Will the the family have art supplies, puzzles, games, books and video tapes? Have the children ever made puppets, a tent, or played store or hide-and-seek? Do they have dress-up clothes to act out stories, or fairies, or dance? Do they like to help with the laundry, or mending, or shopping, or in the kitchen, or make apple sauce, or cookies, or help prepare the supper? Do they have bicycles, a city bus, go to work with Dad or Mom, or explore the neighbourhood? Do they have 'movie night' with popcorn or favourite weekly TV shows? I am so eager to bring my wealth of experience to this family and share my lifelong skills with these young children.

"James," I am feeling solemn and confident, "I am glad that you know that I am as good at what I do as you excel at what you do."

"Eleanor," he responds with warmth and sincerity, "I am so pleased that I can ask for your expertise when my family needs positive input at this time."

"Now, instead of saying 'Bye for now.' I can say 'See you soon.' Hurrah!"

How splendid that childhood competition can ripen into a respect for our different talents and welcome enriching possibilities.

Kevin was all for it. "An all expenses paid trip to England? To do the work you love to do? With room and board and tour guides thrown on? What's not to love!"

* ** *** ****

Living with the families of my brothers was better then a visit. A visit is better than a phone call. A phone call is better than email. Email is better than a letter. A letter is better than nothing. But, for some of the time in my life, nothing was better than the pressures, the memories, the repeated patterns of that earlier teasing and competition.

It sure feels good to have two brothers to talk to.

I don't feel the competition any more. I am not wrestling with self-doubts. I don't depend on their approval anymore. I know that what I do, I do well.

When we were children, listening to their teasing made it hard to think clearly. I continually felt indecision. It seemed risky to share my real thoughts. What if they laugh at me? What if I start to cry? Will they believe me if I want to say something important? Will they respect me if I see things differently than they do? 'Two-against-one' was a constant imbalance. 'Boys-against-girls' was an unequal pressure. 'First-Born-Son' was an automatic advantage. It was easier and safer to withdraw.

Now they listen respectfully while I clarify my thoughts. I don't feel that inner strain. They even support me in ways I could never have imagined back when we were young.

When I married and moved out west, I thought that getting far away might be better. Away from the rest of the family felt less risky. I needed to find out who I was and what I thought and felt and believed without the continual comparison. Without the continual put-downs. Without the cloud of self-doubt.

Yet, now that we can talk and remember, maybe what I am feeling, however private and personal it seems to me, is valid. My childhood impressions have shaped me. Misunderstandings, fears, turning points, confusion, self-doubt all reverberate and ricochet through the years. As an adult I can read and learn and journal and reconsider, ask my parents and relatives questions, better understand early child development, realize the impact that 'society' and the media, religion and family history had on my attitudes and expectations, gender role and perceptions.

Prejudice is a powerful thing. If someone labels me as one thing, how can I ever convince them otherwise? Am I who other people say I am? Or is there something pure and wonderful inside me that will be what it will be? No matter the obstacles or restrictions or deficiency, I want to become 'Me.' I see it, as springtime approaches, when I go to the root cellar to get potatoes. The sprouts reach towards any tiny pin-hole of light. Even the garlic bulbs and onions in the refrigerator know it is springtime and send out tiny green shafts. If these simple vegetables know deep inside themselves what they were created for, can't I 'know', too? Can't I seek and reach and continue to strive? Can't I sense blockage and feel agony if anyone or anything negates my 'Self' as it is just beginning to open like a marvelous flower blossom?

Although my siblings and I were side-by-side in childhood, only some of the sequences were shared experiences. Mostly, we saw and heard things differently, were shaped by different forces, came to different conclusions. But, now we can look at each other with respect and, with effort, have empathy and understanding for the ways our paths intersect and weave, are similar and differ.

What a relief to break out of the isolation. What kind hearts my brothers have. How amazing to feel brighter and more confident.

I always used to wish I had an older brother. Now I have brothers who are older. I don't need their validation anymore, but it sure feels good to know their encouragement is there.

REFLECTIONS

> A musician must make music,
> an artist must paint, a poet must write
> to be at peace with himself.
> What I can be, I must be.
>
> —*Abraham Maslow*

Chapter 8
Friday, January 2, 2009
Awaiting Son: Nicholas

I expect to pass through this world but once.
Any good therefore that I can do,
or any kindness that I can show to any fellow creature,
let me do it now, for I shall not pass this way again.
—*William Penn*

* ** *** ****

Anticipation

Kevin left at 2:00am.

He likes to go early. He parks our SUV on the road parallel to the highway, facing the oncoming traffic. While he waits, he listens to the radio station, talks on his ham radio and blinks his headlights when he sees the bus coming around the bend.

Avola is too small to have a bus station. You have to flag the bus to get on and ask the driver to pull over to let you off.

The Greyhound isn't expected until 2:30 and with the wintry weather, it could be hours late.

Nicholas is coming home! And he's bringing his sweetheart with him!

I'm too excited to sleep. The house is scrubbed clean. The fire is cozy warm. The Christmas tree lights are plugged in. The two bedrooms upstairs are ready. Meals are planned. The 'To-Do' list is all crossed off.

There is nothing to do but wait.

Nicholas! and Joanna!

It will take them eight hours to travel from Vancouver. Three days ago, Joanna flew up from her family's Christmas in Florida. Can you imagine? Florida to British Columbia? In January? She must be a brave young lady! They must really like each other!

I met her two years ago when I visited the Bonnie Hills Church College where they both were studying. I know she's pretty: tall, lean and athletic. Her long, straight, thick, auburn hair and a quick smile highlight her welcoming manner. I know she's smart: you can tell the first time you listen to her. I know she has high ideals and achievable goals from the things Nicholas has told us about her. Will this be 'The One' for him? Will she complete our family? I feel like I have been waiting for her ever since Nicholas was born.

As I often do when alone, quiet and waiting, I allow my mind to drift back in time and retrace the steps that led to this moment: Nicholas is coming home! And he's bringing his sweetheart with him!

I stay home to load more wood into the stove, boil a kettle for mint tea, curl up on the couch wrapped in my sky blue eiderdown bathrobe and settle in, full of hope, to wait. I slowly turn the pages of the Christmas photo album. Kevin and

I made five matching copies for ourselves and the children. It is a bridge to many happy memories.

Satisfaction

The first few pages of the Christmas Album illustrate the nine Christmases before Nicholas was born. 1978, Kevin and I were newly weds in our little log cabin, the next winter was my first pregnancy, then the Christmas in Ontario when Elise was a baby. Waiting for Michael, the fun of having toddlers for Christmas and the move into town are all preserved on the pages of the Album. Community Christmas Concerts captured with the camera count the celebrations during the next three years.

I could see that the dream that Kevin and I were working towards was becoming more fulfilled with each turn of the page. "I want to get married (1978), go out west (in a VW van), build a log cabin (which was frigid, then we moved into town), have a bunch of kids (so far we have a girl and a boy, but now three will make it 'a bunch'), teach them about the Lord (Sunday school in Avola is thriving), volunteer in my community (both Kevin and I have several roles), and then write a book about it (by now I had started by writing for the newspaper)."

That was my dream. It is gradually becoming reality.

Our garden harvest every summer included strawberries and rhubarb, lettuce and spinach, peppermint and asparagus, kale and Swiss chard, peas and beans, raspberries and blackberries, cucumbers and zucchini. In the autumn we gathered in the roots and vines: potatoes, carrots, beets, onions, squash and pumpkins. The wood shed was full. Kevin's job on the railroad was steady. We bought our 4-room house for $5000, right across the street from the playground.

So many special circumstances surrounded the arrival of Nicholas, our third child, to our family. It seemed that Providence smiled on us when the sacred connection I shared with my husband brought the spark of life to fruition.

"What is a name that means 'bringing together'?" I asked Kevin. "We have been two adults and two children. We have been two boys and two girls. But now, we will be a family."

"This child is connecting us," I commented to my husband. "If this is a boy shall we call him 'Lincoln' as in 'links'? or 'Brooklyn' like the bridge? or 'Elmer' you know, for the glue?" I was only half joking. I think that picking out a name is one of the most enjoyable parts of being a Mother. "I really do want to choose a meaningful name." Elise was named after my Mother and for the brave fairy tale princess who rescued her eleven enchanted swan brothers.[48] Michael was named for the warrior archangel who conquers the great red dragon.[49] "What do you think of 'Nicholas' as a name... if it's a boy... which of course we won't know until he or she arrives? Nicholas makes me think of generosity and thoughtful creativity and traditions. That's pretty meaningful," I prompt my husband to give it some thought, "and it also means keeping your eyes open for making 'naughty or nice' choices in life."

Unlike my two previous pregnancies, this time I needed my family's help. During the first trimester, every little thing gave me a wave of nausea: shriveled potato peels on the counter top, goopy egg shells, a sticky pot. I just couldn't look at them! Kevin had to clean up after me! During the second trimester, I got cravings. There was nothing I could do about that while we lived in the cabin ten miles from town. But now, with a 24-hour truck-stop near the highway, I could ask Kevin to "please bring me a hamburger... with extra onions!" As my belly grew larger during the third trimester, contractions interrupted me from lifting books to return to the library, carrying firewood, bending and stretching to hang up laundry. Elise (who was now seven) and Michael (who was now five) pushed the vacuum cleaner, loaded the laundry basket, carried the groceries.

Homeschooling was going well. I had also been volunteering for the neighbourhood children to come to our house twice a week for playschool and on Sunday mornings for a two-hour Sunday School. I was not sure if I could continue to do all of those things when the new baby joined our family.

When the snowbanks started to melt, Dearma arrived. The Greyhound came at 2:30 in the afternoon. Elise and Michael hadn't seen her for two years. They decided to try to trick her. They wore each other's snowsuits. "She will think that pink is for the girl and brown is for the boy," little Michael cleverly suggested. But she recognized them right away. She jumped right in to our family life: read aloud, brought order to the house, provided meals, relieved me of duties, helped me pass the time. We thought up extra projects while waiting for the baby to come!

Dearma had travelled on the bus all the way from Colorado Springs, Colorado. She had just left the deathbed of her own mother. Now she would witness the birth of her grandchild. It was a meaningful time in her life.

Dr. Lam placed the Little One in Dearma's arms. Then the nurse examined, measured and weighed him. "Now Papa," she said and handed him to Kevin. "Hello there, Buck-shot!" he exclaimed. "You've got a lot to do when we get home. You've got a big brother and a big sister, a dog and cat, mountains to climb and all kinds of projects to be a part of."

At last, my hungry arms held him. The suspense of hope filled waiting had become joy filled satisfaction. We have a son! The gift of a precious son!

Wonder

Now we unwrap the gift. Who is this tiny man? What innate talents will emerge? Where will curiosity lead him? When will he show us who he is? How can I help him on his Quest?

Where are you going, my little one, little one?
Where are you going, my baby, my own?
Turn around and you're tiny. Turn around and you're grown.
Turn around and you're a young man
with babes of your own.[50]

Eager

More hope filled waiting.

Cheerful and cooperative, rosy cheeked and curly haired, Nicholas seemed so easy to take care of.

"He grew in the night," Dearma exclaimed.

"Come see him laugh!" Kevin called to me before he was six weeks old.

"We should have named him 'Buddah,'" I observed his chubby belly a few months later.

"He likes it!" Michael protested against my caution while pushing and turning Nicholas riding across the carpet in the big stainless steel bread bowl.

"It's his first word!" Elise announced feeding Nicholas in his red high chair.

"Bup-ca!" Nicholas declared holding his little yellow sippy-cup in his chubby hands.

Now, there is a special photo in the Christmas Album: Baby Nicholas for the first time on Santa's knee!

Self-awareness

Packing a lunch for my husband, washing diapers, preparing playschool and Sunday School and homeschool lessons, writing grocery lists, paying bills, weeding the garden, folding laundry, monitoring behaviour, baking bread, reading bedtime stories: I was giving to everyone and neglecting my own needs.

'Heart. Spirit. Mind. Body.'[34] I was aware of providing stimulation, nourishment, activities and encouragement for the children. But, increasingly, inside, my Self was whining, 'What about me?'

I realized I needed to provide for myself, or run dry and collapse.

What does my Body need to maintain a healthy balance? Food, water, fresh air and sunshine, exercise and enjoyment of the five senses. OK. How can I get those things in a realistic way?

What does my Mind hunger for? How can I learn, try new things, seek ways to satisfy my curiosity? What resources are within reach? How can I set aside time for my own interests?

What satisfies my Heart? Music, crafty projects, people, conversations, hugs and smiles. How can I collect these? How can I store up supplies 'for a rainy day' so that I have embroidery thread and fabric, cassette tapes and records, telephone numbers and friends?

What can I do to nourish my Spirit? Inspirational poems and lyrics, pictures and books. Where can I go? Who will teach me? What will I find to answer the longing for something to believe in?

My life got a whole lot better when I put my Self on the 'To-Do' list!

Team Work

Time goes so fast when the children are small. Each golden day brings development, treasures, explorations. Elise (Grade 3) and Michael (Grade 1) went on the school bus for one year when baby Toby joined the family. With a toddler and an infant, I knew I couldn't give all four of them the attention they needed.

That was the winter when Grandma D came. It took two pages of the Christmas Album to share all of the happy scenes: each of the four children with Santa, Kevin pulling them on a sled, me rolling out cookie dough with lots of helpers, Elise on ice skates, Michael doing stunt-jumping into deep snow, the little boys piled high with wrapping paper and ribbons. And there is Grandma D in her red Christmas dress, surrounded by all four children with their dolls and teddies dressed in the red flannel night gowns and PJs that Grandma D and I made for them. So many happy times!

The following year, in 1989, the laws about homeschooling in British Columbia changed. We were no longer required to use the government provided curriculum, which seemed so time consuming. Instead, I could feast on creativity and allow for the children's interests to lead the way. I designed lessons based on monthly themes. Each month we explored reading, writing, spelling, math, science, geography, art, music and of course, Bible verses relating to one of the Seven Days of Creation.[51]

One memorable moment gave me confidence that my efforts were building a strong educational experience for all four children. One task challenged each person at their own level. It was possible to find that sweet spot where something new is just within reach, neither too easy nor too difficult.

"What colour is this?" I asked three-year-old Nicholas.

"Red," he correctly answered.

"Now, go find the red ball and give it to Toby," I sent him on a mission. Toby, just past one year old, willingly became the recipient of a pile of colourful objects to play with in his playpen.

"Elise, you write a list of all the words that mean 'red.' Michael, you spell 'red.' I am going to type the word in French! Who can do the task in the time it takes for Nicholas to return?"

"Scarlet, crimson, ruby, cherry, and if 'pink' is OK, then rose and blush, O and brick-red, that's a colour!" Elise was quick with words.

"How about you, Michael?"

"r-e-d"

"Correct, and I have 'rouge.' Let's do it again!" So the morning went.

Orange, rust, fiery, golden... blue, aqua, turquoise, sky-blue, navy, royal, denim, deep-sea blue, indigo... purple, lilac, violet, mauve, magenta, burgundy... Elise was a reader and a writer with an ever-expanding vocabulary. Michael dutifully spelled the root word. I bent over the typewriter with the two-finger hunt-and-peck method. Nicholas was the star player running to fetch and carry. Toby got buried in a mound of stuffed teddies, trucks, towels, blocks, balls and books.

Loyalty

I turned the page to find more treasures in the Christmas Album.

Dearma came to visit and we had Christmas in July. Grampa Hinkle sent cross-country skis. Shirley chose beautifully illustrated books. Grandma D sent educational toys and games.

Aunt Julie sent especially thoughtful gifts at Christmastime. When Toby and Nicholas were three and four years old, she gave them both a set of armour: breastplate, shield, sword and helmet. So many scenarios were reenacted by these Guardians,

Protectors, Defenders, Princes, Town Criers. With the addition of the red velvet cape that Aunt Julie had made several years ago for Michael when he was eager to play dress-up, a truly regal presence was achieved.

Empathy

Although I loved to be the teacher, sometimes Nicholas had lessons to teach me. I used felt shapes to teach the A-B-Cs to each of the children, but, when Nicholas was learning his letters, it seemed OK to him to turn or flip each shape. After all, a cup is still a cup no matter if the handle is to the left or right, or the cup is right-side-up or upside-down. Why isn't it OK to do that with letters? But a 'Z' on it's side in a 'N.' And 'b' and 'd' and 'p' and 'q' are all the same shape flipped and turned this way and that. An 'E' and '3' are another pair. I had to think of a way to teach him.

To make matters a little more confusing for both of us, he wrote with either hand. His printing was every-which-way. He seemed so earnest, not rebellious, not lazy, not careless. He wanted to cooperate. I didn't want him to be weighed down with shame or embarrassment or a punishment. I needed him to see that there was only one 'right' way. But I didn't want to spill any tears.

"You be the 'teacher.' I'll be the 'kid.' OK?" I suggested. I sat on the floor with the little green chalk board, white chalk poised for dictation. "What letter shall I make?"

"How about a 'T'?" He liked this role play.

"A capital 'T' looks like this. And here is the little 't.' Hey, look, a Dad 'T' and a Lad 't'!" I might have discovered the key that I needed. "Let's do some more!" I smiled and eagerly awaited my next challenge. Nicholas was a good Instructor.

We went through a few pairs at his prompting. "Hey, these ones look the same!" I pointed out. "'Look: 'S' and 's' then 'O' and 'o' also 'M' and 'm' and 'W' and 'w'... the Dad and Lad letters match!" I was doing well! Then we got to a tricky one.

"Next is a 'P.' Can you do that?" Nicholas gave me the next assignment.

"OK. 'P' is the big one," I proudly showed him. Then I deliberately made a 'b.' "Is that right?"

"No, no, try again," he gently coached me.

I did not erase the error. I wanted to see through his eyes. 'd' I wrote next, looking at his face for a reaction.

"That's not it," he corrected. "Try again."

A-ha! He *can* see the difference, I thought.

"I don't get it," I pouted. "I don't want to do this any more." I made a frown and felt sorry for myself, like he had sometimes tried to be excused without finishing the lesson successfully.

And then it happened.

Nicholas gently put his hand on my arm, looked right into my eyes, gave me an encouraging smile, and with a warm voice and comforting tone he said, "It's OK. You'll get it. You can do it. Here, I'll show you."

Indeed, he was my teacher that day.

Belonging

One of my favourite parts of homeschooling is bedtime!

During the years when our children have gone to school, bedtime is a lot more pressured. They have to get up, wash up, eat up, pack up, bundle up and hurry up to walk up the hill to the school bus... on time! So, bedtime sounds like, "Hurry up! Brush your teeth! Get going! Now! OK, I'm done reading to you. Lights out! Now go to sleep!" And a little later, "Hey! Be quiet up there! No more talking!"

But, when we homeschool, bedtime became much more relaxed.

'I wonder...' leads to fascinating questions which leads to research which leads to learning. Toby was a champion. "Mom, I wonder how my heart works?" or "I wonder what makes earthquakes happen?" or "Do you think people will really travel to Mars?" And while I attempt to answer, I also have a question of my own. "Do you save these questions to postpone bedtime? Are you really so curious? Or are you tricking me?" Toby answered from his bunk bed. "When I start to go to sleep, I am quiet and still, so I think about things. I'm too busy in the daytime to wonder about things." And I was so glad to have these precious moments extend.

'Story back rubs' was another special custom at bedtime. I told a story and poke and paint and sculpt and soothe with textured strokes on the young child's back. "I'm going to plant a garden. First I pull out the weeds (little pinches), then I rake the soil smooth (strong fingers raking lengthwise), then I poke a hole (poke-poke-poke) and push in each bean. Now the rain sprinkles down (little finger raindrops) and then the sun warms the earth (press firmly down with wide hands) and soon the little seeds begin to grow."

Or else I mix and knead bread. Or roll out pie dough. Or paint a scene. Or run all over town doing errands.

"Tell me a story of your life," led to family history.

"Tell me about when I was a baby," allowed me to say out loud how very much I love each family member.

I loved to sing like my Daddy did.

I loved to tuck them in tightly like my Mother did.

Sometimes we planned out tomorrow. Sometimes we remembered yesterday. Sometimes I asked them questions.

"Did you ever feel ___ today?" Excited, scared, angry, mean, grumpy, confused, sorry for yourself, generous, lonely, proud, tired, silly, peppy, curious, kind? I remember in my childhood how each of my siblings experienced the same event with different emotions. It seemed important to gently talk them through. It's OK to have feelings and let other people know how you feel.

Going to sleep after a cozy bedtime was much more relaxing. Waking up when you're ready was much more satisfying. Eating at a leisurely pace, going outside, doing chores, helping with meals, all became woven together with formal lessons and assignments for the 'school' part of the day.

As homeschooling became more popular, Kevin found a book that helped me see the pattern we were already finding. "Homeschooling Burnout" by Raymond and Dorothy Moore stated this formula: 'one-third academic, one-third family business, one-third community service.'

Yes, there is evidence in the Christmas Album that our family was living this ratio. We were involved in so many volunteer and home-based-business ventures which enriched and strengthened our homeschooling lessons.

Sacred

Christmas time was no longer dreary and lonely. With a family of creative children, we decorated the house, tree and cookies. We read aloud and enjoyed singing carols. 'Christmas Shopping' was almost unknown in our family. We rarely went to the city of Kamloops (two-and-a-half hours to the south). Every two weeks we all went to the grocery store, hardware store, pharmacy and Thrift Store in Clearwater (one hour to the south). It was possible to order items from the Sears catalogue. Grandparents sent generous store-bought gifts. But, to and from each other, we made gifts: potholders, place mats, calendars, bags, puppets, pillows, hats, decorated boxes, hand made books, sewing, or other crafts.

Nicholas surprised me with this poem.

WHEN JESUS LAY
Nicholas, age 7

When Jesus lay in the hay
The sheep gave Him a blanket.

When Jesus lay in the hay
The cow gave Him her manger.

When Jesus lay in the hay
The cow gave Him nice warm milk.

When Jesus lay in the hay
The dove cooed Him to sleep.

When Jesus lay in the hay
The mice went, "Squeak! Squeak! Squeak!"

Endurance

Somehow the strain on my body made changes. For a little over ten years I had been either pregnant or nursing or both for a total of 90 months with only a gap of 36 months without eating for two (or three). Somehow the strain of having my husband working the night shift for ten years wore away my stamina. Somehow the strain of continuous interrupted sleep to keep the fire going or to look after children was erosion within my body. Somehow I became a statistic, one of the women who experiences 'clinical depression.'

Of course, I didn't know what that was or how to ask for help. I put one foot in front of another. I fed my kids and cleaned my house and read aloud and supervised school work and chores. But I was bone tired. My body felt like I was carrying a huge mattress every time I moved. It was too hard to decide what to wear, so I stayed in PJs all day and night. It was too hard to decide what was for supper, so we had scrambled eggs or grilled cheese sandwiches. It was too hard to go outside to play. It was too hard to pay attention. The annoying noise and frequent squabbling was fraying my nerves. Life was one big long endurance test.

One day I announced, "That's it! I quit! I'm taking the day off! Someone else can be 'The Mom' today!"

To my surprise, eight-year-old Nicholas went to lay on the couch and governed the others by distributing tasks. Getting attention with a little clapping sound, he pointed his finger and said, "Elise, you feed the dog. Michael, go feed the chickens. Toby, take out the compost."

It was an image of myself that I did not know was making such a big impression.

I asked my counsellor. I got information. I spoke with my Aunts on both sides of the family. I asked my Mother. I spoke with my husband. Depression is a pretty common thing. Medication can be very helpful. In the end I decided that it was the same as needing a hearing aid, or a pair of glasses, or an elevated shoe, or any other device to help solve a physical problem. My body needed something that it wasn't getting. So, I could give myself what I needed.

It felt good to feel good again. No longer did I have to be a grumpy old bear or a droopy old sloth. Normal activities were satisfying. Sleep was welcome. The world had colour and was no longer gray.

Exploration

Travel became a priority. There is so much to explore on Planet Earth. Nature. The Works of Mankind. Hiking in the mountains. Canoeing down the river. Bicycles and skis, ice skates and diving boards. Aunts and Uncles and Cousins and Grandparents in Ontario and Colorado and Florida and Pennsylvania. Amtrack and VIA, airports and taxis, subway and city buses. Ticket stubs and journals. Phone calls and email. It seemed that planning a trip was always on my mind.

We went to museums and demonstrations, backwoods and downtown, symphony and garage bands, an art gallery and an old man's rock collection. I wanted to prepare our children to be able to go anywhere, understand what they were looking at or listening to, participate on this planet in whatever way they choose.

And people travelled to visit us, too. For our 25th wedding anniversary, Dearma and Papa-Joe drove all the way from Florida to tour the Banff-Jasper loop. They invited Nicholas, Toby and I to join them! We feasted in the gorgeous mountains, rivers and towns, toured the Athabasca Glacier and went on the ski gondolas and river rafting. A second batch of company came: Kevin's brother, Richard, and family. We showed them how the country cousins live with drives up the mountains, tours of waterfalls and lakes and bonfire cooking.

And then: the New Millennium! Two children grown and gone. Two children still at home.

Service

When the time came, I couldn't agree to send Nicholas alone to the Bonnie Hills Church School and leave Toby home alone. If they travelled together the following year, that seemed better to me. So I made a complex plan for their last year at home.

We would homeschool while travelling for five months, then finish the school year at the Clearwater high school. We would be guided by Dr. Raymond and Dorothy Moore's ratio for homeschooling: one-third academic, one-third family business, one-third community service.

I had expanded from volunteering in my community and writing for the newspaper. I had recently completed the Provincial Adult Instructor's Diploma, developed a series of Homeschooling Seminars[34] and started my own business. With a portion of my inheritance from my Dad, we could combine speaking engagements with visiting relatives.

Nicholas was sixteen and a newly licensed driver. Toby was eager to return to places we went when he was small and participate in more activities.

'Mr. Reliable,' Kevin stayed home, continued working on the railroad and was involved with his volunteer interests.

First, by Greyhound we rode for 63 hours across the prairies to Toronto. We lived for one month on an educational farm. September, like a cornucopia, spills corn and tomatoes, apples and peaches. The boys learned to care for the animals, served guests and visited relatives and places Kevin and I knew from our youth.

We spent a short time in Ottawa and an overnight in Montreal and then we boarded the train to travel south through the autumn glory of Vermont and into the depths of 'Ground Zero' in New York City to stay nearby with my brother, Andrew, and his family.

Next, the boys attended classes for one month in the Bonnie Hills Church School.

Elise lived on campus, working full-time at the Museum. She was rewriting brochures and tour notes, scanning old photos into a digital archive and working on the web page.

She planned to finish her Master's Degree at the University of Western Ontario in London, Ontario.

Michael planned to finish his BSc in Biology at Bonnie Hills College that spring. He had a very busy and varied life on campus. He worked in the Dining Hall and helped cater for large gatherings. He enjoyed karate and took part in drama productions. He played Schroeder in 'You're a Good Man, Charlie Brown' and had a role in another Shakespeare play.

In November, Nicholas, Toby and I celebrated Thanksgiving in Colorado where my sister, Julie, now lives in our childhood home. Then finally, in mid-December, we were back home.

No matter how you measure it, our 30-day trip (estimated 20,000 km / 12,000 miles) was a success. We worked on a farm in Kitchener, participated in a TV studio audience in Toronto, toured museums in Ottawa and New York City, attended classes at the Church School. We helped out at a wedding, a baptism, cooked suppers, babysat, decorated and performed live music for a Christmas play. We passed through 6 provinces and 21 states. We wore shirts with the slogan, "Not all who wander are lost." It seemed appropriate. It is a wonder of Providence that all the details worked out so well.

After Christmas, there was one more month to fill with homeschool learning. We prepared a display to show the Clearwater high school Principal. Maps and brochures, postcards and photographs, journals and writing assignments were samples of our travels, activities and educational efforts.

We built a 'Time-Line' to illustrate 'Forces Shaping Canada 1812-1912.' It was a 40 foot long mural, divided equally into decades, with maps and diagrams, portraits and coloured labels indicating various kinds of development during this period of history.

Toby did research to write mini-biographies about the Prime Ministers. Nicholas wrote other mini-biographies of explorers, scientists, and well-known Canadians.

We watched videos, used the internet, CD encyclopedia, and research materials such as atlases, index, charts, first person accounts, National Geographic articles.

It was a 'Last Hurrah!' for homeschooling in our family. And it was 'Golden.'

Reliable

Where does the time go?

First Elise, then Michael, and it wasn't long until Nicholas and Toby got ready to leave home to attend the Church boarding school. Stimulating courses, thought-provoking professors, religious instruction, dormitory life, Dining Hall, dating with chaperons, and the major and minor differences between living in Canada and the USA were interesting challenges they met and mastered.

I felt the pressure. What did I need to accomplish before they left? How could I possibly prepare them for the fast-paced world, technological advances, erupting social change, shelter them from harm, yet inform them of the hazards? How could I maintain communication with my children as they fledge the nest, travel across the continent, live in a place and with people who are both familiar and foreign to me?

Kevin's practical training in 1st Aide, radio skills, mechanical ability, safety awareness and bushcraft were all conveyed to the boys coupled with those character qualities which I so admire and depend on: honesty, determination, loyalty, reliability. They became acutely aware of the role their Father played in their lives.

"These tools and knowledge will have no value if you don't practice and become familiar with them. If they're dusty or not sharpened when you need them, or you keep them in a box or only have them for show, then they are a waste," Kevin shared his values. "These tools and skills could do damage if used in haste, anger or to dominate others. Your self-control will determine whether you either kill or heal. Inanimate objects are neutral. They are made 'good' or 'bad' by the hands that use them."

Releasing his sons, Kevin gave them lasting guidance. "Be aware of your own intentions and motivations in your daily decisions and actions. You can help yourself survive and you can also decide to help others who might need your aid."

Kevin spoke solemnly. "I have given you all that I can in hopes that you will come to know 'what it is to be a man.'"

Diligently, I instructed them from my knowledge: research skills, travel experiences, the arts, healthy choices in the kitchen and awareness of their own personal ethics. I also shared a glimpse into the culture they could expect when they would come to live in the Church Community.

"Here is Wisdom collected over four thousand years and preserved for two thousand more!" I invited them to consider their own Bible reading with this perspective. "There are pieces here that will keep you oriented on your Journey. If you are familiar with the teaching here, you will have a good map, a light ahead when you are uncertain, a foundation to build on, and the freedom to expand and take your place as the Lord calls you."

With a trembling voice I continued. "I hope that someday you will have the gladness that we feel right now: seeing your own children succeed and walk tall and enter new places and do new things. We have given you many things, but we never know how they will be used. And it is with very much deep happiness that we see how you are using what you have been given by us and by your Heavenly Father, too, Who alone is the One who made, guides and loves you."

Confidence

Now there are fewer photos on each Christmas Album page. No more cute toddlers. No more dress-up clothes.

The time came for the departure of our two sons. Waiting in the airport, my heart was overflowing with both hope and dread.

Through their eyes, the wide and wonderful world awaits.

Through my eyes, pitfalls and quicksand and booby traps and hazards abound.

No parents, no chaperons, no rules can ever prevent access to 'drugs, sex and alcohol.' Each young person has to face these decisions on their own. Driving, money, trends, attitudes, tattoos, employers, tobacco, even simple things like stunts on the diving board, can irreversibly change the course of a person's life.

There are so many things a parent will never know. There are so many things a parent hopes for, waits for, gives up control over.

If I had chosen a career, I would know I was getting better with increased salary, promotions and recognition, awards and heavier responsibilities.

I have chosen the domestic, Mothering Path. I will never really know if I did my job well, except with little glimpses of grown children's successes, participation in wholesome living, fragments of conversations, clues about their choices as the years go by.

Waiting in the airport. They are eagerly about to launch. I am about to begin the dreaded 'Empty Nest.'

Respect

Telephone calls and email, digital photos and the school web page made the miles and months seem a little more tolerable.

Elise graduated and travelled in Sweden. Michael graduated and zipped around England. Nicholas and Toby were exchange students in France.

Each of them took roles in theatrical productions or helped back stage. Music and volunteering, sports and employment expanded their experiences and sharpened their appreciation for the skills they had brought from home.

"I got an interesting email from Nicholas today," I mentioned to Kevin at suppertime. "He's turning 18 pretty soon, and since he has been living in the dormitory for half a year, making his own decisions about many things, he wanted to tell us what he's thinking about."

"Tell me about it," Kevin knew that I had governed the children with rather specific standards, yet, that my ultimate goal was to equip them to make healthy, wholesome decisions on their own, even though they might differ significantly from our lifestyle.

"Well, it's kind of a pledge. He seems to be able to see himself as a child, the effort we made, and, now it is as though he's standing on a plateau, he can look back and ahead along his own life Path." Kevin was interested.

"He starts out by being very respectful. It's actually heartwarming to hear him appreciate the effort we have put into raising our family. He says he's 'lived a healthy, active, fun filled life, full of good things' and that he's 'blessed to have good parents who haven't had a divorce.' He's thankful for the opportunities that are available at the Seer-Church school. It's the kind of message I've always hoped I would someday have from our children as they reach adulthood! He says he doesn't want to be rebellious, or throw out everything we've taught him. He just wants us to know he is making his own decisions and not all of them will be identical to the decisions we made when we grew up."

I continue, "Let me read you this part. 'I have kept good grades and kept working my hardest in school, maintained healthy friendships, done well with keeping a good reputation, not got in any trouble with the law ever. And none of that is going to change. Since I respect you and Dad, I want you to tell me what you think and how you feel before I make decisions, but I want them to be my own.' Don't you think that is an amazing message?" I just can't get over how wonderful it feels to have this result after all the years of parenting I have tried to do well.

There are so many things I decided not to do, yet, I want my children, not to follow my way exactly, but to think through their own decisions. Kevin was an on-going example of integrity and honesty. I taught them to say 'oops' and admit it when they made a mistake, instead of getting angry and swearing or blaming someone else. If possible, then we found a way to fix the mistake. I love hearing that when they go to work everyone is amazed that my kids finish the job by cleaning up after themselves. I hope their wives and husbands will appreciate that one little part of parenting that I tried to pass along.

'The Empty Nest'

The last four pages of the Christmas Album have no children in the photos. Only Kevin and I.

But, there are also wedding photos to add to the pages! Yes! First Michael wed Deborah, then Elise married Phil. After a year of college Nicholas moved to Vancouver and Toby is in the architecture program in Atlanta!

It got pretty quiet here. However, I had time and opportunity to pursue my own interests.

I have been waiting and dreading this for years. What shall I do with my time, talents and all the boxes of treasures I have collected for children's activities? I have already had a taste of 'depression.' Sleeping all day and awake at night, watching TV for hours and hours (and hours), immobilized on the couch, talking on the telephone to anyone and everyone... It's no fun and not a sustainable way to be.

I don't want my kids to feel sorry for me, or remember only those dreary times when I was too tired to come outside and watch them do a 'tricky-trick' or too grumpy to think clearly or muddle-headed and angry at every interruption or misbehaviour.

It took me a little while to appreciate the benefits of being home without daily 'Mom' duties. When I eventually figured out a healthy balance, I wanted them to know.

* ** *** ****

email from Mom to all of my children November 30, 2008

I am so happy!

Today is the last...LAST... L-A-S-T day of November and I have finished the month with zero depression or days in bed all day or insurmountable exhausting unsolvable problems...yay!!!

It has been dark, but warm. Yesterday was a slight snow fall. I have been out for my daily run (I can run for 16 minutes with no tired feelings!)

Toby: Max (your dog) is my personal trainer!

Mr. Fitness, Michael: I never, ever believed the magazine articles that said that exercise was a solution to depression. Well, ta-da!

Elise: I am having two girls come and stay next weekend in your old room. We will decorate cookies.

Nicholas: you will laugh: there is a new channel for Christmastime on our satellite dish that is a continuous burning fireplace... and music!

To this I will add... Now that I have my own car, I can go to Clearwater when I want to. I am a Brownie leader again! It is so much fun to remember all the times when you were a little Brownie, Elise. I bring my guitar and sing with them, too. On the same night, there is Christmas choir practice! We will have three performances. It is fun to be with some of your old teachers here who always ask how each of you are doing.

So, you all have matching Christmas gifts in the mail. Dad and I worked on them together which was very satisfying and I hope you will enjoy them.

Anyways, I just wanted to tell you all that we are doing great and sending you lots of love as you enter the Christmas time of year filled with traditions. Now you are launched out and will decide how to express your beliefs and love and make meaningful family moments for yourselves.

Tradition

And that 'matching gift' I mentioned is the Christmas Album of family photos I am flipping through tonight. 30 years of Christmas memories. 30 years of family times. 30 years of traditions. In these wee-hours of winter darkness, I wait, filled with hope. Nicholas is coming home... and he's bringing his sweetheart with him!

And now, it is now.

The weather forecast for the morning is expected to be just exactly a perfect kind of day: Very cold, clear weather with the mill pond frozen flat and clear and smooth. There is a dusting of powdery, sparkling, rainbow crystal snow to shovel off.

Instead of a full-sized Christmas tree, I went into the woods to cut branches. I have four kinds: cedar, spruce, fir and pine. One for each of my children. The greenery is tied with a red bow, hanging in the living room from the centre beam with tiny white lights and silvery ornaments.

> I am missing Toby because this winter I am wearing the
> boots and snow pants that he outgrew.
> I am missing Michael (and his lovely wife) because everything is more fun when they are around.
> I am missing Elise (and her tall husband) because
> she used to make the 3-D puzzles of castles and
> cathedrals that Aunt Julie liked to send.
>
> I am missing my Dad and his wife, Shirley and also
> Grandma D who have all left this world. And Len.
> I am missing Papa-Joe and Dearma because
> I cut the evergreen branches like we used to
> do for Christmas when I was small.

I am missing my children's spouses because they haven't been here for the winter yet, and it would be so fun to have their good times turn to memories to add to the rest.

But one I will not be missing: Nicholas is coming home... and he's bringing his sweetheart with him!

I have woolen layers for Joanna to wear so she can stay bundled up because it's so cold. Kevin made chocolate brownies, waiting their arrival. The Christmas music is ready to play. Branches above the windows are decked with red and gold balls, angels and stars.

Self-Sacrifice

It is so strange to be a Mother. Instant time travel seems to be part of the experience. I look at a newborn and see a young man, wonder what career path, who he will choose to marry, anticipate holding his babies in my arms.

I wait for this 21 year old young man, my son! I so clearly recall the moment when I first brought this beautiful, cheerful, precious baby home from the hospital. I floated him in the bathtub. He went all soft and relaxed because it was like living in the womb. It seemed to me that through our eye contact I knew that he could remember the comfort and peace from before birth. I always wanted to protect him as long as possible to see how it would affect his character to be without pain or fear or shock.

I hoped this baby would have some special qualities to bring to the world that other children might have forgotten because they had been treated roughly and their world was filled with yelling, or hungry for love, or unpleasant surprises.

I was amazed that from the time he was very young, he has had the most authentic ability to sense what others might need, when I am tired and worn out, or when guests come to stay, or when a little child feels sad.

I remember when my Mother showed me Psalm 139. I cannot think of a single dot that would improve what the Lord God the Creator of the universe made on the day He began to 'knit you together in your mother's womb.'

Some people think that being a parent involves a lot of self-sacrifice. And what have I given up? Travel? Entertainment? Wardrobe? A fancier house or car or TV or hair style? It all seems entirely incomparable. Sleep. That is one thing I gave up. And a new coat. I gave up a spec and was given four precious children. Above value. Beyond measure.

Reunion

I hear the truck in the driveway! I hear the doors slam! I hear voices! I hear boots stomping on the porch! I hear the door creak open!

And into our family comes Joanna. And I know she's 'The One' because the item she carries is the matching copy of the Christmas Album. And she knows all the family stories.

No more waiting. Only Hope filled with Joy.

REFLECTIONS

The grand essentials in life are:
Something to do,
Something to love,
And something to hope for.
—*Joseph Addison*

Chapter 9
Tuesday, January 5, 2010
Father Emil Sasges: Reverend

The curious paradox
is that when I accept myself
just as I am,
then I can change.
—*Carl Rogers*

* ** *** ****

August, 1984

One summer day, when I answered a knock on the door, I stood face-to-face with a Catholic priest. His warm brown eyes, bearded smile, slow moving gestures and the book he reached to offer me, all signalled kindness, generosity, trust and welcome. But the black and white clerical collar felt like a barricade. I had never in my life spoken to a Catholic priest.

In the same instant, while I was reading him, he was reading me. "I've heard that you are teaching Bible stories to the children in Avola. Perhaps you will find this helpful." He gave me a colourfully illustrated children's book. I invited him in. And that is how I first met Father Emil Sasges.

Kevin and I had recently moved our family from our log cabin in the woods, into a four-room frame house in the town of Avola. Now that transportation was no longer a problem and I could walk anywhere in town, opportunities opened up for me to volunteer. I asked for the use of the one-room log schoolhouse. I invited all of the children to come from 10:00am until 12:00 noon for Sunday School.[52] And they came.

Kevin continued to patrol the railroad tracks during the night and was home all day. Elise and Michael made friends with the children who came to the playground across the street.

News of my Sunday School spread up and down the valley. Seven different denominations donated flannel board figures, pictures illustrating Bible stories, books, project ideas and craft supplies. I spent several days sorting the materials and filing them in sequence. I hadn't expected to have the support of the local travelling Catholic priest!

Father Sasges was something of a 'living legend.' That first day he came to our house, he and Kevin had a lengthy conversation about his airplane crash.[53] In 1969, as he tried to land his tiny aircraft on a mountain meadow with a storm coming in, a gust of wind flipped it, tore off a wing and he was stranded for three weeks. The experience of his survival realigned his Faith Journey. Depending on God became a life-and-death reality.

Other times he came to visit, he had lengthy conversations with me about my beliefs, my desire to serve the Lord and teach the children. As I came to trust his gentle manner, focused listening and wise counsel, I confided in him. I knew I was not the only women approaching 30 with two preschoolers running around and a husband on night shift. I knew I was not the only woman having difficulties in marriage and with children and balancing self-worth. I didn't know that the exhaustion and frustration are part of the reality. I was always mad at myself.

The ever-present sense of isolation during the years in the cabin were not entirely overcome. Although we had left behind the rugged log cabin lifestyle after five years and two babies, and I now had the advantages of indoor plumbing, electricity and telephone, propane stove and hot water, neighbours and playmates for our children, as well as worthwhile ways to volunteer, there was still a gnawing hunger within me. Without a church and the sense of belonging that I used to feel as a child when we lived in the Arbor Hills Church Community, I still felt that I was 'homeless' and wandering, searching, really, since I had deliberately left the Church Community, and I had never found anything satisfying to replace it with.

Cautiously, I shared bits and pieces of my beliefs. There were so many teachings in the Seer-Church I had been raised in that were different from other forms of Christianity. There was an underlying warning to avoid both Catholics and Protestants. That's why the Church Communities were formed. If we kept our children away from other influences, built schools to instruct them in the doctrines, and lived by a specific standard, that would practically guarantee that the Church would grow and the people would live 'as in Heaven, so upon the Earth.' But, since Kevin and I decided to live away from the people who believed and lived by the teachings in The Seer's Books, there was really no safe place for me to go for instruction, answers to my questions, or to worship. It had been nearly ten years since my husband and I left the Church Community. I was trying to be 'Self-Sufficient' in both the garden and do-it-yourself lifestyle as well as providing spiritual guidance to my own children. It was challenging and enjoyable but also exhausting and lonely.

June, 1986

In the early summer, when the wild roses were just finishing their abundant, fragrant blossoms and the wild strawberries could be found, tiny and red, I took a trip by Greyhound to Valemount to learn from Father Emil Sasges, attend Mass and try to sift through my own thoughts, feelings and faith. There were so many ways that we seemed to have similar beliefs.

Hungry to participate in the Sacrament of the Eucharist, yet not being a Catholic I could not. Father explained to me that while the whole Christian Church is broken and divisions exist, this is the way it has to be.

My heart was aching as I walked alone, struggling and discouraged, yet determined to search and reach and learn and continue my Journey. I asked the Lord to help me know what to do, some way to sense His guidance. I breathed deeply from a goblet-shaped wild rose and tasted a tangy sweet wild strawberry. In this way I participated in a fraction of the sense of unity and belonging I knew was available in the Holy Supper.

September, 1986

The adults in Avola were asking for Sunday School, too! I did not feel at all qualified to teach adults. I invited pastors from the seven denominations which had offered support to the Avola Sunday School to come and take turns leading worship, answer our questions and give us some instruction. One church donated old hymn books. I brought my guitar.

Father Sasges played the guitar. I was so pleased to discover that we knew some of the same songs. When he taught me this song, I felt a heavy weight lift. God is not primarily wanting us to 'have the right doctrinal answers,' to wrestle with words, or flip pages in a scholarly book, or dream up theories, or argue the minutia of semantics, or walk the lofty halls of philosophy, or quarrel for centuries about theology. He is 'Father,' and as such, He wants to gather His children in His arms. He is 'Shepherd,' and as such, He wants to provide and protect, guide and comfort. That's it. That's all. Except for one thing: If He is my Father, then 'Who am I'? If I agree to participate in this relationship and walk into the place reserved for the 'Child,' then a wave of welcome surrounds and uplifts me. I do not have to struggle for my place. I am not in competition with anyone. I do not have to fear abandonment.

Do you know who you are?
Can you see with My eyes?
Have you heard what I said in My Word?
Do you know who you are?

If I am the Shepherd then you are a lamb
that I carry in My arms as my own.
And if trouble is nigh I would rather die
as I did so you'd never be alone.

If I am the Father then you are the child
and all that you need I will give.
Let your heart be at rest, I'll do what is best
for I've said I have come that you might live.[54]

This one song seemed to be the answer to my lifelong Quest. And another chorus confirmed the 'calling' I seemed to be guided by throughout my life. A 'calling' to serve the Lord was not exclusively reserved for men! It was universally summoning each one who seeks to follow the Lord. Welcoming. Accepting. I have been searching for Him. He has been calling me!

Here I am, Lord, Is it I, Lord?
I have heard you calling in the night.
I will go, Lord, where You lead me.
I will hold your people in my heart.[55]

This was a new world view for me. God the Creator, Infinite, Eternal, Omnipotent, Omniscient, Omni-Present was also All Loving, and continually calling. Everyone. Each of us. Me. And, He had a mission: He wants to deliver loving kindness on earth, and this is the way: through our hands. My hands. I am part of God's work!

I taught Sunday School to the children in Avola for nine years, homeschooled our own four children for fifteen years beginning each day with family worship, I read and asked and studied and learned from many religions and branches of Christianity, but never decided to belong to any one group.

Father Sasges was assigned other parishes near and far. I had no expectation of ever seeing him again.

June, 2009

Our children were grown and gone. There was not a single child left in Avola to teach. Now I was hungry with a pain that is hard to describe. What is there left for me to do?

The Lord can make amazing things happen if we just follow tiny promptings. In June 2009, I learned that Father Sasges had returned to the North Thompson Valley! Instead of his previous assignment, visiting all the towns for 200 miles, his duties were to serve only two towns north of Avola: Blue River and Valemount.

In 2008-2009, I had been volunteering in Clearwater as a Brownie Leader and I also taught songs to the Girl Guides. They planned a camping trip to Blue River, 25 miles north of Avola.

I went, but I had few responsibilities beyond leading songs at evening campfire time. I asked to be excused on Sunday so I could attend Mass.

Somehow, my heart was open. My eyes feasted on the gestures of worship as the priest's hands were folded, lifted, open in blessing, made the sign of the Cross. My ears soaked in the prayers, songs, chants and Scripture verses.

When I got home from the camping trip, I shared my gladness with Kevin, "25 years ago Father Sasges came to our house and helped me sort out my tumbling mind and heart. 25 years ago he was about the same age that I am now! Today, he is nearly 80 years old. Today, his voice seems to nourish my spirit again."

July, 2009

At about that time, Kevin's railroad supervisor offered him a company truck, so I had the use of our vehicle. I was free to go to church! Every Sunday I eagerly drove to Blue River to attend Mass on Sunday afternoons.

"Kevin!" I burst into the house with happy news, "I was invited and made welcome to read aloud from the Word during worship! You *know* how much that makes me happy!!!"

* ** *** ****

I started to meet weekly with Father Sasges. First, out tumbled my life story. I told him about 'The Doll in the Oven.' I told him about 'The Day on the Cliff.' I realized how these two incidents had begun the crippling self-doubt that had plagued me all my life. I told him how Kevin and I met and how we felt the Lord's guidance, about our wedding and our decision to travel west and live the 'Back-to-the-Land' lifestyle. I told him about my parents and how the knowledge I had of my Dad's and Mother's broken marriage constantly haunted me. I feared other men. I feared my own autonomy. My fears were impacting my relationship with my husband with no logical reason. It had been exhausting. I told him what we believed about marriage. I told him how Kevin, as a teenager, had seen the damaging effects of alcohol and adultery and violence against women and had no intention of moving away from his marriage vows to me. I had recently asked for help with depression. I had recently been in a car accident. I had recently quit my job. It was a time in my life that was mostly shadow.

I also shared many positive aspects of my life, including how Kevin and I had raised our family, my volunteer and home-school teaching and how we were continually striving towards serving the Lord.

"Kevin isn't interested in the academic studies of religion like I am," I explained. "When we met, he had two posters. 'Happiness is seeing a sunrise and knowing Who to thank.' and 'By the work one knows the Workman.' He lives his faith in his actions. He is a 'Good Samaritan' always looking for ways he can help people. I cannot begin to tell you how glad I am that I am married to this particular man. I am so proud of his accomplishments. I am so glad I can trust his good judgment. I am so safe and well provided for and respected."

Talking with a Catholic priest was a huge relief. I knew there was nothing 'bad' that he had not already heard. I knew that he could give me hope because he knew the way out of the swampy jungle of emotions and confused thinking. I knew I could not shock him. I knew he would not abandon me. I knew he would keep my story confidential. Better than a counsellor, who only deals with psychology, the priest could also guide me using Scripture, share the wisdom of his personal experience of the Journey and draw on his many years of coaching others.

With all of my stories told, I now wanted to study and learn. I asked Father questions which lead down many paths, but with an experienced Guide, everything began to make sense.

Barricades were cleared away. One-by-one obstacles vanished. From my youth I have loved and desired to serve the Lord. I loved going to church (the songs and ritual, the sense reverence), but the part about 'belonging to a Church' had never seemed necessary to me (the attitude that 'my Church is better than yours' really upset me). Now I could understand, feel and experience the reality of the Church as a kind, generous, nourishing Mother. Small 'c' catholic means: universal. I have been seeking this for a very long time.

Every Sunday, when the clock told me it was time to go, Father would say, "To be continued," so I knew I was not asking for more time than he was willing to give me. So many hours of conversation, so many pages of reading, so much journalling resulted in so many questions answered, so many blockades dissolved.

August, 2009

I went on a trip to visit my Mother and Papa-Joe, who now lived near our original family home in Colorado. First, I stopped in at the Bishop's office in Kamloops and asked for a copy of the 778 page 'Catechism.' I decided to read the whole thing. In secret!

I didn't know what I was going to find! I had been warned in my childhood not to ever go into a Catholic Church. The statues and objects, the reverence for Mary, the Crucifix and saints, the Latin chanting and old fashioned customs all seemed to be fearfully strange.

I turned each page of the Catechism, expecting to come to some dreadful doctrine that I would find repulsive. It was difficult to begin. I had so much respect for Father Sasges. I didn't want to find some insurmountable conflict. But, I also didn't want to keep coming and being influenced by him if, indeed, there were toxic underlying beliefs. Better to make an exit sooner rather than later. I felt drawn to go forward, but I had to be ready to walk away.

Page after page, new chapter, new topic, checking the footnotes and Scripture references... I never came to anything disagreeable! I was astonished. I did see places where a little twist or a tiny turn of definitions caused the various Christian denominations to split off and veer in different directions. But, the original definition of each topic seemed clear and wholesome to me.

It was hard to read a 700 page book in secret! I read on the Greyhound. I read in the airport. I read flying high over the landscape. I read on a blanket under the trees in the mountains of Colorado. I read very early in the morning. I read very late at night. My Mother was well-read in Bible study, but, I did not want to have her input until I knew my own thinking.

When I got back to Canada and showed Father Sasges that I had finished the entire book (much to his surprise) I spoke with a bright face, a sincere tone of voice and steady eye contact. "I feel like I have opened a treasure chest full of sparkling gems and ropes of pearls! I have thrust my hands deeply into this vast wealth, this collection of brightly coloured clear thoughts. Each reflected beam of light makes all the other jewels sparkle all the more. I am so happy and well fed!"

And then, I needed to bring my husband up-to-date on what I had learned.

First, I made flashcards, listing all the churches I have visited and all the resources I had read.

"Kevin, as you know, over the years I have attended church services in several denominations, trying to find a place I could worship and learn and belong: United Church, 'Bible Only' Christians, Evangelical, Anglican, Pentecostal, Baptist and Seventh Day Adventist. You have heard me come home upset and confused and unhappy." He nodded his head, remembering my lengthy research and pacing anxiety.

"I have read a little or a lot from the Mormon, Tao, Baha'i, Swedenborgian, Mennonite, Jehovah's Witness. Each is interesting to know about, but none seem to satisfy my heart. I have friends who believe: New Age, Buddhism, Reincarnation, First Nations. But, I don't belong there, either." I showed him each of the flash cards with each name or topic.

"I have taught Sunday School here for a total of nine years. I have homeschooled our four children for fifteen years with family worship frequently. I love to teach because first I have to do research and learn. I have also learned from watching TV programs, sent away for courses, borrowed video tapes. I get magazines and newsletters in the mail. But it is not the same as being with other people. The smiles and hugs and conversations and connections are important, not just the doctrine and teaching." I could see that Kevin was listening. "I can't only have ink on paper. I need real people."

"I know that God is everywhere and I can worship Him anytime. But, by myself, I feel so alone and sad and hungry. I want to sing... with other people. I want to learn... with other people. I want to kneel and stand and smile and look forward to next week... with other people." My tone of voice conveyed the yearning I felt.

"Visiting the Catholic Church and having time with Father Sasges to answer my questions has become very important to me. When he talks I can hear him. When I talk he can hear me."

With his signature smile, Kevin quietly interrupted with his own observation. "That's why they pay him the big bucks!" We both laughed, knowing that 'Big Bucks' was not Father's motivation any more than Kevin's volunteer work could be measured with a stack of dollars.

Wanting to express my earnest message to my husband, I continued. "I have decided that 'Nothing' is not an option. And, although I am just as surprised as you are, I am going to pursue the possibility of finding nourishment in the Catholic Church. I have read this entire thing." I held up the thick, blue Catechism for him to see what I had been reading while on my trip. "I have not felt that old anxiety and conflict with any of it." Kevin flipped through the pages, noticing all the bookmarks, underlined places and notes in the margins.

"I don't think I have to give up anything I already believe! I think I do get to replace the things that I don't believe with better ideas. I just want you to know that I am taking this seriously and something new might be around the corner."

From that time on, I faithfully relayed to Kevin what I was learning and exploring and gaining.

September, 2009

I asked Father Sasges for his email address. He checked his email every Wednesday at the library.

It was the beginning of a valuable correspondence. We could continue our Sunday conversations. I could follow up with further ideas, questions, let him know what I was reading, ask him to bring me information on topics I needed to clarify.

There was so much I was familiar with, so much that was new. I only had little glimpses about Catholics from movies. It was embarrassing how much I knew about the Catholic Church because people made fun of it.

October, 2009

Now I began to ask specific doctrinal questions: What about the Pope? Why is Mary so important? What is the meaning of all the objects used in worship? What is the 'Liturgical Year'? I don't understand all the parts of Mass? Why are there more books in the Catholic Bible? What does it mean to be a 'saint'? What is this Catholic idea called 'Purgatory'? I asked him everything else I could think of.

It was way different to talk with someone who understood and believed and lived all of these things, much different that an encyclopedia article.

I did not offend him with my questions. I was eager to learn, to weigh new things against what I already believed and test inside my heart to see if they were wholesome ideas to continue with and build them into my life.

Some new things I could see clearly right away.

The frequent use of objects, statues, stained glass windows and other ornamentation is of value when trying to instruct the people who could not read during all the centuries before the printing press. The five senses are each doorways to the heart. Not only the intellect is to be nourished during worship. The Rosary and other symbols help the people remember the stories, characters, sequences and teachings.

'Saint' is the word for a person who is in Heaven. Hell is not about being 'good' or 'bad' but about being 'unrepentant.' Purgatory is a Greek word meaning to purge and clean. It makes sense that the people who die and are going to Heaven need to pause and have a cleansing period before entering the brightness of that place.

The Catholics have more books in the Bible than the Protestants simply because they include some Greek books, not only the traditional Hebrew texts.

I have always veered away if a religious conversation gets started about 'the Devil' or 'Satan.' It always made me feel like some religions are based on fear. But Father used the name: 'the Father of Lies.' That seemed to me to be a healthy way to speak.

I also love when Holy Communion is called 'the Source and the Summit.' It just fills me with hope. Everything good comes from and returns to the Lord through this simple participation. I want to approach the Summit and then return from the Source to enter my daily life cleansed, enriched and reoriented, thankful for the Gift.

Some things make me really happy.

The Liturgical Year brings a cycle of Scripture readings and songs which lead the people through the year to better understand and celebrate the prophecies of the coming Messiah, Jesus' birth, life, teachings, His last days, the Crucifixion, Resurrection, Ascension and Pentecost. It makes it easy to learn and teach and review each year and experience Jesus' life story again.

"Father Sasges says the most basic thing when I ask him about Mary," I opened the conversation with Kevin when I got home one Sunday. "He looks me straight in the eye, giving me something that is very precious to him and says, 'Become as a little child.' It is a new sensation for me. He says, 'She is your Mother.' I have never had that thought. There is no big doctrinal debate. I have tried it to see how it feels. It makes me relax and feel less anxiety."

I am beginning to see that whatever you believe about Mary influences what you believe about Jesus... and whatever you believe about Jesus influences what you believe about Mary.[56]

"I have told Father Sasges my whole life story. When we had family worship in Colorado my Mother said, 'The reason you are learning how to read is so that you can read the Word.' Then, when I was a teenager I was so disappointed when I volunteered to teach Sunday School in the Church Community and I was told that since I was a female, I was not allowed to read the Bible verses aloud. I had to decide whether to stay with that restriction, or listen to my own inner sense." Kevin likes it when I sound content and calm.

"Since I have come here, I read, lead hymns, teach, participate in myriad ways. Even lay people can bring the Eucharist to shut-ins and help serve during Mass. There is a service led by a lay-person which sometimes is the option if a priest cannot attend. Only the Consecration of the Host is exclusively for the priest. I understand and accept why the male priesthood is in place permanently. Women are not priests, but they have an honoured role. The Catholic Church recognizes great women teachers and saints, and there is so much respect for Mary." I pause to collect my thoughts.

"I'm still new at this, but I am getting used to it. I told Father Sasges today that I feel like the opposite of petrified wood." Kevin looks puzzled. "When mineral deposits replace the fibers of wood, they become stone. Now I am having the hard parts of myself removed and replacing them with living, vibrant strands which connect and bring life."

I could watch daily Mass on TV! At home, in the quiet, with such frequent input, I could read along, learn the patterns, soak in the message, learn the responses, test my observations, begin to feel that precious, nourishing sense of belonging. If I had questions, I could send Father an email!

November, 2009

Some topics were harder to understand and accept.

I wrote Father Sasges a letter.

* ** *** ****

I am noticing a pattern in my response whenever you direct my attention to each new territory.

Risk
Resistance
Trust
Responsibility

You say, 'Mary' and my immediate reaction is: 'danger!' This is something I have been taught is 'medieval,' too 'Catholic,' worshiping an idol, non-essential, a distraction... It seems too great a Risk!

You say, 'do you sense the Real Presence in the Eucharist?' My immediate reaction is, 'people killed for this, nations go to war, divisions and hatred, prejudice and power lie in the answer to this question!'

You say, 'Rosary' and I think: 'is it for good luck?'

You say, 'saints' and my first reaction is: 'ghosts? dreamers? visions? messages? out-of-touch with reality?'

Every time, with one word, you direct my attention to new territory. Every time, my reaction is the same: 'No thanks, I'm fine how I am. I don't want to go into this.' New seems dangerous.

Then I look again at my Resistance. I recall where, when, from whom, or from what source I got the old information I have. I begin to weigh out the Risks without that first shock of fear.

Perhaps I could enter this new territory if I had a safe passage, a Guide, a trusted source to show the way, a map?

So, how do I know if I am getting trustworthy information? Perhaps I can cross-reference between reliable sources and see if they match? The Word, the Catechism, other Catholic friends, other reading, Father Sasges, the priests who are teaching on

TV, returning to do research about what I have been taught in the Seer-Church I was raised in, compare and contrast, sort through and consider.

I am allowing myself to be influenced by others and letting Trust open the doors. I am still not finished. I don't want to copy anyone, be dependent or partially developed in my mind.

Now it becomes my Responsibility: If there is a difference between what I have been given in the past and have been holding on to... and what I am learning now... which do I keep and which do I say good-bye to? What do I choose? What am I now taking for my own beliefs?

Now that I see this predictable pattern, it doesn't seem so scary.

I don't feel disrespectful, ignorant, threatened, or like I am stupid or lacking in faith or twisted in my thinking.

Risk
Resistance
Trust
Responsibility

I am so grateful that you are NOT putting pressure me.

It seems that when I am willing to step into the new territory, then passageways, corridors, museum-like collections, libraries and volumes and abundantly generous resources come into reach and the possibilities that seemed foreign and risky become welcoming, familiar, bountiful treasures!

Thank-you for your patience.

'Thy Word is a lamp unto my feet and a light unto my path.' Psalm 119: 105

* ** *** ****

One Sunday I arrived for our usual hour or two for studying, asking, listening, and I bluntly stated, "I have figured out the Pope. I don't need to ask you anything at all!"

His bushy eyebrows raised with an expression of question, tinged with an affectionate twinkle in his eye. He could never be sure what his new pupil might come up with.

"I'm glad there is a Pope. Because if he wasn't the Pope, than I would be!" Hastily I added, "By that I mean: It is his job to sort out and make decisions about what to keep and what to discard. I don't want the job! He can have it!"

Since I began to watch 'Daily Mass' on TV, I became familiar with the patterns, the language and sequence of the Mass. I heard fourteen priests give their instruction. "I'm not only relying on Father Sasges," I told my Mother over the phone. "I have many teachers. None of them have said anything that I object to. It all fits together."

Meanwhile, I loaned Father Sasges a slim Seer-Book which was a summary of the doctrine I had been raised with. I did not want to hide anything from him now. After he read it he assured me, "This is 98% good teaching!" That made me feel like I had a pretty good sense inside myself to be able to sort out what to keep and what replace.

"These are the three main things I no longer believe from the Church I was raised in," I was ready to tackle the 'biggies.'

"Number 1: The Seer wrote that the 'soul' is from the father and the body is from the mother. So, I was glad to read #366 in the Catechism, 'The Church teaches that every spiritual soul is created immediately by God – it is not produced by the parents.' That is good news to me!"

Father nodded and indicated I could go on. "The next one will hurt your ears," I hesitated.

"Number 2: The Seer wrote a lot about 'hereditary evil.' He said that since Jesus' soul was from the Father and His body was from His Mother, that He was contaminated by her with her 'hereditary evil.' The Seer wrote that Jesus had to 'put off' and overcome the evils He got from His Mother and that is how He became fully Divine. Also, that the 'hereditary evil' embedded in the soul from the father can never be eradicated or overcome. I don't believe that. But I don't know what to replace it with?" I searched Father's face for hope and guidance.

"You can rest assured that you have stepped away from teachings that are untrue. The Sacrament of Baptism washes away Original Sin and after that, you yourself act and must repent when you turn away from the Lord's leading. Adam and Eve thought they knew better than God. That is what 'sin' is: putting yourself above God." It seemed like Father was encouraging me to step across raging river rapids on stepping stones which he knew were solid and safe.

"Number 3: I have never wanted to belong to a Church which believed 'I'm in and you're out' as if they were the only ones who were going to go to Heaven. I always thought that the Catholic Church believed that. But, the very first sentence of the Catechism assures me otherwise. Listen to this." I flip open to the first page, paragraph #27, and read in a bold, clear voice. "'The desire for God is written in the human heart, because man (meaning mankind - each person) is created by God and for God; and God never ceases to draw man to himself. Only in God will he find the truth and happiness he never stops searching for.' I just love that!" I sink back and relax into this wonderful thought.

Quietly, with a steady gaze, he spoke. "You must proclaim this. People need to hear what you have discovered."

* ** *** ****

Another development in November: I drove to Clearwater to attend Mass there and get to know the people. I also took a trip to Vancouver and Seattle and attended services there.

I sent an email to Father Sasges in late November. "I will know by Epiphany whether or not I am going to say 'Yes' to taking Communion."

I was actually considering joining the Catholic Church!

December, 2009

When winter weather and early darkness might have prevented me from travelling to 4:00pm Mass, a neighbor in Blue River offered me a place to stay overnight on Sundays. Now I could join Father and the others for Monday morning Mass as well. We made Monday our study time and Father invited me to participate in the two-hour silent prayer time called, 'Adoration.' I didn't know what that was or what I was supposed to do. So, I 'became as a child' and observed and followed along as best I could. Two hours of silence?

Father began each session with these two traditional prayers.

"Jesus, I believe in You,
I love You.
I trust You.
I adore You.
I beg pardon for those who do not
believe, love, trust and adore."

Here was a man nearly 80 years old, wise, kind, with over 50 years of experience as a priest beginning to pray with such words. Slowly, deliberately, sincerely, truly asking for something he needed and could not achieve with his own efforts:

"Jesus, meek and humble of heart,
make my heart like Yours.
Jesus, meek and humble of heart,
make my heart like Yours.
Jesus, meek and humble of heart,
make my heart like Yours."

I opened the topic of the Trinity later in December and we both thought: 'Here is a big difference.'

I thought, 'This is the end. I will continue to be homeless, hungry and without a teacher and without a Church. This was my last hope and this friend is so important to me. Now it will all be gone. I am so exhausted by having *nothing*.'

Since June, I have quoted Deuteronomy 6:4-5 and Mark 12: 29-30 over and over again while we were studying. 'Hear, O Israel, the Lord our God the Lord is One.' "I am not willing to trade worshiping One God for worshiping three!"

I felt afraid, like I was entering a labyrinth, like in those adventure movies with dangers on all sides.

But, at the same time, I also had an idea which made me feel bold and confident. In Math, a person can check their answer to a problem. 2+5=7 or 7-2=5. In building, you can check accuracy with a plumb line, a right angle or a level. It seemed to me that I was beginning to be able to check the old ideas I thought were untrue with these new ideas which seemed to be wholesome and good.

'Lord, I believe, help Thou my unbelief!' Mark 9:24

I confided in Kevin. "There has to be a way for mental health and spiritual health to be in alignment. If one set of beliefs makes me feel crazy and the other set of beliefs makes me feel calm and whole, I think I know which one I prefer!"

Another time I told him, "If 'God' is 'real' and He made us and loves us and sees us and wants to be close to us. And if we want to find and follow and love and be close to Him... Then there have to be times and places and people who have experienced that. And if they did experience a genuine 'close to God' moment, then if they tried to tell others or write it down, that would be a wonderful collection of sacred writing to read. Someplace, sometime, it must have been real. Maybe that is what the Bible is. A collection of real experiences. Maybe that is what the 'Church' is. A safe place to learn about these real experiences."

December 24, 2009

Meanwhile, in Avola, several of our neighbours decided to get together once a week to play guitars and sing together. We decided to practice Christmas songs and prepare Scripture readings and invite the townsfolk to come for a Christmas Eve presentation.

I sent Father an email celebrating how the Lord was opening doors and making wonderful things happen.

Kevin lit a candle out in the snow representing 'The Light of the World' and wrote a message for me speaking of his faith in The One Who was born in Bethlehem.

December 25, 2009

Christmas Day! Worship! Hymns! Familiar stories! Deeply meaningful! Gathered with others! Traditions! I felt so happy I could have celebrated Christmas with cartwheels!

December 30, 2009, Wednesday, 3:24pm

email Re: lots to think about
From: Emil Sasges
To: E Deckert

You have come to a momentous stage in your faith journey. I am saying this with all of your current e mails in mind! ...... What you have lived with your neighbours in Avola is an answer to my prayer for some time. As you recall, I have asked you to reach out to others in Avola. Now what you felt impossible & overwhelming to think of has become a reality. It has not only freed you from your isolation, but you testify how your effort has answered a huge need for others as well. .... It has not only set others thinking of "next year" Christmas but also set the stage for weekly group gatherings. .... What a marvel without even knowing of the countless connections there will be on a one-to-one basis!!!!!!!! .... YOUR ENTIRE DESIRE TO SERVE HIM HAS BEEN GIVEN A STAGE ON WHICH TO SERVE and I am absolutely confident you will know the joy of having a "church to use them in."........ YOU HAVE ALREADY EXPERIENCED THE COMMUNION OR INTERCONNECTEDNESS OF SUCH A CHURCH. I see a solid foundation laid in what you have learned from childhood deepened by what you have embraced in your recent studies. Your solid commitment to Kevin deepens my confidence in the authenticity of your Journey & its ever more fruitful unfolding. That candle he set against the darkness will serve both of you well in those times when things are humanly impossible. For the childlike heart even the humble candle is sufficient light...YOU WILL BE A "SUNBEAM FOR HIM" enlightening many lives with the light of Jesus so that many will know a bright dawn and even the brightness of full day.

So I say, do not be afraid of what may seem like an insurmountable obstacle in the Trinity. Your sincere, persistent, humble search makes certain you will find the way as you continue to be led by your faith in Jesus. It will deepen your wonder & praise as you continue to pray: HEAR O ISRAEL THE LORD YOUR GOD IS ONE............... Delight in the rich inner life of that one God proclaimed by Jesus and His Church!!!!!!!!!!! ...... So you feel absolutely free to come Monday or whenever you choose, even for Mass if you are happy to make a spiritual communion with the Lord while others embrace Him tangibly in the Sacrament. Your faith is already mature enough to unite to the mystery of Calvary made present in the Sacrament. I repeat what the angel Gabriel said to Mary as she struggled with God's proposal: NOTHING IS IMPOSSIBLE WITH GOD!!!!!!!! I look forward to seeing you......... May He keep you in peace! Your Brother in Christ.

December 30, 2009

Father loaned me 'The Great Adventure, a Journey through the Bible' DVD. I had never heard such clear teaching. "Do you trust God?" the speaker kept repeating. That is the theme behind all of the centuries, characters and stories. I will watch it over the next three days and return it to him.

The time line helps me understand that it is all one big, long story. I thought all of the Bible stories were about 'good' people who 'obeyed God.' But now I realize that every person has fallen, turned away, gone astray. The important thing is not that they have 'sinned' but that they admit it and turn back, asking for forgiveness. I never saw this before.

All my life I have been trying to 'obey' and 'be good.' Now I realize: I am part of the human race, stumbling, turning away, needing to ask for forgiveness. I am not afraid of my own errors. I am just like everyone else, in need of a Saviour. I cannot do it all by myself.

Father Sasges, as a shepherd, has been able to guide me.

'The Lord is good to all and His tender mercies are over all His works.' Psalm 145:9

I spoke with my Mother on the telephone. "I'm so glad you have a spiritual mentor and steady friend, but, are you sure you are not putting Father Sasges up on a pedestal?"

I had to look hard at my thoughts and impressions. Was I authentically interested in joining the Catholic Church? Or was I seeking approval from a 'Father Figure' and making a significant decision based on a false motive?

I spoke with my husband. He cautioned, "You're only looking at what you want to see."

I had to look inside at the way my mind was working. Well, I thought to myself, yes, that is how I look at a lot of things: Like living in a drafty log cabin at -40°C! Or the soot and sawdust in the living room from feeding the wood stove! Or the racket and mess of raising four children! Or the weeds in the garden! Or the unending piles of laundry and dishes! I'd rather see the potential and what's good about it. Why bother with all the effort if things are going so badly? I'd rather nourish myself on the hope, not wallow in the despair.

"Well, yes," I spoke aloud to my husband, "I realize that through history not every day has been sunny and bright in the history of the Catholic Church... but that is a matter of human error, prejudice, power and pride. The 'Church' I am speaking about is the ideal gem. The intended, clear, precious, wholesome, wonder-filled vessel, a place for the Lord and people to come to know and love one another. A 'Treasure Trove' where manuscripts and art, symbols and meaning are preserved and passed forward in time, ready to share with those who Seek."

I continued. "It is not unlike the word 'marriage.' Or 'mother.' There is the messy, jumble of human weakness with yelling and running late and conflicts. But, there is also the ideal, the original intent, the central, highly valued, sacredness we reach for and sometimes catch a glimpse of. And how sweet it is to experience. That is the 'Church' I am getting very close to being a part of."

January 4, 2010

I dreamed the music from Handel's Messiah "Make straight in the dessert a highway for our God. The crooked shall be made straight and the rough places plain."[57]

After Adoration I quietly spoke to Father. "I trust you more than anyone else in my life."

His immediate reply, "Jesus, Trust Jesus."

I searched within my heart and mind all through the night. I travelled the Path of my life. I lined up the pros and cons, the reality and the doubts. I tried to imagine 'No' and walk away into isolation or 'Yes' and enter the welcoming.

The wise men followed the star to find the Infant Lord. What small sparks of light can I be sure of? Will I bring my gifts to lay before Him?

January 5, 2010

"I'm ready! I can do it!" My eager face and wide smile was as much a surprise at this early hour as my presence standing in the doorway. It was a Tuesday. I had never before stayed for an extra overnight so I could come to Tuesday morning Mass.

Gesturing to come in, holding the door wide open, Father's curious, welcoming eyes took in my parka and scarf, my bright eyes, my buoyant stride and invited me into the warm meeting room.

"I can do it now. I figured it out. I'm ready for my First Communion." Unwrapping my layers, I move to sit on the soft blue couch where I had shared my life story, asked my questions, struggled and prayed with this priest guiding me along the Journey.

"It was the Trinity that was still confusing to me, remember?" The Seer-Church I was raised in taught that there was clearly One God and Jesus was It. All references to the Trinity had been removed from every hymn. The Trinity as the Catholic Church taught it seemed like a contradiction for me. How could One be Three and Three be One? "I figured it out last night, or rather, it popped into my head. 'The Trinity' is like a prism. The white light from the sun has all of the colours in it, but we can't see them until the light beam passes through a prism. The light slows and we can see the brilliant spectrum. The colours were there all the time, but now we can see it. So: the Trinity is like that, too. God has been too distant for people to approach, to comprehend, to love. The Trinity is like slowing down the idea of God so that we can appreciate the marvelous Being that He is. The Father, Son and Holy Spirit were there all the time, but now He has slowed Himself down for us to be able to see more clearly."

His eyes follow my every gesture and expression. His ears and mind follow my thought process.

"It that OK? Have I got the idea now? Is there anything preventing me from my First Communion?"

He's clearly surprised, yet, he has been waiting for me, hoping, leading, allowing me the freedom of time and for my mind to catch up with my heart, so long yearning to belong.

"You know there is one thing you have to do before you come to the Lord's Table."

"Yes, my first Confession. I am ready to do that right now, too."

Standing and gesturing with a wide dramatic sweep of my arm, realizing I have stood on the street corner with the self-important Pharisee I declare, "O Lord I thank you that I am not as other men! Look at that sinner. I am so righteous and not like him."[58]

I had another idea. "You know the story of the Prodigal Son?[59] The younger brother was the naughty one who wasted his inheritance on disgraceful living. He came back home asking his father for forgiveness. Well, I am the older brother. The one who stayed home and was obedient and hard working and never strayed. But, inside, he was jealous and mean and thought he was so important. That's me. He didn't 'do anything bad' so he cannot see his own 'sin' so he doesn't ask for forgiveness. But, now I do. And so I am."

Grinning I sit down again. "I have been that person for a very long time. I never say swear words or drink or smoke. I brag about how 'good' I am, how I never break the rules, how much I love God and read the Word and do good deeds. And yet, by thinking myself so wonderful, I have stolen from God. I have made myself grand and turned away from Him, taking the gifts He has given me as if they were from my own effort. I have eclipsed God with my own 'goodness' and this is my 'sin': to be ungrateful and proud, turning away from humility and unaware of my dependence on Him, acting like I am in charge."

In conclusion I add, "I am one of the ones who messes up. I am one of the ones who needs the Saviour. I am one of the ones who cannot do it all by myself, who needs to be forgiven and who cannot be forgiven until I forgive."

He is silent... letting this jumble of words and the intensity of my conversion sink in. He is weighing everything we have already spoken of, aligning it with the requirements I need to meet before stepping into the Church through the doorway of the Sacraments.

Having heard my Confession, he instructs me to bow my head for the Absolution and for the first time, I hear the soothing, encouraging, strengthening words. Now I am given a Penance. I forgot that this was part of it. A little squeamish (it's so Catholic), I listen intently and agree to the assignment.

Now I know a glimpse of what 'Grace' means and what 'Peace' feels like. Now I know that I must rely on the Lord alone to stand guard at my lips, heart and actions.

Now he turns to me and asks, "Shall we wait? Is there anyone you would like to invite to your First Communion? Sometimes people plan a little reception for this important day?"

"No, I have already thought of that. It is midwinter, I can't ask people to drive so far. My husband will be glad I did this. We spoke together, but he does not want to come to church. I am ready. This has been a long struggle. I would like to do this today."

"Will this feeling fade away? Will you change your mind? This is a big decision."

I said, "I get to be the Little Lost Lamb. You get to be the Shepherd! I am tired of being in the wilderness. I am willing to enter the fold!"

We laughed and he said, "There's nothing in the way now."

I said, "Yes, the rough places are plain and the crooked is straight."

We were both laughing.

"So," he said, "there is nothing preventing you from taking Communion today."

I said, "I know!"

And he said, "And tomorrow is Epiphany"

I said, "I know!" (and it had been impossible until that exact day).

"I am ready."

"OK," and he explains the ritual which will bring me into this world-wide, centuries old, body of believers called the Catholic Church.

He lets the others know the news. It is a bit of a surprise, but as always, it is the priest's decision.

We wait in silence for the priest to prepare his white vestments.

Father Sasges asked me to answer the baptismal vows: renounce Satan, believe in the Father, Son and Holy Spirit and other pledges in the Apostle's Creed.

I am filled to overflowing with gladness and light and warmth and my heart is expanding to wider love for Him. No longer fragmented puzzle pieces, all parts of the Journey make sense and fit together.

'Here I am send me.' Isaiah 6: 8

'Speak, Lord, for Thy servant heareth.' I Samuel 3: 9

* ** *** ****

How could I tell Kevin how clear this was for me?

"Remember when we watched 'The Titanic' movie[60] over New Year's Eve?" I invited his mind to follow mine. "There were three ways the scientists could verify what they had discovered. They had the blueprints. They had the broken moss-covered ship. They had the eye witness account of Rose." Kevin can see my logic. "It's like having a plumb line, a right angle and a level.

They all match. They all tell you the same thing." I am so eager for him to see what I see.

"This is the question I have been asking my whole life: If this 'church stuff' is 'real' then there should be evidence that comes from a variety of sources that all point to the same thing. Well, here are the three things. We have the 'blueprints': which would be the printed Word, the Bible. We have the 'ship' which is the actual physical evidence, that would be the 'Church': the traditions and teachings. And we have the eye witness: our own 'level' headed sense! 'I' am part of the puzzle. It has to be something that 'I' can see and accept. Not just blind faith or obedience which goes against my own sensible 'Self.' I feel like I have discovered a time and place and way that they all fit together. It is very exciting. The text and the data and the experience all match!"

"That is how I feel right now, Kevin, like everything cross-references and fits together. That is why I was able to say, 'Yes' today and enter the fold and no longer be out on my own in the wilderness trying to figure out everything by myself."

'This is the Lord's doing. It is marvellous in our eyes.' Psalm 118:23

January 5, 2010, Tuesday, 2:04pm

email: first surprise
From: E Deckert
To: Emil Sasges

As I stepped out into the sunny day.... immediately in
front of me was an enormous grader 'making all the
crooked places straight and the rough places plain.'

I have much to learn. I have much to be thankful for. But, I am not yearning and hungry anymore.

'I was glad when they said unto me, let us go into the house of the Lord.' Psalm 122: 1

January 6, 2010, Wednesday, 3:11pm

From: Emil Sasges
To: E Deckert

WHAT BEAUTIFUL MILESTONES...........It will take an eternity to tell the whole story ....thanks for letting me see how amazingly you are being led!!!!!!!!!!!!!!!!!

January 19, 2010

Neither awake, nor asleep, I had an experience. It seemed to me to be a mini-miracle.

I described it to Father Sasges.

"I re-experienced Christmas Day, 1958. I was 15 months old, enjoying my gifts, especially the twin dolls[19] my parents gave me in anticipation of the twin babies soon to be born. I felt the shape of the doll cradled in my arms and the little bottle I held to feed the dolly. I felt the 'puddle-duck' PJs and my bathrobe tied around my waist.

"I named both dolls 'Jesus' because everywhere I looked there was Baby Jesus: on Christmas cards, pictures in books and of course the Nativity figurines near the Christmas tree. I took good care of the baby dolls because I loved Jesus. Feed, wash, dress, wrap, carry, sing.

"I heard my Mother calling, so I needed to put the Baby down. I looked for the right place to let Him rest and sleep. Mary put her Baby in a manger. My Mother told me that a manger was a warm box where the food comes from... so I put my baby there, too.

"First, I put the doll on a kitchen chair. Then, I reached up to the oven door handle, gave a mighty pull to open the oven door, and laid the Baby safely inside. Then I trotted to my Mother.

"Frozen in time, I could see the scene. I understand the sacred moment I had at such an early age. Then, I was given a new experience, a message to shield me. 'Little Eleanor, we see what you are doing. We know what is in your heart. We will always be near you to Guide and Protect you. You can trust this part of your Self that wants to serve the Lord. Never let anyone take it away from you. It is authentic. Soon you will hear a loud voice. The other people do not understand what you did. It will seem to them that you have done a harmful thing. But you know and we know that it was a sacred act of worship: serving the Lord Jesus.' I didn't see who spoke, but I think, since I was caring for Baby Jesus, that it was Mary and Joseph."

Father Sasges was silent. Looking intently into my face. "A Gift!" he whispered.

"Yes," I held his gaze. "And it changes my entire life story. Then my Mother turned the oven on, the doll melted and my Daddy yelled at me. To him the dolls represented his unborn sons! To him is seemed horrifying that I could plot their murder! Or was I so early showing signs of insanity? He reminded me and asked me about this incident as I grew up, never letting it be still.

"But now I can see three things:

"First: my actions were authentic (because they could not have been coached or copied).

"Second: my actions were a kind of holy act. I wanted to participate in the story.

"Third: my Dad's interpretation of my actions caused him to mistrust me and hold the possibility that I was crazy. Of course, he was alarmed when the doll melted. He was doing what any parent would do. He didn't do anything to hurt me on purpose. But, it still did damage."

"So, you can forgive your Dad?" Father leaned forward, watching my face.

"Oh, yes, right away!" I reply and hurry to add another new awareness. "And, here's the thing: When Jesus was on the Cross and He said, 'Father, forgive them for they know not what they do.'[61] I always thought that He was talking about the soldiers who were doing their gruesome task at the execution. But, now I think that He meant everyone, all of us, even my Dad, even me. Daddy didn't think to himself, 'I am going to damage my daughter.' I didn't get up in the morning and decide to damage my own children! But, we do things we don't understand. We can't see the future consequences. We don't know until later that we did a 'bad' thing."

"To be continued," Father looked at the clock and prompted me to head for home.

I had a lot to think about as I drove home.

I felt forgiveness pouring like a fountain on generations of my family. "Father, forgive them, they don't know what they're doing." Opa's Dad didn't know how damaging his drunken actions were. He beat on his wife. He beat on his son. Opa ran away to sleep in the neighbour's barn, vowing not to do the same. Opa provided a much more stable home than he had as a child, yet, his strict discipline and lack of experience as a husband and father brought some unhappy interactions with his wife and children. But, he didn't know any better. He did the best he could with the limited example he had as a child.

My Mother didn't set out to break up with my Dad, what ever painful childhood messages she had, she remained steady during many stormy years. She gave us a better childhood than she had. And then there's my Dad. To get what he wanted, he made an exit. He didn't know that his voice would echo inside me for decades, 'What is *wrong* with you?'

Now I live my role as 'Wife' and 'Mother.' I act and decide and impact my husband and children. I have done harm. It happens so fast. It cannot be undone. I 'know not what I do.' I beg to be forgiven.

In the heat of the moment, and filled with 'The Original Sin' of 'Me First' a person cannot see how a tiny turning point will lead to a very different, damaging outcome.

The reaction my Dad had to 'The Doll in the Oven' and 'The Day on the Cliff' has impacted me throughout my life.

My reaction has been, 'Since *you* think this bad thing about *me*, then I have to prove that I am so good and so smart.' It also caused the beginning of this lifelong pattern that I do not trust my own inner 'Self'.

This caused a huge divide deep inside me that left an insurmountable gap that has been confusing and painful.

A little child thinks, 'My Daddy, can't be wrong, so I must have been wrong. I thought I was doing something good but he says it was terrible and bad.' This leaves me damaged as to my own judgment and perception and self-awareness.

Now I see that when I put the doll in the oven, it was authentic. I am so relieved and grateful to have this motivation identified, located, and the damage rooted out. It was never true that I was evil or crazy. Those messages cannot ever be entangled inside me anymore.

The Lord also showed me that I have not been wandering, lost, abandoned, but always led, provided for, protected, guided. He has sent teachers and kept my eager, listening heart open.

The Father created me, so I can trust Him.
There is an 'Eleanor' He intended and planned for.
He wants me to return to Him and not turn away.
The Son is available to me in the Word,
the Tabernacle, the Eucharist.
He can bear fruit through my hands and voice and actions.
He calls me, leads me, knows me.
He is my Teacher, Shepherd and I can trust Him.
The Holy Spirit is my Comforter,
Guide, prompting, available, a quiet calm voice within.
He is drawing me towards wholeness.

'Come to Me all who labour and are heavy laden and I will give you rest.' Matthew 11:28

REFLECTIONS

> Shame needs three things to grow exponentially in your life: secrecy, silence, and judgment. Shame cannot survive expression, empathy, and compassion.
>
> —*Brené Brown*

Chapter 10
Wednesday, January 11, 2012
One Husband: Kevin

I learned this at least from my experiment:
That if one advances confidently in the direction of his dreams,
and endeavours to live the life which he has imagined,
he will meet with success unexpected in common hours.
—*Henry David Thoreau*

* ** *** ****

4:52am

The red digital numbers read 4:52 as I reach to press the button to shut the alarm clock off before it blasts the annoying beep-beep-beep.

Now I have eight minutes to nestle in quiet and cozy to plan my day. This is the very last time I will have to get up at 5:00am. What bliss it will be to sleep until Natures cycles awaken me.

What bliss it will be when there is no need for a clock to pierce the winter darkness and force me from my warm cocoon.

The routine today will be like many others. Feed the fire. Prepare the meals. Wash the dishes. Look after the animals.

But tomorrow: Hurrah! A new chapter will begin. And, Dear Lord in Heaven, Please let it be a long one. Just the two of us, working towards our lifelong dream: 'Back-to-the-Land' in our little log house, on our riverside property, in the snowy mountains of British Columbia, Canada.

"Kevin, it's morning. Today is the day!" I gently nudge and quietly speak.

I slide out from under the down duvet, reach for my down-filled housecoat, step into my comfy slippers and move down the stairs. I pause to peek into the wood stove, call the dog to come outside while I bring in an armload of wood. The bed of coals is deep and glowing orange. No need to wait and watch and blow to be sure the flames will feast on the new birch logs. It feels so good to be warm even after the fire has been burning for five hours.

Thankful for the electric heater in the bathroom, I also plug in the electric heater in the kitchen, just to chase away the morning chill while I make Kevin's breakfast and lunch. Every day I am thankful for electricity that brings me light, hot water and cooking. After those first five years of lighting with candles, or a flashlight, or a kerosene lamp, now the brightness in every room is a wonder. After those first five years of carrying water in buckets, going to the laundry mat, dashing to the outhouse, now the convenience of running water is a luxury. After those first five years of isolation, now the telephone is my favourite thing about moving back to modern living.

We have kept many features of the 'Back-to-the-Land' lifestyle, though. We still heat with wood. We still grow a vegetable garden, preserve food in the freezer, root cellar and pantry to supply our winter meals. Feeding a family of six people is no small feat. We have two full-sized chest freezers loaded with garden produce as well as home-grown chickens, ducks, rabbits, pork and also venison and bear.

By the time he smells the toast browning, Kevin prys himself out of slumber, heads downstairs, dresses in his work clothes and comes to the table. I have everything ready. Onto his warm plate I scoop up a golden mound of freshly gathered scrambled eggs, arrange toasted home baked bread thickly layered with homegrown raspberry jam. In his gray metal lunch box are a pair of home made molasses bran muffins, locally grown roast beef is in the sandwich, carrots from the root cellar and a wedge of rhubarb pie.

"Is this a dream?" I croon as I hand him the plate. "It took a long time, but this is exactly what we were hoping for when we first came out west. 33 years. What a long time ago."

"It's a lot of miles of track. A lot of hammering spikes. A lot of cold and wet and mosquitoes and fighting fire and midnight emergencies and always wearing hot, heavy safety gear," he measures the years.

"I wish the kids were here to celebrate this day with us," I muse as I sip my mint tea. In so many ways their lives were shaped as they learned skills, observed our decisions, participated in this lifestyle. How many times they have helped in the garden, taken a place in the kitchen food production, picked out school clothes at the Thrift Store, made Christmas cards, practiced stunts for my Mother's Day Circus, accepted homemade birthday gifts and Halloween costumes. How many times have they heard their Dad go off into the winter dark, returning with frost on his beard, or come home from the fierce summer heat, sweat washing the soot off his face. "I think they'd like to know that you made it to the finish line. I think they'd be proud of your accomplishments."

But, they are all far away. Grown. Graduated. Married. They are just beginning the long line of years to push uphill to pay the mortgage, furnish and repair the house, make decisions about raising a family, prepare a zillion meals, provide family customs. "Kevin! Our youngest child is older now than we were when we started!" The courtship, the wedding, the VW van outfitted as a camper, the trip out west from our childhood homes in Ontario to these rugged mountains, finding land, building the little log cabin, that first winter of hardship, the years of ever increasing stability, the parenting, the community service... it has been a wonderful life. Our four children have set out to make their own decisions, different from ours, but just as ambitious.

"We lived our dreams. They have to reach for theirs." Kevin always has to help me focus on the big picture, when, as a Mom, I want them all nearby.

Yes, we certainly have lived our dreams! After five years and two babies out on the homestead in our first cabin, we moved into the town of Avola so our kids could go to school. But that was the year the elementary school closed. Homeschooling became a way of life.

After three years in town, Mr. and Mrs. Gibson offered us their land! And so, we continued our 'Back-to-the-Land' lifestyle on their two-and-a-half acres beside the river. Wood heat, gravity feed water, rich soil in the garden supplied an abundance of fruits and vegetables filling cellar, freezer and pantry. This was the life we dreamed of 33 years ago. This is the reality now.

It has been eight years since the youngest left for school. I am getting accustomed to the 'Empty Nest' which has brought not only the sadness of no longer having my children nearby, but has also brought many benefits I wasn't expecting.

But, today will be my last day of staying home alone. Tomorrow my husband will be here with me!

5:45am

As Kevin gears up for his last day of work on the railroad, I sigh. Both anxiety and gladness fill my heart. I hate to see him go out into the cold, focus on the highway, stay alert to safety while he works. I count the hours until I can expect him home safe. I am so very glad that this day has finally come: Today Kevin will be retired!

"I love you. Be safe. Come home."

"I always do."

He starts the engine, unplugs the block heater, sweeps the snow from the truck, stomps back inside for another kiss, and then, he's off. It takes one hour to drive to the Tool House in Clearwater, then the eight hour work day and the last one hour drive to come home. If everything runs smoothly, I'll see him at 4:00 this afternoon.

I go to the kitchen window to blow kisses as he rounds the bend and vanishes into the snowy darkness.

How shall I mark this day? For 33 years I have kissed my husband good-bye, never knowing if he will return safe and sound. Rivers flood, rocks slide, trees come crashing down, grass catches fire, frost heaves, tracks buckle, bears, moose, cougars, coyotes, de-railments, faulty equipment, dragging chains, the crack of a cable snapping, highway hazards, washouts, ice jams, mud slides, extreme cold, extreme heat, extremely long days to rebuild after derailments... and then the potential hazards of chemicals, fuel or cargo spills... all of this he has faced, all of this could have cost life or limb.

I watch the clock as I move about my morning routines, always a little anxious, yet, I can hear his voice on the radio scanner as he calls off the landmarks as he makes his way south. “I have reached my destination,” he announces and I begin to relax.

7:00am

Now I have my reading time. It will be pitch black until 7:30 when Max, the dog, my faithful personal trainer, will pace and whine and tell me 'It is time to go jogging.'

I reach into a box of treasures and pull out my Journal from that first year in the cabin. How much is the same? How much has changed?

I feel like we have each and 'Twogether' walked along the Path of the 'Hero's Journey.' Young. Determined. Idealistic. We had a dream. How would we cope when difficulties arose? How would old childhood hurts influence each of us? Would our words and interactions hurt or heal? How would we nurture and protect each other during illness, disappointments and grief? Would our World View be enough to weather life's storms? As the kaleidoscope of circumstances shifts, would we be able to chart our course towards our goals? Or abandon each other when the going got tough?

“I want to get married, go out west, build a log cabin, have a bunch of kids, teach them about the Lord, volunteer in my community, and then write a book about it.” I constantly remember that as a young bride, this was my pledge.

The central resource we seem to always circle back to is: Trust.

I feel like the wealthiest woman in the world with this underlying Trust.

Looking back at the photos of Kevin and I, twenty years old, one month married, loading up in our VW van in 1978, I can see that we have indeed continued to aim for the same goals.

I see that the stability, however winding the Path, whatever other choices I could have made, the sacrifices and endurance were worth it. He is a Champion. Some get a medal. Some have their name on a plaque. Some make that first million. Some see their name in lights.

I am a Champion, too.

I am still wearing my wedding ring.

* ** *** ****

Journal entry
January 31, 1979

Before this whole month slips away, I need to record the progress and changes we have come through.

Christmas brought us 'home' to the McRae family for a happy day together, then they all came down to visit us on December 26th. It was a wonderful thing to have guests in our own home. We nibbled on the goodies from Kevin's Mom and had tea.

The next day the weather changed very cold and it proved to be my last day to work at the restaurant. On the 28th the temperature was so low that the van wouldn't even begin to turn over. So my worries became realities sooner than I expected!

The weather stayed very bitter (-40°C) for three weeks! During this time we kept the fire going all night by getting up every one-and-a-half hours to refuel! My last pay cheque was carefully budgeted. We planned to buy food to last one month – but it looks like it will easily be two.

Kevin spent a long hard day at cutting birch with the hand saw during the cold while Howard's chainsaw was being repaired. He ended up sick for five days. The wood was then my responsibility and I learned how hard I could work. Wood hasn't ended up to be too much of a problem. In two days we can cut enough to last about a week – that's hand cutting. Also, Red McRae brought two loads of mill end lumber. That has helped a lot. Kevin got to borrow Howard's chainsaw at last (Sunday, January 28th) so we're in good supply for awhile.

Finally, on the 18th our VW van was started. Warm weather, recharging the battery and some friendly persuasion got the old dear running for one last trip to Kamloops. It only sold for $100 but that covered the cost of the parts for the jeep that Kevin is hoping to fix up, a wrist watch, a root cellar book and the bus ticket back to Avola.

While Kevin was in Kamloops, I stayed in Avola and as always enjoyed my visit with Fran and Archie, Cheryl and the kids. Bonnie and Jack have remembered the songs I taught them in August – and I haven't been there to sing with them since Christmas! We have had some nice times with Annika and Karl also, New Year's Eve party and dinner the next day. We celebrated living one month in our new house with a tea party here with Grant, too. They have given us rides to Clearwater and Avola occasionally, although Kevin has hitch-hiked more often.

Progress has been made in our new home and our skills since we moved in on December 22nd Wow! We have a second wood stove from Howard all hooked up. Annika gave me an old shelf to use as a kitchen cupboard. Our table is built from the wood under the bed in the van. Kevin has built himself a desk from the mill ends Red brought and also a wood box, and most beautiful of all: a corner shelf where the Word, sacred books, reference books and lovely seven branch candle stick are in the eastern corner.

I have become quite handy with the splitting maul, although not always confident. My fire lighting skills have much improved and I have learned a lot about baking through trials and some errors. Granola, bread, cookies, bran muffins, cake, casseroles, baked beans, cornbread, and yeast bread have delighted our tongues and tummies.

Kevin has almost completed work on the out house and built a fast and fine little sled for hauling about three armloads of wood. He has greatly improved his skills with pen and ink, water colours and the birthday present I couldn't resist giving him just now: oil pastels. Our other project together has been reading out loud from the Word. Starting with Genesis we were both pretty familiar with the stories until we got to I Samuel. We completed II Kings this afternoon!

Our feelings and attitudes have changed a lot this month, too – from depression, frustration and almost giving up (over no job) to joy in this short time we have together to share, learn and enjoy. Now we wait hopefully and patiently for the next necessary step.

* ** *** ****

I can see it all!

I can also see gaps between how I really felt and what I wrote. I tried to smooth over the fear and doubts, the unending battle with the cold, the anxiety about 'what's next,' the pain of isolation and lack of friends.

The first gap that I didn't write about in this Journal entry is the new wood stove that Howard brought. He brought some lengths of chimney, but there was a piece missing. We needed a piece to adapt from six inch in diameter to seven inch pipe. So, the high hopes of New Year's Eve were dashed the next day when we tried to assemble it. Without transportation or any more cash, when would we ever be able to install this heater? What a big difference it would make with the larger wood box, four times larger than the cook stove we were using. Kevin had to hitchhike up to Avola, ask Fran for some work he could do for pay, hitch a ride all the way down to Clearwater to the hardware store, buy the missing piece, then install the chimney. But what an improvement! Now, the larger firebox held more and larger pieces of wood. We could sleep for about four hours before feeding the fire. Bliss!

My fragile, stormy, easily confused feelings were too difficult to write about at the time, too. As they say, 'The honeymoon was over.' Ideals and dreams had met the harsh reality of the Canadian winter. I wanted to be brave, to trust the Lord, my husband and my own decisions, but there is never any guarantee. During the early part of our marriage, I wanted to be like Ma in Laura Ingalls Wilder's 'Little House' books. I wanted to say quietly, 'What ever you think best, Charles,' just like she said to her husband. But really, I was clenching my mouth shut, lonely, hungry, slowly, slowly counting the days until... until what? What could improve our situation? Warm weather was sure to return. But what good would that do with no transportation? And we won't have transportation until we have money. And we won't have money until Kevin gets a job. And he can't get to a job without transportation. What a labyrinth!

Those short winter days and long January nights of bitter cold in 1979, to save kerosene, we decided to stay in bed until daylight (7:30-8:00am), to eat only two meals a day, to go back to bed at 4:30pm when it got dark. It was almost like solitary confinement to have such restrictions. The monotony of melting snow for water and going into the forest with the hand saw to cut more wood was like a heavy weight. All of the effort made no real improvement. The inside of the cabin never went above freezing, no matter how hot the fire snapped and crackled. 40° below was just too powerful.

And then there was the day when hope resurfaced! The temperature rose to only -15°C. Kevin could start the van! I waited to see what he would decide: keep it, return to the possibility of transportation: people, money, resources, food? Or sell it: for how much, to buy what?

The day he drove away to Kamloops to sell it, I had to try to keep my mind from racing ahead. "Maybe $1000? Maybe $500? We'll have money for food, to pay for gas when we ask for a ride, to start saving for another vehicle. Maybe I should have gone with him to oversee the purchases? But, I trusted him. He could see the priorities.

I did not write about how disappointed I was when he returned. A bus ticket! A book! A watch! No food! No cash! Our only link to town was gone.

Of course, Kevin had high hopes for the old yellow Jeep he had traded for back in September. Maybe the parts he brought home would make it run again? But, no.

Time moves so slowly when there are no people, no obligations, no resources, no plans, no telephone, no television. 'What can I do with what I have?' became my motto. Of course there were the chores: wood and water, water and wood. There were the boxes of books to read, as long as it was light enough to see. There was the radio, as long as the batteries would last. Kevin watched the wind-up clock so he could turn on the news and hear the weather report. We both looked forward to the evening radio play called 'Sears Radio Theatre' on the Seattle radio station KIRO. To keep up our spirits, we started the custom of playing a game of dominoes after supper. The winner got to stay in bed in the morning while the loser had to get the fire going, scoop the snow and boil the water for oatmeal. We also read the Bible aloud to each other.

But, we made it through that first, terrible January, 1979. Eventually spring did return. Time brought employment, income, another vehicle and children; everything we dreamed of. Wonderful chapters. Sweet memories.

From the start, Kevin made a special word for us: 'Twogether.'

In the spring of 1979, Kevin and I were like the birds and animals and even insects awaking from winter dormancy. Kevin found work. I stayed home alone in the cabin. It was so quiet I could hear the ants gnawing on the hollow core of the cedar logs. I had to sweep up little pyramids of sawdust every day. One day a spider dropped to the table in front of me. I overturned a glass jar to capture it. A second spider! Again I captured it. It was fascinating and repulsive at the same time to watch them challenge each other, circle and gesture, each one daring the other to a duel. When Kevin came home, we watched them. I knew that larger birds and animals face-off and compete for territory. But I had no idea that even spiders quarrel and vie for dominance. After that, when Kevin and I felt grumpy with each other we would break the tension with laughter by saying 'Spiders-in-a-Jar' to signal a truce. Surely we have more brains than a spider and can solve the problem.

Our situation became stable. By the following January, Kevin had work and we had a vehicle, I was pregnant. Our only daughter was born in the summertime. When winter came again, although we had spent the summer building a warmer house, it was not finished and I realized that the cabin would not be a place to have an infant, so I travelled back to Ontario with her for the winter months of 1980-81.

Before babies, I was able to volunteer regularly in the Avola school. 1982 brought a winter-born son. In 1983, I started a 'Moms and Tots' playschool group.

Somehow I realized that, 'What ever you think best, Charles' was not the method of marriage that I wanted to live by. It was not helpful to always 'agree' and never speak up with my own observations, suggestions and questions. If I didn't let Kevin know what I was thinking and feeling, or doubtful, or confident about, how could he ever know who 'I' am? Although I felt anxious that my Mother's independence seemed like part of the cause of my parents' break-up, I began to carefully explore new territory, expressing differing opinions. And, mostly, Kevin liked it! He didn't want to be married to a picture of me! He wanted to know 'Me.' I didn't want to be in competition with him, like I was with my brothers. We encouraged each other to excel in our various activities, congratulated each other when new opportunities arrived and shared information about our friendships, employment, volunteering and interests.

We moved into Avola in 1984 and the five years of isolation were over. Propane cook stove and hot water tank! Washing machine and telephone! Indoor plumbing and a refrigerator! However, I was dead set against having a television!

Kevin did a lot of bartering. Furniture and rides to town, truck repairs and firewood, snow shoveling and errands were a kind of currency with our neighbours, especially the elderly. Kevin helped a fellow build his wood shed. In trade, he came home with a small black and white TV. I was furious. I bundled up the kids and went outside to play in the snow. I didn't want it!

A few minutes later, quietly, a little timidly, Kevin called to me from the doorway. "I think I should tell you: 'The Wizard of Oz' is just starting."

I was inside and glued to the tube in a blink of an eye!

For ten years, Kevin worked alone all night, patrolling the railroad tracks, watching for rock slides or any other danger before the passenger train came through. He left about 10:30pm and came home just after 7:00am. We laughed, although it wasn't funny, at how many times the rain came pouring down just as he tied his boots to leave. One man in the wilderness on a tricycle pedaling along the train tracks in the dark, no matter the season or weather, I tried not to think about it!

I tried to provide a warm nest to return to, a welcoming voice, listen to his adventures, appreciate his difficulties, respect his character qualities, and make good food. 'The way to a man's heart is through his stomach,' was an old saying. 'Kissin' don't last. Cookin' do' was a Mennonite favourite.

Since we lived in town, vendors sometimes came door-to-door. Encyclopedia? Vacuum cleaners? Life insurance? Cleaning products? Make-up? Frozen prepared foods? The only one I was eager to do business with was the Fruit Truck! Cherries! Peaches! Pears! Plums!

I discovered, while nursing Michael in the wee hours of the morning, that 'The Waltons' was on TV at 2:00am! I had something 'just for me' to look forward to! And, when I bought 60 pounds of cherries to preserve, I realized that it would be tricky to do all of that work with the children interrupting. I had a reason to be up from 2:00am until morning: pitting cherries.

And, so it was, that Kevin came home one morning at dawn, just precisely as I was bending to slide five cherry pies out of the oven!

"Shh! I will give you pie for breakfast if you don't wake the children!"

"I could smell this marvelous aroma as I came walking home... but I didn't dare hope," he whispered to me as he sat down to the feast. I can still remember his smile and the look in his eyes! It was a once-in-a-lifetime Golden Moment. Twogether.

Two more sons arrived. The move to the Old Gibson place brought us to our final home location. Now the years were filled with children's activities, gardening for our food, exploring the mountains, meeting people and volunteering. Our dream was richly, abundantly, happily coming true. Each little decision, each opportunity, each friendship, each new skill and expression of artistic talent had such satisfaction, always against the backdrop of that first solitary, cold, despairing winter.

The Church School in Pennsylvania looked attractive. We sent the first, then the second high school student. When our children began to leave home, I was filled with dread. What if the lonely winters come back to weigh me down?

When it was time for the younger two sons to leave for the Church School in 2004, I hit a very deep depression. I just couldn't see any other life than 'Wife and Mother.' With all four children grown and gone and Kevin gone to work all day, there just didn't seem to be any gladness in only the 'Wife' role.

I went to New York City to be the Nanny for my brother for the winter of 2005-06. Children! Outings! Learning! People!

When the year was up and I came back to the mountains, I had a few hours of employment each week as a Nanny and Parent Educator. Then I started a weekly newsletter and volunteered with the Girl Guides and Brownies. My contact with Father Sasges brought new, rich meaning to my Life Journey, a daily prayer routine, the televised Mass to learn from, the 'Sense of Belonging' that is so crucial to a satisfying life.

All of this winding path lead me to a lot of soul searching. What is my purpose if it is not to be a Mother? How is it possible that what I love to do most and have become very skilled at doing is gone after 'only' 24 years? The years to wait until Kevin retired seemed very empty. And, when we finally reached the goal of 'Retirement,' would we end up as 'Spiders-in-a-Jar'? Tension? Companionship?

I didn't know much about getting older. I observed my parents. Each seemed so much more comfortable in their second marriage. Dad and Shirley had charming little interactions in their home, enjoyed outings in the city, experienced trips to Italy and Greece, England and holiday resorts in the USA. They seemed so glad to spend time together.

Mother and Papa-Joe went boating, to baseball games, played Bridge, went to church. He took her to Scotland and Alaska, into the mountains on old-time narrow gauge railroad train tours, and they visited their grandchildren. They seem so content together. When they came to visit us or we went to visit them I noticed a satisfaction I had never sensed between my parents.

I wondered, "Now that we have made it through the rather stressful first 30 years of marriage, could I have this second comfortable relationship with my same husband?"

But today... TODAY... at last... a new chapter will begin. I won't be alone all day anymore. My husband, my friend, my partner will be with me day and night.

7:30am

Look at the time. Max is pacing. My trusty dog never lets me forget to get up and go at precisely 7:30 each morning. I pull on my felt-pack winter boots, zip up my parka, mittens, scarf, hood. Yes, I bundle up to go for my daily jog. It keeps those Christmas pounds from staying around for long.

I like to keep regular habits, that way I can fit things together in the day, both necessities and enjoyable hobbies. While I trot along, I let my mind scan over the years, recall the other Januarys, celebrate the realization of the marriage vows that have kept my husband and I on course for all of this time. It's quite a story we have written Twogether.

Sometimes, while jogging, I have a flash of an idea. Yes! I know how I want to mark this 'Now I'm Retired' day. Actually, it is a double idea.

First, I will celebrate and congratulate by setting out a memento reminding Kevin of each of his children. Also, a mysterious parcel has arrived in the mail from our children. I saved it for him to open on the actual First Day of Retirement.

Second: When I first woke him up, I said, "Don't you think it would be a marvelous celebration of this day if we put the alarm clock in front of the tire and crush it?" But, Kevin's sensible logic didn't think it was so funny. However, with a camera, I could stage multiple scenarios: 'Destruction of the Alarm Clock!'

8:15am

After my jog and the chickens and dog are fed and watered and I fill up the wood box on the porch, I'm done outside for awhile. I like to eat breakfast after my jog, so I wash the dishes from last night while my eggs boil. Soft boiled eggs and toast is my favourite breakfast.

A pretty table setting will be part of our celebration. First, the red and white checkered table cloth I've had since our wedding, then the dishes reserved for holidays: the white plates with blue rim, red hearts and green curly ribbons.

I will make a display on the cedar chest. First, the parcels: one from our children, one from me. Now for the momentoes from the children.

It's easy to find the card Kevin made for Baby Elise while were in Ontario. I remember how heartbreaking that winter was. I was warm and well provided for, but I missed my husband. My parents were splitting up and my siblings all had to get packed and move out. This card was like a life raft for me to cling to. Hope. We had a stable marriage, although our cabin was too cold for the Baby. Today, this hand-drawn card will be the centrepiece. He wrote it as a pledge for the future. Now it is his lifetime achievement award.

Precious ... Lady...

A father to be true must
be a priest and a doctor,
a teacher and a farmer, but mind,
I could be none of these
without your mother.

Much Love,
Your Father, Kevin

Next, a framed portrait of Michael skiing on the mountain top is to remember the helicopter ride Dad and Lad took together to help a mountain guide set up his cabin. Harold, Kevin's Dad, passed along outdoor skills to Kevin. Over the years, Kevin deliberately gave his sons instruction and experiences in the mountains.

What to bring to the collection to connect the heart with Nicholas? His birth was especially memorable because my Mother was in attendance, shortly after she had been with Oma as she passed away. I dug into a box of memories and found the tiny white baptism gown I made for him so long ago.

The youngest, Toby, arrived when our family was actively pursuing the homeschooling lifestyle, gardening and volunteering. We were an active bunch. One day, Kevin left the family to attend to an emergency on the railroad. When little Toby asked questions to try to understand Kevin's activities, we brainstormed and I wrote down a list of Kevin's roles.

Husband, father, brother, friend.
Railroad worker, truck driver, fire fighter.
Mountain guide, snow mobile operator, host.

Mechanic, carpenter, plumber.
Gardener, hunter, butcher.
First Aid attendant, Highway Rescue, Search and Rescue.
Ham radio, computer, geo-cache, GPS.
Water Board, Cemetery Board, Parks Board.
Machine operator, inventor, maintenance.
Journeyman Tracker, First Aid Instructor, Search Manager.

With careful lettering, I make Kevin a card with one of my favourite quotes.

> Whatever you can do,
> or dream you can,
> begin it.
> Boldness has genius,
> power and magic in it.
> —*Johann Wolfgang von Goethe*

Yes, this display will be a suitable tribute to this amazingly talented and dedicated man.

9:00am

Now, for the second project: 'Destruction of the Alarm Clock!' I already have a list of ideas. The little digital camera I have will display the pictures on the computer screen so we can laugh and laugh. I'll start inside. I make a tag with red numbers '5:00' and tape it onto the dreaded alarm clock! Quickly I move from one idea to the next: fill the washing machine with billows of soapy foam (snap a picture as if I was tossing the alarm clock in to gyrate and spin), close to the water (what if I flushed it down the toilet?). Into the kitchen, I place the alarm clock on the cutting board (butcher knife at the ready), boil in the crock-pot, spin in the blender, destroy it in the firey wood stove. Outdoors now, I lean the shot gun up against a stump and place the alarm clock in front of the bull's eye. In the driveway, I lay the clock down just where the tire will crush it, bury it in a snow bank, mash it under my boot, shatter it with the axe, send it out with the trash. With no sounds of approaching engines, I step for a moment onto the train tracks.

There's one more place I'd like to go: up on the highway bridge. There's a sidewalk. I'll be safe. What a dramatic view: dropping the alarm clock from this height into the icy river below.

With a gleeful chuckle I return down from the bridge hill.

10:20am

And, what's this? A truck is approaching! Out of the passenger side I can see: Kevin! Quickly, I refocus the camera and 'snap!' the actual moment of retirement is captured. It is 10:20am! Kevin is FREE!

I feel like I've been holding my breath! Kevin is HOME! I am so happy I don't know what to do. 33 years and no significant injuries. I just keep looking at him, touching him, listening to his happy voice. Kevin is HERE!

"The guys took me out for breakfast. We didn't even go to work. They all signed a card!" Kevin is overflowing with the story of his last day. "I put my keys in the middle of the table and said, 'There's just one problem. I need a ride home,' since I've been driving the company truck." I wait for the rest of the story. "I'll take you home, 'Old Timer'... He called me 'Old Timer!' But I guess that's true. Those new guys will have to figure it out now!"

Kevin reaches into a pocket. "Look! They pitched in cash and gave me a gift card for outdoor equipment!" And that was just the start. An envelope from our children holds another gift certificate. The parcel from them is a pair of Bushnell binoculars, something Kevin has always wanted to own.

"Wow! That goes with the telescope you bought recently!" I congratulate him.

"What are you going to do with all that money?" I am curious.

"I've been looking at possibly improving our sound system with a Bose speaker," he replies, "and an Ipod." Wow! We never had those back in 1978!

"There's one more present," I have a twinkle in my eye now. I made a long strip of adding machine paper to count down the days 55 – 54 – 53 – 52 until 0 when he can open it. Kevin unwraps it and laughs out loud. It's a clock, but all of the numbers have spilled and scattered randomly along the bottom. "It's to celebrate that for 33 years your life has been governed by the clock. Now you don't even have to wear a watch!"

I show him the alarm clock destruction photos. We just keep talking and laughing and recounting the funny details.

Now we are right back where we started. January. Twogether. But now, instead of dreaming of what lies ahead, we have the satisfaction of achieving our goals. Hurrah!

"Kevin! I feel like I want to plant a flag on the top of the mountain!" I speak boldly and gesture with a stance.

"Do you know what? I just had an idea," I sit down face-to-face, intently making eye contact with my husband. "We have something right now that neither of our parents ever had! Your Dad died before retirement and my parents divorced. We made it! We made it from sixteen-years-old until today: still married. You made it through 33 years with no injuries!" Up again, I cannot contain my overflowing joy. "I don't know what to do! I'm so happy!"

All these years, I have been like a kite flitting this way and that. All these years he has been the steady reliable one, feet firmly planted on the ground. If I did not have him, I would be just a stray piece of paper, blown into a tree. If he did not have me, he'd be standing there, still, all alone.

5:00pm

Supper is a significant satisfaction. Garden harvest, 'Back-to-the-Land' abundance, with the addition of plentiful store-bought supplies too. It is wonderful to know that his retirement income will also be steady.

"Dear Lord in Heaven, Please protect us as we continue the Journey."

9:00pm

As we snuggle down under our hand-stitched quilt, a quieter kind of happiness fills my heart. Kevin knows all of my stories, the places I've lived, my people, my hurts, my talents, my flaws. I am still learning about him. We will never run out of things to talk about and do together. This new chapter will bring unexplored opportunities and bright adventures.

"Kevin?" I am feeling nostalgic, "Today I was reading pages of my Journal from 1978-79... remembering that first bitter cold January. Here's a part I want to read to you. 'As I looked into his eyes I could see the future: children, well stocked pantry and root cellar, rows of jars of jam, herbs and onions hanging, freezer full of garden produce, Christmas tree, reading aloud, singing, outings with children.' Now I can write the mirror image of that day. 'As I looked into his eyes I could see the past:

babies, outings, work to develop the land, volunteer projects, educational activities, trips.' We've had a pretty good life. Maybe I will finish writing that book I keep talking about. We have had a lot of Januarys!" I muse as I switch off the light.

"Kevin? We have a future together now, too, don't we?"

"We most certainly do!" His voice is warm and gentle.

"Will we travel? Make new goals? Do you have a 'Wish List'? I'm a little disoriented without the same routine and priorities we have had for so long. Is everything significant in the past?" I hesitate.

"I will be right here. This is where we live. This is our home. We are still Twogether." It seems like I've heard him say these words before.

"Kevin?"

"hmmm?"

"I'm so glad I found you."

"Me, too."

"You know what?"

"What?"

"'One' is my favourite number!"

"Why is that?"

"It is the number of husbands I have had!"

I hear his little chuckle.

"Kevin?"

"hmmm?"

"I think I just made a new word for us!"

"And what would that be?"

"Twomorrow!"

"That's a good thing."

REFLECTIONS

The Mission of My Life

God has created me to do Him some definite service. He has committed some work to me which He has not committed to another. I have my mission. I may never know it in this life, but I shall be told it in the next. I am a link in a chain, a bond of connection between persons. He has not created me for naught. I shall do good; I shall do His work. I shall be an angel of peace, a preacher of truth in my own place, while not intending it if I do but keep His commandments. Therefore, I will trust Him, whatever I am, I can never be thrown away. If I am in sickness, my sickness may serve Him, in perplexity, my perplexity may serve Him. If I am in sorrow, my sorrow may serve Him. He does nothing in vain. He knows what He is about. He may take away my friends. He may throw me among strangers. He may make me feel desolate, make my spirits sink, hide my future from me. Still, He knows what He is about.

—Cardinal Henry Neuman

* ** *** ****

If you enjoyed *10 Days in January*
...1 Husband, 2 Brothers, 3 Sons, 4 Dads...
watch for future titles Eleanor Deckert is working on:

10 Days in February ...I'd rather be someplace else...

10 Days in March ...and then I'll volunteer...

10 Days in April ...high hopes and a detour with cancer...

10 Days in May ...plant, nurture, wait...

10 Days in June ...one thousand dollars...

10 Days in July ...first fruits...

10 Days in August ...so many times 'good-bye'...

10 Days in September ...learning...teaching...

10 Days in October ...glad, sad, mad, scared...

10 Days in November ...maiden, sister, mother, crone...

Titles currently available through Author's web page:
www.eleanordeckert.com
also at Chapters-Indigo stores
or order directly from Friesen Press:

10 Days in December ...where dreams meet reality...

Endnotes

[1] Bible verses quoted: Psalm 11:4, Zechariah 2:13, Psalm 95:6, Psalm 27:4, Matthew 6: 9-13.

[2] Judges 16:4-30.

[3] Source unknown.

[4] More will be told of Little Eleanor in future title "10 Days in November" by Eleanor Deckert.

[5] 'Happenings in our Home' Grammie's journal.

[6] William Penn was granted a huge tract of land in 1681 by King Charles II of England. A Quaker and pacifist, Penn governed his colony with religious tolerance. Persecuted sects established religions communities to live, worship and educate their children in Pennsylvania.

[7] Lennart Nilsson's photos of life within the womb. 1965 Time Life Magazine.

[8] 'America the Beautiful' lyrics by Kathrine Lee Bates first published in 1895.

[9] This is an old campfire song of unknown origin. 'The New Song Fest' compiled by Dick and Beth Best.

[10] 'The First Lord's Song' from HMS Pinafore, by Gilbert and Sullivan.

[11] An American folk song of uncertain origin.

[12] Elizabeth Cecilia Clephane 1868.

[13] USA Patriotic song, Lyrics by Samuel Francis Smith, 1831. Melody the same as UK's 'God Save the Queen.'

[14] 'Farewell to Shady Glade' Copyright 1966 by William Peet, Houghton Mifflin Co. Boston.

[15] Old Dutch nursery rhymes Hardcover – 1917 by H. Willebeek Le Mair.

[16] Listen on You tube 'Debussy plays Debussy: Golliwogg's Cakewalk' (1913).

[17] Listen on you tube: 'Pathetique' by Betthoven; 'Nocturne E flat major' by, Chopin; 'Fur Elise' by Beethoven; 'Claire de Lune' by Debussy; 'Liebstraum' by Liszt.

[18] '10 Days in December...where dreams meet reality...' by Eleanor Deckert© 2016 relates the full story of how Kevin and I met, wed, travelled west, found our land and built our cabin in the Canadian wilderness.

[19] See photo on the back cover '10 Days in January.'

[20] African-American spiritual folk songs: Deep River first collected in print in 1876. Swing low sweet chariot earliest recording 1909. Michael row the boat ashore preserved with music notation in about 1863.

[21] The portrait of Len and Sylvia is on the author's web page. www.eleanordeckert.com '10 Days in January' Chapter 4.

[22] Numbers 6: 24-26.

[23] Luke 2: 29.

[24] Source unknown.

[25] Langston Hughes.

[26] William Arthur Ward.

[27] Henry David Thoreau.

[28] Flanders and Swann recordings are available to listen to on youtube.

[29] These comedy sketches are also available on youtube.

[30] Geoffrey O'Hara, 1917.

[31] Don Raye and Hughie Prince, 1941.

[32] See Wikipedia article for more history about the 'year 2000 problem.'

[33] Search for 'video BBC 2000 Today.'

[34] More homeschooling information, decisions, charts, curriculum, and Seven Predictable Patterns® seminar content will be shared in the future title, '10 Days in September...learning...teaching...' by, Eleanor Deckert.

[35] Thomas: John 20:24-29. Benjamin: Genesis 43:29.

[36] 'Toby Tyler, or ten weeks with the Circus' by, James Otis Kaler was made into a 1960 Disney movie.

[37] Psalm 150: 6.

[38] Written by John W. Peterson. https://www.youtube.com/watch?v=szbslSkPE9Y

[39] Recorded by Sharon, Lois and Bram.

[40] Dona Nobis Pacem: Traditional. This is my Father's World: Lyrics by Maltbie Davenport Babcock and music by Franklin L. Sheppard.

[41] Revelation 21: 1-4.

[42] Both stories by Rudyard Kipling.

[43] Texts mentioned regarding Mary: Luke 1-2, John 19: 25-27, John 20.

[44] How Fran and Archie helped us get started, is in Book 1, '10 Days in December...where dreams meet reality...' by Eleanor Deckert© 2016.

[45] 'When We Were Very Young' A.A. Milne 1924.

[46] 'I am the Good Shepherd' John 10:11, and 'Behold the Lamb of God' John 1:29. Palm Sunday Matthew 21: 1-11, Mark 11: 1-11, Luke 19: 28-40, John 12: 12-19.

[47] Children's songs: source unknown.

[48] 'The Wild Swans' by Hans Christian Andersen, 1838.

[49] Revelation 12: 7-8.

[50] Excerpt from song by Malvina Reynolds and Alan Greene adapted by Harry Belefonte, 1958 Clara Music Publishing Corp.

[51] More details about the 'Seven Days of Creation' homeschooling curriculum developed by Eleanor Deckert will be found in future title '10 Days in September...learning...teaching...' by, Eleanor Deckert.

[52] More information about the non-denominational Sunday School in Avola will be shared in '10 Days in September' and '10 Days in March... and then I'll volunteer...' by Eleanor Deckert.

[53] Read the interview with Father Sasges by Eleanor Deckert published in the North Thompson Times newspaper at http://www.clearwatertimes.com/ourtown/271259961.html

[54] I copied the words and guitar chords from Father Sasges' collection of 450+ songs. This song had the name Barbara Pires, although I cannot find a way to confirm this person wrote it.

[55] Dan Schutte.

[56] Catechism of the Catholic Church 1999 English edition #487.

[57] Isaiah 40: 3-4.

[58] I am paraphrasing Jesus' parable in Luke 18: 9-14.

[59] Luke 15: 11-32.

[60] 'Titanic' 1997, directed by James Cameron.

[61] Luke 23: 34.

What Readers are Saying

"... a remarkable piece of writing... it is so descriptive, it feels like I am in the room."

—Kathy, Social Worker

"...you have conveyed a difficult journey."

—Anne, author

"...thanks for pouring your heart out again."

—Peter, electrician

"It is encouraging to realize that your family is like all of ours: bright days and dark, knit together with the occasional threads of the strife – but always thrumming with love."

—Editor, Friesen Press

Review

Readers experience effective writing which is colourful, personal, emotional and frank. Deckert demonstrates her gift for detail, is dedicated to utter transparency and satisfies the reader's curiosity with her warm, descriptive style.

From early childhood through marriage, parenting and the empty nest, Deckert focuses on her relationships with her father, brothers, husband and sons, as well as father-figures who enter her life while she struggles to remain self-aware, mindful of her own spiritual Journey and psychological well-being.

By sharing the puzzle pieces of her life, Deckert challenges readers to examine for themselves the core question: How do I become my most authentic 'Self'?

—Editor, Friesen Press

About the Author

Storytellers inspire hope again, and again, and again.
—*Walt Disney*

My childhood was simply beautiful and my parents provided richly textured experiences for my siblings and I. Like Noah's Ark, I loaded up valuable skills and traditions to carry into my future to include while raising my own children.

My childhood was also shadowed by negative messages which carried into my future the agony of self-doubt. If you can't trust your 'Self,' the world is a very confusing place.

It is my hope that sharing my story will prompt readers to sort through their own cargo, realize that renewal is possible, and feel encouraged to believe that even during life's struggles, helpful resources will be provided. It's all worth it.

It is the Hero's Journey.

CPSIA information can be obtained
at www.ICGtesting.com
Printed in the USA
LVHW101117200119
604570LV00010B/101/P

9 781460 297100